Gender and Labour in Korea and Japan

Bringing together for the first time sexual and industrial labour as the means to understand gender, work and class in modern Japan and Korea, this book shows that a key feature of the industrialization of these countries was the associated development of a modern sex labour industry. Tying industrial and sexual labour together, the book opens up a range of key questions:

- In what economy do we place the labour of the former "comfort women"?
- Why have sex workers not been part of the labour movements of Korea and Japan?
- Why is it difficult to be "working-class" and "feminine"?
- What sort of labour hierarchies operate in hostess clubs?
- How do financial crises translate into gender crises?

This book explores how sexuality is inscribed in working-class identities and traces the ways in which sexual and labour relations have shaped the cultures of contemporary Japan and Korea. It addresses important historical episodes such as the Japanese colonial industrialization of Korea, wartime labour mobilization, women engaged in forced sex work for the Japanese army throughout the Asian continent, and issues of ethnicity and sex in the contemporary workplace. The case studies provide specific examples of the way gender and work have operated across a variety of contexts, including Korean shipyard unions, Japanese hostess clubs, and the autobiographical literature of Korean factory girls.

This book provides a compelling account of the entanglement of sexual and industrial labour throughout the twentieth century, and shows clearly how ideas about gender have contributed in fundamental ways to conceptions of class and worker identities.

Ruth Barraclough teaches modern Korean history and literature at the Australian National University. She is currently working on her book: *Korean Factory Girls: Capitalism and the Seductions of Literature*.

Elyssa Faison is an Associate Professor of History at the University of Oklahoma and the author of *Managing Women: Disciplining Labor in Modern Japan*. Her current research interests include issues of citizenship and national belonging in imperial and postwar Japan.

Gender and Labour in Korea and Japan

Sexing class

**Edited by
Ruth Barraclough and
Elyssa Faison**

LONDON AND NEW YORK

First published 2009
by Routledge
2 Park Square, Milton Park, Abingdon, Oxon, OX14 4RN

Simultaneously published in the USA and Canada
by Routledge
711 Third Avenue, New York, NY 10017

Routledge is an imprint of the Taylor & Francis Group, an informa business

First issued in paperback 2011

Typeset in Times New Roman by
Value Chain International Ltd

British Library Cataloguing in Publication Data
A catalogue record for this book is available from the British Library

Library of Congress Cataloging in Publication Data
Gender and labour in Korea and Japan : sexing class / edited by
Ruth Barraclough and Elyssa Faison.
    p. cm. — (Women in Asia series)
  Includes bibliographical references and index.
  1. Sexual division of labor—Korea (South) 2. Sexual division of labor—
Japan. I. Barraclough, Ruth. II. Faison, Elyssa, 1965–
  HD6060.65.K6G43 2009
  306.3′615095195—dc22
                                                        2009002033

ISBN 10: 0-415-77663-5 (hbk)
ISBN 10: 0-415-67358-5 (pbk)
ISBN 10: 0-203-87436-6 (ebk)

ISBN 13: 978-0-415-77663-9 (hbk)
ISBN 13: 978-0-415-67358-7 (pbk)
ISBN 13: 978-0-203-87436-3 (ebk)

Contents

Notes on contributors

Ruth Barraclough teaches modern Korean history and literature in the Faculty of Asian Studies at the Australian National University. Her research at present focuses on two topics: Korean kisaeng (courtesans) and sexual slavery in high art; and Red Love in the global 1920s. She is currently finishing her book *Korean Factory Girls: Literature and the Seductions of Capitalism*.

Heather Bowen-Struyk's research focuses on Japanese proletarian literature in the 1920s and 1930s (and implicitly what we can learn from it today). She has published widely in journals such as *positions: east asia cultures critique* and *Tembo*, as well as *The Asia Pacific Journal: Japan Focus* online. She is currently working on an anthology of Japanese proletarian literature in translation with Norma Field (*Literature for Revolution*), an edited volume based on the 2008 Kobayashi Takiji Memorial Symposium at Oxford University, and a manuscript tentatively titled *Beyond "Red Love"*. Since receiving her PhD in 2001, Bowen-Struyk has taught at a number of universities including the University of Chicago, Notre Dame, Loyola University Chicago and her alma mater the University of Michigan.

Haeng-ja Sachiko Chung is an Assistant Professor of Anthropology at Hamilton College in New York State specializing in the Korean Diaspora and contemporary Japan. She is currently working on her book project on Korean nightclub hostesses in Japan as an SSRC-JSPS Long-Term Postdoctoral Fellow at the University of Tokyo Department of Cultural Anthropology. Her research interests include sex work, emotional labour, and postcolonialism.

Elyssa Faison is an Associate Professor of History at the University of Oklahoma specializing in modern Japanese history. Her book *Managing Women: Disciplining Labor in Modern Japan* (University of California Press) appeared in 2007. Her research interests include gender relations, labour history, and the histories of Japanese colonialism, citizenship, and Japan's family registration system.

Jong Bum Kwon is currently a Lausanne Postgraduate Fellow in the Department of Anthropology at Willamette University in Salem, Oregon. His dissertation, *In the Crucible of Restructuration: Making and Unmaking "Workers of Iron" in the Transition to a Neoliberal Democracy in South Korea*, examines the culture and politics of labour and social protest in the aftermath of the Asian financial crisis (1997). His research interests include: transnational social movements; violence, trauma and social memory; police, security and neoliberalism; and intentional communities.

Hwasook Nam is an Assistant Professor in the Henry M. Jackson School of International Studies and the Department of History at the University of Washington, where she holds the James B. Palais Endowed Professorship in Korea Studies. Her research focuses on postcolonial labour and gender history in the context of South Korea's economic development and struggles for democracy. Her book *Building Ships, Building a Nation: Korea's Democratic Unionism under Park Chung Hee* was published by the University of Washington Press in 2009.

Chunghee Sarah Soh is Professor of Anthropology at San Francisco State University. She is the author of *The Chosen Women in Korean Politics: An Anthropological Study*, *Women in Korean Politics*, and, most recently, *The Comfort Women: Sexual Violence and Postcolonial Memory in Korea and Japan* (University of Chicago Press, 2008). Her research takes a historical-comparative and psychological perspective of critical anthropology on such topics as gender and sexuality, women in politics, social/cultural change, social inequality, human rights, and life history.

Series editor's foreword

The contributions of women to the social, political and economic transformations occurring in the Asian region are legion. Women have served as leaders of nations, communities, workplaces, activist groups and families. Asian women have joined with others to participate in fomenting change at micro and macro levels. They have been both agents and targets of national and international interventions in social policy. In the performance of these myriad roles women have forged new and modern gendered identities that are recognizably global and local. Their experiences are rich, diverse and instructive. The books in this series testify to the central role women play in creating the new Asia and re-creating Asian womanhood. Moreover, these books reveal the resilience and inventiveness of women around the Asian region in the face of entrenched and evolving patriarchal social norms.

Scholars publishing in this series demonstrate a commitment to promoting the productive conversation between Women's Studies and Asian Studies. The need to understand the diversity of experiences of femininity and womanhood around the world increases inexorably as globalization proceeds apace. Lessons from the experiences of Asian women present us with fresh opportunities for building new possibilities for women's progress the world over.

The Asian Studies Association of Australia (ASAA) sponsors this publication series as part of its ongoing commitment to promoting knowledge about women in Asia. In particular, the ASAA women's caucus provides the intellectual vigour and enthusiasm that maintains the Women in Asia Series (WIAS). The aim of the series, since its inception in 1990, is to promote knowledge about women in Asia to both the academic and general audiences. To this end, WIAS books draw on a wide range of disciplines including anthropology, sociology, political science, cultural studies and history. The series could not function without the generous professional advice provided by many anonymous readers. Moreover, the wise counsel provided by Peter Sowden at RoutledgeCurzon is invaluable. WIAS, its authors and the ASAA are very grateful to these people for their expert work.

Louise Edwards (University of Technology Sydney)
Series Editor

Acknowledgements

The editors would like to express their gratitude to the people who have contributed to the creation of this book. First and foremost we would like to thank the contributors, who brought their intellectual passion to the project and have stayed the course over the three years it has taken from conference to hard cover. As well as sharing in the task of editing, the contributors' enthusiasm for the entire venture has supported us enormously. The project began with a conference on labour and gender hosted by the Department of Japanese and Korean Studies at Sydney University in 2006. We would like to acknowledge the generous support of the Korea Foundation and the Japan Foundation in enabling us to bring the participants "down under". At the conference we benefited from the critical feedback of our discussants, Laurel Kendall, Hagen Koo, Vera Mackie and Elise Tipton. Laurel Kendall in particular gave us the theme that brought the book together, and continued to advise us both on the subject of our essays and on the challenges of editing. She has been a true mentor. This book would not have come about were it not for the perspicacity and guidance of Louise Edwards, the editor of the Routledge Women in Asia Series. Louise has been the ideal editor: generous with ideas and deadlines while setting high standards for the manuscript. We are grateful to her for the opportunity to bring the work of these contributors together in this volume.

1 The entanglements of sexual and industrial labour

Ruth Barraclough and Elyssa Faison

The histories of labour and class in industrial societies have always been entangled with the development of modern expressions of gender and sexuality. The working class and wage labour – both categories generally presumed male – have depended on female bodies, heterosexuality, and normative visions of the family for their articulation within social and political discourse. This has been true in industrializing Japan and Korea as well as in the West. The essays in this volume span the twentieth century and focus on various forms of industrial and sexual labour in Japan and Korea. The phrase "sexing class" in our title refers to the ways that sex, gender, labour, and class are inextricably related categories in the stories that are told in this volume. In some cases, especially in the essays that deal with sexual labour, "sexing class" refers to the classed nature of sex work and the deployment of various forms and meanings of sexuality within the sphere of "work." In other instances, "sexing class" indicates how biological sex, and the constructions of gender that emerge along with it, contribute in fundamental ways to the production of class and worker identities. That is, "class," "worker," and "labour" do not exist outside the realm of gender, but are constituted through interactions among gender formation, experiences of work, structural conditions of labour and family, and the politics of nation. Sex, gender, sexuality, labour and class cannot exist independently of one another.

Read together, the essays that follow allow us to examine three themes that have been central to the writing of labour history globally: colonial legacies and the ethnic tensions they have engendered; the central place of the family in considerations of labour; and sexuality – particularly how prostitution, which has become a central feature of modern industrial societies, is or is not considered wage labour, and how metaphors of prostitution have been used to discuss wage labour more generally. This collection of essays substantiates the interconnectedness of industrial and sexual labour by focusing on how working-class masculinities and femininities have been produced at the junction of these social and economic worlds.

Colonial legacies

Colonial relationships have been central to defining Western class and gender formations (McClintock 1995, Stoler 2002) just as Western semi-colonialism in

Japan and Japan's colonization of Korea created the conditions for the formation of a modern working class, and for industrialization itself. Japan has been subject to forms of semi-colonial domination by Western powers not once, but twice: first during the Meiji era (1868–1912) when Western powers forced unequal treaties on the country, threatening the prospect of outright colonization and driving the new government to rapidly modernize its economy, its military, and its political institutions. During this era, textile factories employing mostly female labour spearheaded industrial development, while prostitution became subject to the exigencies of the new capitalist system in the form of *karayuki-san*, young women sent abroad by their impoverished families to engage in sex work.

The second time occurred at the end of the Asia-Pacific War, when American forces representing the victorious Allied Powers occupied Japan for seven years. During these years (1945–52) the Supreme Commander of Allied Powers (SCAP) oversaw a restructuring of Japan's economy. The *zaibatsu*, or financial cliques, that had dominated Japan's wartime economy were dismantled, while land redistribution resulted in a drop in tenantry and the eradication of a widespread pattern of absentee landlordism. Meanwhile, labour unions that had been suppressed during the war enjoyed a renaissance, their leaders were let out of jail and new laws put into place to protect the rights of workers to organize and to strike. Under a new postwar constitution, women gained the right to vote for the first time, and sexual equality became a legal, if not a practical, fact. With the onset of the Cold War, however, American anti-communist policies began to dovetail with the long-standing antipathy of Japanese wartime leaders (the less militarist of whom continued in positions of power after the defeat) to socialist and communist thought, and to the labour movement that was associated with it.

In between these two periods of Western semi-colonialism, the Japanese state itself embarked on a fifty-year process of imperial expansion. Japanese imperialism began with the acquisition of the island of Formosa (present-day Taiwan) as part of a peace agreement ending a war with China in 1895, and by 1910 Japan had annexed the Korean peninsula outright. Throughout the 1920s and 1930s, Japan's colonial policies created a class of Korean wage-labourers, many of whom had been displaced from smallholding and tenant farming due to colonial land registration policies. The changing political and economic landscape of Korea created incentives for Koreans to find work in the metropole (Japan proper), and other parts of the expanding Japanese empire. And by the late 1930s, as Elyssa Faison and Chunghee Sarah Soh discuss in this volume, Korean women were being recruited as industrial workers within Japan, and as forced sexual labourers for Japanese soldiers in China and other part of the empire. The effects of the colonization of Korea and the subsequent labour migration to Japan accounts for the significant Korean minority population living and working in Japan today. The essay by Haeng-ja Chung in this volume examines gendered and ethnicized forms of labour in Korean hostess clubs in Japan, pointing to the continued salience of colonial history, as well as the continued mobilization of Korean sexual and erotic labour for Japanese interests.

A focus on the gender politics of labour history also allows us to challenge some of the truisms about the colonization experience, and glimpse episodes of transnational class collaboration that inform the spirit of this book. Thus, Chunghee Sarah Soh discusses the critical collaboration between Japanese and Korean feminist activists that helped launch the campaign for Korean "comfort women" reparations. We might go further to conjecture a genealogy that connects the transnational campaign by and for those Korean women who were caught up as comfort women with earlier Korean strike tours of Japan in the 1920s that raised money for Korean workers on strike in Japanese factories in the colony. For example, when the all-women's union of the Kyŏngsŏng Rubber Factory went out on strike in July 1923, their supporters included union groups in Japan (Lee 1978). By connecting sexual labour with industrial labour we are also able to cross imperial lines to trace networks of solidarity with working women at the very beginning of colonial industrialization.

Gender, labour, and the family

Scholars have recognized the role of the state in promoting the modern configuration of the family (centred on a monogamous heterosexual couple and their offspring) in order to sustain the reproduction of labour at least since the publication in 1884 of Friedrich Engels' *The Origin of the Family, Private Property and the State*. The family, and women's place in it, has defined both men's and women's class positionalities and place within the wage labour system from the beginnings of industrialization in Asia as well as the West. Feminist scholar Heidi Hartmann has famously argued that modern forms of patriarchy are upheld by the sexual division of labour, which has at its foundation the notion of women's work within the domestic sphere (Hartmann 1976). Joan Scott and Louise Tilly have demonstrated that the expansion of political rights to women did not correlate with expansions in women's employment in wage labour, and have suggested that the economic needs of the family unit, rather than individual political rights, have dictated the possibilities for women's wage labour under capitalism (Scott and Tilly 1975). More recently Carol Morgan has argued that "women's secondary position in the workforce was naturalized as employers expressed their hiring preferences according to predominant ideas about manhood and womanhood, often designing new technologies with the sex of the worker in mind" (Morgan 2001: 11). In Korea and Japan, too, industrialization and modernization saw the normalization of the nuclear family, the intensification of gendered divisions of labour based on the family system, and new ideas about femininity and masculinity that shaped men's and women's roles within the family, in the industrial workforce, and as members of labour unions.

The Japanese emphasis on the "good wife, wise mother" ideology for women starting at the turn of the twentieth century dictated that females in the wage labour force should be young and unmarried, and that women's wage labour should constitute a temporary stage in a woman's life before marriage, childbirth, and the maintenance of a household – work that should be a woman's primary duty in adulthood (Faison 2007). As Elyssa Faison argues in her essay in this volume, the Japanese state promoted these same patterns in colonial Korea. This domestic ideal of womanhood combined with policies of assimilation that colonial authorities used to legitimize and solidify their rule of Korea ultimately limited the ability of the wartime imperial state to conscript female labour. While the exigencies of total war led the Japanese state to conscript Korean men to work in Japanese coal mines, in factories, and as soldiers in the Japanese Imperial Army, and to coerce lower-class Korean women and girls into sexual slavery for the Japanese military, relatively few Korean women were recruited to work in factories in Japan. Practical reasons such as the low number of Koreans who possessed enough knowledge of the Japanese language to allow them to function efficiently in Japanese factory settings were part of the reason for the failure of the Japanese state to mobilize large numbers of Korean women for work in the metropole. But an equally significant factor was that the ideology of sameness that proscribed a domestic womanhood for educated women (in Japan and Korea) denigrated female wage labour and work outside the home. In other words, by insisting that middle-class Korean families replicate the domestic structure of Japanese families in the name of assimilation, the Japanese state made it impossible to recruit much-needed female labour except within the terms of idealized womanly roles: such labour could only be cast as temporary employment undertaken for the good of the nation (the Japanese empire) by unmarried women.

The idea of a living wage has also contributed significantly to the importance of family structures in determining the form and possibilities of the wage labour market. In the twentieth century, the promotion by labour organizations and certain state bureaucracies of a living wage explicitly posited the wage earner as a male household head. The living wage thus subordinated women, children, and other dependents as those supported by this wage. Labour unions have been strong promoters of the living wage of the male-headed family in the West as well as in Asia throughout the twentieth century, and as a result union attention to the concerns of women wage workers has been meagre. As Michele Ford and Kaye Broadbent have noted, and as the essays in the present collection bear out, women "have been peripheral to union concerns and largely excluded from union hierarchies" (Broadbent and Ford 2008: 2).

Sizeable union movements in Japan and South Korea have upheld gender norms that discriminated against single women as well as married women, even as they challenged the political and economic status quo. This book explains this gap by examining how femininity and labour came to be defined as antithetical in Japan and Korea. Ruth Barraclough's essay shows how in Korea the gender ideologies forged in colonial industrialization that declared a conflict between ideal womanhood and manual labour have haunted working-class women in the second half of the twentieth century. Barraclough's chapter takes the writings of working-class women as its archive to examine the sexual politics of poverty among working-class women in 1970s South Korea. This chapter connects the struggle of working-class female authors to be considered writers with their struggle to be considered feminine in South Korea's social world that defined them by the taint of labour. Here we see the immense cost of embracing a working-class identity, and the gulf between manual and cultural labour that these proletarian authors and their publishers sought to overcome. Barraclough argues that female working-class writers tell a compelling story about the culture of late industrialization: the intimate effect of the class divide, what it was like to be alone in the capital and sexually curious, and to be hungry for literature but without the space or time to read. The questions that tormented these women about their own capacity as writers are in this essay turned into important questions about the limits of representation in the overlapping worlds they inhabited.

Likewise, Hwasook Nam's chapter delineates the challenges facing working women as they attempt to participate in predominantly male labour unions. But Nam's essay goes further in helping us to understand how tightly woven into the organization of industrial work are discourses of family, especially when it comes to women. Nam's work reveals how structural features of industrial workplaces and labour unions require women (workers or union leaders) to be interpolated first as part of a family unit, and only secondarily as skilled workers or effective organizers. The protagonist of Nam's essay Kim Chinsuk, an unmarried woman hired as a welder who eventually rose to a position of leadership within the Korea Shipbuilding and Engineering Corporation (KSEC) Union, initially confounded gender expectations. As an *agassi*, or young unmarried woman, Kim was not a likely candidate for the more physically demanding, rougher jobs at the shipyard. Women in such positions tended to be older, married women (*ajumma*). These *ajumma* were the widows of men killed in work-related accidents, or the wives of men injured during their military service. Such women could be allowed to take the more demanding and higher-paying shipyard jobs only because they were related to men who were no longer able to provide for the family. As Nam tells us,

> These *ajumma* workers represented an extension of family, rather than an intrusion into the male workers' world of women as workers *per se*. The presence of such women workers did not disturb the prevailing notion of male worker/family head, entitled to a family living wage, but rather had the effect of reinforcing it.

Kim Chinsuk's exceptional story is not, however, the story of a working woman who transcends the gendered discourses that have conditioned the possibilities of her labour; rather, it is a gendered narrative of a different kind – one that invokes the familiar (if less common) image of the woman who sacrifices family and personal happiness, "selflessly devoting her life for the public good." Nam shows us the costs involved in the labour movement piety that allows only an asexual and selfless model of female leadership. Here we see how the processes of industrialization lead to an erasure of gender with a simultaneous intensification of gender difference. That is, Kim seemed to transcend gendered norms to win her initial welding position and the support of male co-workers for her position as a union leader, but subsequently found herself redefined on the factory floor as a heroic exception who embodied a more rarefied image of womanhood, the selfless seeker of justice.

If the story Hwasook Nam tells us about the union leader Kim Chinsuk is exceptional, however, the wives of "Daewoo men," and the men themselves, discussed in Jong Bum Kwon's contribution to this volume, are perhaps more representative of gendered workplace norms. In the wake of the 1997 Asian financial crisis, Korean companies undertook restructuring initiatives encouraged by the International Monetary Fund, and thousands of workers found themselves without the factory jobs they and their families had come to depend on. Women were much more susceptible to the lay-offs partly because unions had little history of supporting women's interests or protecting women's jobs, but also because women's factory jobs tended to be located in smaller, light manufacturing concerns that were less able to survive economic downturns (Broadbent and Ford 2008: 2, Moon and Broadbent 2008). But Kwon reminds us that men were the central figures in the national discourse of post-financial crisis restructuring. Kwon's analysis of laid-off striking Daewoo workers indicates quite clearly that women, and women's role and position within the family, are central not only to defining women as workers (as Nam's essay shows us), but are also central to the construction of male worker subjectivity. Women, in the case of the Daewoo workers' strike, "were engendering agents … integral to the constitution of normative masculine identities for unemployed men. It was the women who redeemed the men, enabling them to reclaim their identities as respectable husbands and fathers." Women aided men in the redemption of their masculinity and the reclamation of their role as male breadwinners. Kwon's chapter illustrates how the 1997 Asian financial crisis and its devastating aftermath in South Korea, along with the simultaneous decline in authority of militant working-class politics, were also experienced in Korea's "Confucian capitalism" as a profound gender crisis.

Sexual labour and the problem of prostitution

For critics of labour relations under capitalism the problem posed by the prostitute is succinctly summed up by Heather Bowen-Struyk in her essay for this volume: "The sex worker occupies a complicated labourer-subject position that distinguishes her from the female factory worker precisely because what she is selling, sex, is understood within a system of sexual desire rather than paid labour."

Prostitution – in this case female paid sexual labour – has frequently been used as a metaphor for male wage labour, especially in its slave-like and underpaid forms, and in terms of the often compromising use of the body that attends both prostitution and industrial work (Roediger 1991). In her intriguing analysis of Hayama Yoshiki's short story "The Prostitute" (written in 1925), Heather Bowen-Struyk demonstrates, in her essay in this volume, how male writers of Japanese proletarian literature used the female body and the figure of the prostitute as a vehicle to express the abject plight of the working classes – but without allowing the discomfiting reality of female subjectivity to encroach upon their narratives of male class consciousness in formation. Bowen-Struyk examines how Hayama's male protagonist, brought by two men to visit a disease-ravaged woman whom he assumes is being prostituted, sees in her the oppressive reality of the working class. He reaches an "epiphany," Bowen-Struyk tells us, "possible only by the window opened by sexual difference and heterosexual desire." Hayama's short story is, as she puts it, "an example of the process of 'sexing class' because of the way that it renders class (politics) visible through the trope of gender/sex." That is, Hayama's male subject only comes to class awareness by having a visceral experience – at once arousing and repulsing – of the working class embodied by a woman who may (or may not) be a prostitute. Bowen-Struyk shows that the socialist realist commitment of proletarian literature founders in the presence of sexually available lower-class women, who appear in their fiction as the embodiment of the enchantment of capitalist relations.

Prostitution, however, has also been central to the story of industrialization in far less metaphorical ways. One key feature of the advance of industrialization in Korea and Japan was the associated development of a modern sex labour market. The historian Song Youn-ok's pioneering work on sex labour in colonial Korea has established that brothel and factory recruiters in 1920s Korea shared the same procurement practices, offered similar bonded labour contracts, and were competing for the same pool of potential workers (Song 1997). As Korea became increasingly enmeshed within an imperial economy, and the number of Korean men working in mines and factories in Japan increased, the regulation of a (ethnic) sex labour market to "service labourers" became a key component of colonial industrialization (Song 1997: 185–6). Fujime Yuki, writing on the history of sex in modern Japan, has demonstrated that the imperial state and the military's role in organizing and managing female sexual labour in what has become known as the wartime "comfort woman system" emerged out of the state's long involvement in managing prostitution in Japan (Fujime 1997, 1999). In her essay in this volume, Chunghee Sarah Soh offers a genealogy that traces the history of certain militarized forms of women's sexual labour in Korea, linking the pre-colonial *kisaeng*, the wartime Korean comfort women used by the Japanese military, and the South Korean Army's systematization of its own "comfort woman" system during the Korean War. All of these forms of female sexual labour, Soh argues, have been defined in official and public narratives by the dominant masculinist discourse that "treats women's sexual labour as stigmatized yet customary." It is this masculinist discourse, she claims, that defines "comfort woman" only in terms of the national shame and victimization that came at the hands of Japanese colonial masters. Such an understanding erases the South Korean government and military's perpetuation of similar systems of controlling women's bodies, and instead defines sexual labour only in terms of an apolitical capitalist consumer culture.

Sexual labour and the history of colonialism come together again in the final essay by Haeng-ja Sachiko Chung. Chung's ethnography of Korean hostess clubs in Japan turns on its head the feminist epistemology of Japanese "hostess clubs" to reveal how much tedious labour goes into the libidinal economy. What has been for other feminists a site of dramatic female exploitation is for Chung part of a wider ethnicized economy that transforms the club into a site of working-class Korean entrepreneurship. Part ghetto, part niche business, competently run by managers, waiters, and cooks, Korean clubs in Japan provide a complex site for an examination of the interplay among labour, gender, ethnicity, and eroticism. Chung retires the hostess from her starring role in the club to reveal how male workers are also a necessary part of the labour force in a successful club. She skilfully shows us that gender and ethnicity never mean one thing: there are many ways to be "Korean" in Club Rose just as there are multiple overlapping gender, age, and ethnic hierarchies within the club. Throughout Chung's essay we never lose sight of the wider economy within which the club must compete. Although operated by Koreans, and selling a "Korean aura" via Korean dance and food, it must "pass" as a Japanese club, where the real business of "hosting" is done in the Japanese language.

Industrial labour and sexual labour are rarely discussed together, but as we argue, they are both central to shaping modern gender and worker identities. Based on the understanding that capitalism in Japan and Korea encompasses a labour market and a sexual economy connected both to a residual history of indentured labour and emerging notions of modern gender relations, we argue that sexuality and labour must be analyzed together if we are to understand the lived history of capitalism in Korea and Japan in the twentieth century. By connecting a discussion of the labour of sex work with the question of what happens to sexuality in factories and other sites of industrial labour, the contributors explore how sexuality is inscribed in working-class identities. The chapters insert concerns about sexuality, desire, poverty, and social mobility into an analysis of working-class identities and the people who seek to shape them, to examine how sexual and labour relations have shaped the cultures of industrialization in Japan and Korea.

References

Broadbent, K. and Ford, M. (2008) *Women and Labour Organising in Asia: Diversity, Autonomy and Activism*, London: Routledge.

Faison, E. (2007) *Managing Women: Disciplining Labor in Modern Japan*, Berkeley: University of California Press.

Fujime, Y. (1997) "The Licensed Prostitution System and the Prostitution Abolition Movement in Modern Japan," in *positions: east asia cultures critique* 5, 1 (Spring): 135–70.

—— (1999) *Sei no rekishigaku* [The history of sex], Tokyo: Fuji shuppan.

Hartmann, H. (1976) "Capitalism, Patriarchy, and Job Segregation by Sex," *Signs* 1, 3 (Spring): 137–69.

Kim, E. (1998) "Men's Talk," in Elaine Kim and Chungmoo Choi (eds.) *Dangerous Women: Gender and Korean Nationalism*, London: Routledge, pp. 67–117.

Lee, H. J. (1978) "*Ilcheha-ŭi Yŏsŏng Nodong Munje*" [The situation of women workers in the colonial period], in *Han'guk Nodong Munje-ŭi Kujo* [The structure of labour problems in Korea], Seoul: Kwangminsa, pp.131–79.

McClintock, A. (1995) *Imperial Leather: Race, Gender and Sexuality in the Colonial Contest*, New York: Routledge.

Morgan, C. E. (2001) *Women Workers and Gender Identities, 1835–1913: The Cotton and Metal Industries in England*, London: New York.

Moon, K. H., and Broadbent, K. (2008) "Korea: Women, Labour Activism and Autonomous Organising," in K. Broadbent and M. Forde (eds) *Women and Labour Organising in Asia: Diversity, Autonomy and Activism*, London: Routledge.

Roediger, D. R. (1991) *The Wages of Whiteness*, New York: Verso.

Scott, J. W. and Tilly, L. A. (1975) "Women's Work and the Family in Nineteenth-Century Europe," in *Studies in Society and History*, 17 (January), 1: 36–64.

Song, Y. O. (1997) "Japanese Colonial Rule and State-Managed Prostitution: Korea's Licensed Prostitutes," in *positions: east asia cultures critique* 5, 1 (Spring): 171–217.

Stoler, A. L. (2002) *Carnal Knowledge and Imperial Power: Race and the Intimate in Colonial Rule*, Berkeley: University of California Press.

Yi, O. J. (2001) *Han'guk Yŏsŏng Nodongja Undongsa 1* [A history of the Korean women's labour movement, vol. 1], Seoul: Hanul Academy.

2 Sexing class: "The Prostitute" in Japanese proletarian literature

Heather Bowen-Struyk

> "Instead of a prostitute I saw a martyr. It appeared to me that she represented the fate of the entire exploited class." – Minpei, in "The Prostitute"
>
> (Hayama 1925)

"The Prostitute" (1925), by Japanese writer Hayama Yoshiki, was highly regarded in its time and continues to be among the most frequently discussed and anthologized stories from the period of proletarian literature in Japan (ECD *et al.* 2007).[1] "The Prostitute" is a provocative account of a young sailor coming into class consciousness through an encounter with a degraded prostitute. The story is typical of a type of masculinist proletarian literature that tended to foreclose issues of gender/sex and sexuality in the service of class consciousness. In "The Prostitute" the male protagonist struggles to affirm his masculinity and save the exploited woman. He can only do so, however, by overcoming sexual desire and finally seeing the woman as an emblem of her class instead of as a woman. Yet as the protagonist himself reminds us, he can only come to this resolution *because* she is a woman. This complicated process – where sexual desire must be overcome so that the obviousness of sexual difference can allow for an epiphany regarding class difference – is what I am calling "sexing class." This essay will explore the process of sexing class through a close reading of "The Prostitute," a short story that continues to fascinate readers with its erotic-grotesquerie, revolutionary possibilities, and sexual mystery.

Before 1926, the Japanese proletarian literary world consisted of several dozen writers committed to advancing radical politics, but there was no one writer who was so outstanding that he or she could not be ignored by the mainstream literary world. At least, that is, until "The Prostitute" was published in November 1925, followed by Hayama's grotesque "Letter in a Cement Barrel" in January 1926. Hayama Yoshiki also had the honour of being the first proletarian author to be discussed in the *Shinchō* literary round-table, the prestigious forum of the central literature clique, the *bundan* (Kume *et al.* 1926; Uranishi 1994: 6). At the other end of the literary spectrum, modernist Shinkankaku-ha (New Sensationists) writer Akagi Kensuke found in "The Prostitute" "a ray of hope" (Akagi 1925: 84). Akagi's proposition of a new romanticism inspired by works such as Hayama's never gained currency in the fight to overthrow the *bundan*, but it is noteworthy that he enlisted Hayama's story to demonstrate effective alternatives to what he saw as the decay of bourgeois realism. And members of the *bundan* were themselves fascinated by Hayama.

"The Prostitute" begins as the narrator self-consciously recalls a strange experience from his youth, while he assures the reader that truth is stranger than fiction. He was drunk, he tells us, wandering around the fashionable streets of the port of Yokohama in his sailor's clothes when suddenly he was hailed by someone promising him "the kind of fun a young man can have" if he has some money. The narrator-as-a-young-man, Minpei, then followed three men, one of whom is referred to as Slug, to an abandoned warehouse where they presented to him a dying, naked young woman. Saying, "Go ahead and do as you like," Slug leaves. The young man is overcome, not by passion but by compassion, and after a tortured self-examination, he offers to save the young woman and take her away. She laughs at him, telling him that the men are taking care of her. Minpei tries to put up a fight when the men return to tell him his time is up, but then realizes it is useless. He leaves only to return later, slightly more inebriated, to question the men further. It seems the woman was not a prostitute, but a horrible freak show staged to make money to pay for medicine for her and for the men. Finally Minpei comes to feel solidarity with both the woman and the men. "The Prostitute" ends:

> Now a light robe was draped over her body. She was probably sleeping. Her eyes were closed.
>
> Instead of a prostitute I saw a martyr.
>
> It appeared to me that she represented the fate of the entire exploited class.
>
> Tears welled up in my eyes. I walked quietly so as not to make a sound, and when I got to the door I handed Slug one yen. As I handed it to him, I grasped his shriveled hands with all my might.
>
> Then I went out the front. As I took a step down the stairs, the tears welling up in my eyes fell in drops.
>
> July 10, 1923, Chigusa Prison (Hayama 1925: 18–19)

Before the protagonist's eyes, the sleeping woman transforms into a symbol, "a martyr" who "represented the fate of the entire exploited class." And thus the story becomes a proletarian allegory.

"The Prostitute" is an example of the process of "sexing class" because of the way that it renders class (politics) visible through the trope of gender/sex, and the ensuing "contradiction" referred to by Paula Rabinowitz as "the repression of gender and sexuality by its invocation" (Rabinowitz 1991: 64). Perhaps it will seem ironic that the foreclosing of sexuality/gender takes place by foregrounding sex/gender and sexuality as tropes to render visible class antagonism. However, it is because the body of a degraded woman signifies the misery of her sex, and moreover the misery of her sex is clearly visible in a way that the misery of her class might not be, that makes it a poignant and transferable figure to represent the suffering of an entire class.

Sexing class is a strategy frequently employed in radical literatures throughout the world of the 1920s and 1930s. Paula Rabinowitz writes of US proletarian literature that "in order to be legible ... the narrative of class struggle relied on the metaphors of gender differences" (64). Rabinowitz also writes that US "male writers saw female sexuality – the coding of woman as a desired and desiring body – primarily as a metaphor for class conflict, whereas women built narratives of female class consciousness out of the political relations embedded in sexuality" (91). Women's bodies have been troped in radical fiction to signify misery, but their fictional minds rarely understand the source of the misery. Regarding English Socialist writings, Janet Montefiore has written, "The rhetorical trope whereby a woman's body personifies a class is a common feature of the Socialist writings of the thirties" (Montefiore 1996: 94). Montefiore writes that in revolutionary fiction, men typically grow and develop in class consciousness while "the female victims can only signify misery, not understand it. Their used, degraded bodies represent the suffering of their class, just as their narrow minds represent its emotional deprivations" (94). Indeed, Hayama's eponymous prostitute represents the misery of a female victim so that the male protagonist – and the reader – can come into consciousness. As evidenced throughout this volume, "sexing class" was practiced in Japan and Korea as well, where the inequalities of gender could be put to work representing the inequalities of class.

"Women" (as tropes) were available for class-conscious narratives in Japan in the 1920s and 1930s precisely because they were already so visible in mass media, from images of the urbane modern girl to exposés on the lives of exploited female textile workers. In her study of women's journals in the 1920s and 1930s in Japan, Sarah Frederick signals the concern that the women writers and editors of the sometimes proletarian women's arts journal *Nyonin geijutsu* (1928–31) had over the way that they, too, were participating in the troping of women:

> [M]any of the participants worried that women were simultaneously being used as the icons par excellence both for commercialism (as readers, consumers, and subjects of representation in journalism) and for the labour movement in the form of the factory girl. Observing the extent to which women and female categories had become larger-than-life representatives of the perception of social change, the editors and contributors to *Nyonin geijutsu* struggled with how best to be activists without simply reproducing those categories.
>
> (Frederick 2006: 158)

In the early twentieth century, female waged workers outnumbered male workers in Japan. In 1909, women were 62 percent of the "entire factory work force." They continued to be the majority of the waged work force throughout the 1920s: "Their proportion stood at 52.6 per cent as late as 1930 – a rather high figure when compared with other late industrializers, such as France, Italy, and India" (Garon 1987: 13). However, in the context of labour politics, working women were frequently treated as objects of pity rather than as a prospective proletariat (Faison 2007, Tamanoi 1999). Sheldon Garon writes that "most surveys and exposés after

1895 highlighted the plight of respectable farm girls who were caught, stripped, and beaten, or of women workers burned to death because the owners locked the dormitories every night" (Garon 1987: 15). In her study of socialist women in Japan, Vera Mackie writes that "the convention of writing about women as objects of pity and compassion continued into the 1920s, particularly with the publication of Hosoi Wakizō's book *Jokō aishi* (The Pitiful History of Female Factory Workers) in 1925" (Mackie 1997: 108). Hosoi's book, among others, insured that women workers were visible as victims, not as a potentially revolutionary proletariat.

"The Prostitute" is a fascinating intervention into this literary culture because not only does it participate in the masculinist proletarian imagination already described, but it also includes the muted narrative of the exploited subaltern. On the one hand, this story is an allegory of the downtrodden lumpen proletariat and the image of the prostitute functions as an allegorical figure. The transformation of the prostitute into a powerful symbol becomes for some readers the meaning of the story. However, as Maedakō Hiroichirō noted in 1926, it depends on how you read it: "what is stronger, the last eight lines or the rest of the story?" (Hayashi *et al.* 1926: 25). It also holds true that the woman protagonist in the story holds her own beliefs and asserts her own subjectivity, although it clashes with the narrator's subjectivity creating a dissonance within the story.

Sexing class, as we will see, means two overlapping things: one, the way that sexual difference (not just gender difference) is an effective trope for rendering visible class difference; and two, the way that sex – sexual difference, female sexuality, and heterosexual desire in particular – is sacrificed or elided in the service of the formation of class consciousness and a class conscious narrative. As a result of the sexing of class, the protagonist is able to see, for the first time, the oppression suffered by one class for the benefit of another. However, the muted voice in this narrative reminds us that rendering class visible through sex is not without its costs.

The conflict between class consciousness and sexual desire

The story opens at an intersection at the entrance to Chinatown. The pimp-like man referred to as Slug and his two buddies call out to Minpei on the street, "Hey there, young man," but Minpei does not know what the man wants "since he's not a woman" (Hayama 1925: 3). Slug then offers him "the kind of fun that only a young man can have for two bits" (3). Minpei decides to accompany Slug and his buddies. From this first encounter, Minpei is interpellated as a certain kind of man, a young man looking for something that a woman might have to offer, and Minpei will later struggle to redefine his masculinity against this position.

After being led on a disorienting walk through the back streets of Chinatown, Minpei is brought to an expansive, dimly lit warehouse. His first thought is that he has been led there to be killed for material for a Chinese medicine, rumored to use fresh livers. As his eyes adjust and he sees that the "clump" before him is actually the naked lower body of a woman, it seems his suspicion about the place's danger is confirmed, until Slug tells him, "Go and have a look. Go ahead and do as you like. I'll be on the look-out around here." At this point, Minpei takes a look at the "corpse that sighs. … Each breath was wrung from her chest as though it were her last" (7). Later, he notes to himself that he prefers to think of her as a living corpse (8). This near-corpse of a 22- or 23-year-old woman is lying naked, half-hidden by a beer box lid, and it turns out that she is the attraction for which Minpei was brought to the warehouse.

He confronts "a very cruel scene" before him, one marked by grotesquerie:

> There was filth around her shoulders and the pillow that looked like vomit from when she was able to eat, and it was strewn about in chunks mixed with dried blood. Her hair was congealed in it. And her [twelve characters censored] was sticky. An acidic stench arose from her head area, and from her limbs there radiated the kind of putrid odor peculiar to cancerous tumors. The grotesque odor made me fear whether a person's lungs could endure such a stench. Her eyes were wide open. Those eyes seemed to be looking at me. But probably they weren't looking at anything. It appeared, of course, that she didn't even know that I was standing in front of her naked body. I stood near her feet, entranced by the pitiful sight. I remained standing, with two distinct thoughts in my head:
>
> Here is a pitiable human being.
> Here is a pitiable woman. (7)

The "two distinct thoughts in [his] head" are not so obviously distinct at first; she is, after all, both "a pitiable human being" and "a pitiable woman." Why they are distinct is clarified when he tells us that the development of class consciousness is possible only because she is a woman: "I have a confession to make, a really painful confession. If the person lying there naked hadn't been a woman, if it had been a naked man, then would I have stayed so long? Would I have felt so moved?" (8). The implication is no, he would not. This epiphany is possible only by the window opened by sexual difference and heterosexual desire.

As Minpei stands before the woman he struggles with conflicting forces within himself: he must overcome any sexual desire in order to salvage his moral sense. He thinks to himself that this woman cannot resist, either legally or physiologically, and that "even this woman would be better than a corpse to fulfill one's sexual desires" (8). He wonders how many men have come here before him and how many of them have been able to walk away because, "The brakes are hard to apply on this road" (8). When she finally speaks to him, he will again struggle against the embarrassment of sexual desire, because he knows that if he wants to think himself any different from the men before him, then he must convince her that he does not desire her.

As Minpei struggles to suppress his sexual desire, he begins to see the woman as an exploited labourer: "This woman who had battled against all of life's hardships had sold the last dregs of her labour power, and now she sold the one thing that should never be sold, her chastity, in order to survive" (9). He sees her plight as analogous to the killing of a person to make the precious and expensive Chinese medicine: "To save a person the medicine cannot but kill another person. Similarly, in order to fill her stomach, she, like every member of the proletariat, bit off her own arms, sexual organs and even nerves. She extinguishes herself in order to live. There is no other way" (9).

Given the gruesome condition she is in, it might seem surprising that Minpei continues to struggle with sexual desire. But it is crucial that he confront and overcome his desire in order to translate desire and sexual difference into class consciousness. He cannot feel class solidarity as long as he sees her as a potential object of sexual desire. He thinks to himself: "I didn't feel even the slightest sexual excitement towards this woman, I thought. But actually that was mistaken. I was looking. Looking is only looking, but what is that? I was making excuses to myself" (10). And later, he thinks: "As long as she was a woman, of course it was possible that I might feel some impulse. However, that wouldn't be appropriate in such a situation. This woman was reduced to skin and bones. And she would soon be resting eternally" (10). Minpei recalls how his eyes and nose were bombarded by the putrescence emanating from her body. Nevertheless, he sees before him a prostitute and he was brought there to "do as he pleases," so despite protestations of upright intentions, he struggles to overcome his sexual desire.

We need not know whether Hayama was actively conscious of the way that sex and/or gender place the relations between people into hierarchies. Nevertheless in this story class is rendered effectively through the metaphor of sex because the power relations that hierarchize sex are readily visible.

Can the woman speak?

Because the woman in the narrative has no name, and moreover, because she is not even really a prostitute, we are left without anything to call her except "the woman." And, perhaps that is appropriate because in this story the woman is meant to stand in for her whole sex, all more or less degraded, as well as the entire exploited class. However, when I ask, "Can the woman speak?" I recall Gayatri Spivak's challenge to elites regarding the voice of the subaltern (Spivak 1988). "The Prostitute" offers its own answer to this question: yes, the subaltern (woman) can speak, but her speech is disturbing and mostly unintelligible, and the protagonist is happiest when she allows him to act as ventriloquist to her thoughts. In wider society the proletarian Minpei would hardly be elite, but his voice reigns over this narrative. The woman's speech is ultimately the most destabilizing element in this story. Indeed all signs of her subjectivity – that she looks back at Minpei, for example – threaten the tenuous ongoing struggle between class consciousness and sexual desire.

Minpei had "wanted to know if she could speak or not" (9), but had given up the idea when he noticed that her eyes were indeed tracking his movements: "I was surprised. Then – this is so stupid, but – I blushed bright red. I reconsidered, and thought that perhaps I just felt that her eyes followed my actions" (9), and so he waved his hands in front of her face "just as doctors frequently do on someone's deathbed" (9). Her blink confirms that she does actually see him. His blush signals to her, to him and to the reader that he had previously had the unselfconsciousness peculiar to those accustomed to thinking themselves invisible and untouchable. So long as she did not see him, he was free to gaze at her according to his own desires, but he is discomfited by the possibility that she, in turn, sees and judges him.

When she finally speaks, it is anticlimactic: "'Don't be too hard on me, you hear?' she uttered. There was no power in that voice, and she spoke in bits, but it was not the voice of someone on her deathbed" (10). From the first moment that she speaks, the woman begins to uproot Minpei's expectations; in this case, it is the assumption that she was on her deathbed that she contradicts. He prompts her several more times, but when she turns her head to look at the ceiling, he takes the opportunity to gaze at her once again freely, although not without shame: "I was extremely afraid that she would see where my eyes were looking. To be frank, at that moment I was being a brave, humanistic (*jindōteki*) and ascetic youth. There was no discrepancy between my mind and body. That's why I didn't want her to know that I was looking at her OO with scorching eyes. Why was it only my eyes that I could not overcome?" (10). (The "OO" in the citation indicate characters that were censored, a practice that allowed even radical or overly explicit language to be suggested without needing to be printed. In this encounter with the woman, there are multiple instances of such self-censorship, suggesting to the reader that the spectacle is un-writably obscene.) Contradictions aside, Minpei reasons that if she saw him looking at her, then she would think that he was like all the rest: "I feared that then my present heroic, humanistic actions and logic would snap and come tumbling down. I was ashamed" (10). Her gaze threatens to undermine the fragility of his position.

Minpei had wanted to hear her speak in order to affirm his sense of self, in particular his sense of himself as "a brave, humanistic and ascetic youth":

> I wanted to hear how many fellows had come into this room and done how many cruel things, or perpetrated how many mean, shameful acts to this woman, my pitiable compatriot. I wanted to show off my good nature by declaring that their actions should be cursed. (10)

Minpei wants to be affirmed as a certain kind of masculine youth – specifically, of higher moral caliber than those who would exploit this woman – and yet this subject position is difficult for him.

Minpei also wants to hear her speak in order to affirm the monologue of her history that he voiced for her at the end of the second section of the story. He imagines what she would say:

> "Ah, I want to work. But there is no one who will take me. I contracted tuberculosis from breathing the textile refuse in the air, from the high temperature, and the dry air in the factory. I was thrown out because I contracted tuberculosis and could no longer work. But there was no place that would take me.

However if I didn't work, then my elderly mother would no longer be able to go on living with me. ..." So she probably looked for work for a number of days, wandering around town from factory to factory. Still, there was probably nothing. "I'll sell my chastity." And hadn't she thus spilled out the final drops of her life energy? She then became even less able to work. Until, finally she had come here in this state, given up even the hope of living, and was waiting to die. (9)

The story he imagines is reasonable; perhaps it is even a familiar story to readers in the 1920s in Japan. However, the narrative of "The Prostitute" will challenge any certainty a reader might feel with regard to this woman's story because she will refuse to confirm it.

Her speech disrupts Minpei's pleasurably moralistic masculine position:

Finally, she answered in a small voice.
"You want to ask me some things? It's painful for me to speak, but if you're not going to do anything else, I'll talk to you for a little while."
I blushed bright red. Damn! That girl yanked me up by the roots. Again a hot shudder ran through my body.
What the hell did I want to find out by making her talk to me? It's all already perfectly clear, isn't it? And what will become of making her gasp out painfully even if there is something I don't know?
I resolved to save her. (11)

Minpei wants to demonstrate his noble feelings; he wants to hear her confirm the story of suffering that he has imagined so that he could have the pleasure of denouncing those who have defiled her. He wants to do her the favour of showing sympathy or pity; but instead she shows him that it is she who is doing him the favour by speaking through her pain. His intention was not to cause her more pain, only to appease his own conscience, but as a result he feels himself to be "yanked up by the roots." He repeatedly demonstrates that his masculine subject position is fragile and dependent upon the woman affirming his shaky view of the situation.

The woman, who in the beginning appeared to have no power to resist, is surprisingly able to resist Minpei's offer of help. When Slug's friends return, Minpei panics and quickly offers her anything she wants. She responds that she just wants to be left in peace, and Minpei is deflated: "The heroine of a tragedy, she betrayed my expectation" (12). Every time she speaks, she confounds expectations by asserting her subject position. She refuses to become the near-corpse that he imagined, and although apparently dying, she resists even his offer of help. He will not be able to regain his dignity until he returns and the prostitute, having fallen asleep, plays the role of the mute symbol that he first imagined her to be.

The sexual difference between Minpei and the prostitute is translated into a gendered relationship in which he imagines that he is empowered while she is powerless to resist. Minpei comes into consciousness by seeing her as an exploited labourer "who had sold the last dregs of her labour power," but he does so by acting as a ventriloquist for her history. He offers his assistance from the purport-edly secure position of masculine savior to the apparently powerless female, but she talks back. By drawing out her words and actions, I have tried to demonstrate that, surprisingly, the narrative does not suppress the woman's subjectivity. Only Minpei, who cannot fathom her words and actions, and the reader's complicity with Minpei, suppresses her subjectivity. The woman's subjectivity is ultimately undermined by a reading that sees her as a symbol of the oppressed class. In order to see her as such a symbol, we must forget that she actively refuses to play that role when it is offered.

However, her speech is partially irreconcilable with the narrative. Minpei is, after all, a sympathetic protagonist, the story that he imagines for her is not unrea-sonable, and his desire to help her is perhaps not entirely self-serving. Her speech therefore remains something of an enigma in the story, a trace of female worker subjectivity that resists easy reconciliation with the narrative. We have already seen that the story ends as Minpei has an epiphany and comes to see "a martyr instead of a prostitute," a "symbol of the entire oppressed class." This ending has the power to suppress the woman's subjectivity simply because it becomes so much more important to be thinking about an entire class than a single, sick woman. This ending also has the power to render the meaning of the woman and the meaning of the story into the trope of the prostitute, but that would be misleading.

The politics of misunderstanding

In a last-ditch effort to save the woman, Minpei tries to fight for her and finds himself trading punches with one of the other men. But when he takes advan-tage of having knocked a man down to turn to the woman and say, "Let's go," she confounds him one more time by yelling at him: "Young man, you're a fool. You might have killed him. That man and a couple of others have been taking care of me. What a problem" (13). When he questions her, she responds, "Young man, these men haven't defiled me. Someday when you're a little older you'll understand." And Minpei feels, "At once, I fell from a hero to a fool" (13). He suddenly becomes weak as the stench assaults his nose and the exertion and hot humidity take their toll. He apologizes for the "misunderstanding": "Brothers, I don't want to fight with you. I misunderstood. It's my fault" (14). In fact, Minpei has not yet understood what he has "misunderstood." However, already we see that "misunderstanding" offers a resolution that allows Minpei to walk away.

However, Minpei is unable to resist returning to the warehouse that night to see the woman one more time. He is still unwilling to "buy" her, he thinks to himself as he fondles the borrowed one yen in his pocket, but he "just wanted to see her one more time." He "thought it would be fine to go check on her for 'just five min-utes'" (17). As we saw earlier, when he returned for one more gaze she is sleeping, covered by a robe. And it is now that he has his epiphany that "she represented the fate of the entire exploited class." Not coincidentally, he is able to overcome his sexual desire when she has been covered up. Finally, she is silent and motion-less long enough for him to indulge in his troping of her. His sexual desire no longer threatens to undermine his moral subjectivity, and his sympathy and class consciousness come to the fore.

Up to this point we have no reason to suspect that the woman is not a prostitute. However, immediately before his epiphany, Minpei confronts Slug, and Slug explains to him what has been going on, thus finally clarifying what the woman's speech was unable to make clear. Slug tells him that they are not pimping the woman, and that she is not a prostitute. They have been reduced to the farce of this grotesque freak show because they are all sick and need medicine.

In fact, when Slug first addressed Minpei on the street, he asked him if he had money for "admission" (*kenryō*), and Minpei responded that he was ready to accompany the men since he had paid his "admission fee" (4). But since the story is called "The Prostitute," surely most readers simply assume it is a code for seeing a prostitute. Minpei seems surprised to be brought to a warehouse and rather than thinking that it is a likely or unlikely place for a prostitute, he instead questions his own safety. By the time the men tell him to "do as he pleases," Minpei does seem convinced that she is a prostitute, and it is on these grounds that he is able to assume the morally superior subject position and offer to save her. The narrative has taken him from the assumption that he is going to a show, to the assumption that he is going to a prostitute, and he does not seem to realize at that point that he has been brought to a grotesque freak show.

Slug tells him, "This woman isn't made to prostitute. There are guys who would do that, but we stand guard, if there's anyone like that, we throw them out." He continues that Minpei was purposefully selected from the crowd because of the way he held his head up high as he walked through the streets. As the narrator recalled walking about the showy Yokohama port amidst the well-dressed passers-by and foreigners, he felt shame that he did not know then that he looked like a fool. Twice he asserted that he did not yet know to which class he belonged, in order to explain how he could have been so foolish: "If I had had consciousness, I would not have purposefully played the fool" (2). He had walked through the fashionable streets wearing his sailor's overalls without any class consciousness, and he had no sense that he looked ridiculous with his chest puffed out. It was, ironically, his lack of class consciousness that made him an ideal audience member for the freak show. Minpei's response is narrated internally: "I had completely misunderstood. What kind of a shameless punk was I" (18). It is important to note, however, that the narrative emphasis of the story is not on unveiling the "misunderstanding" of the woman's prostitution. On the contrary, it is almost irrelevant that she is not really a prostitute as Minpei still needs her to be a prostitute in order to come into consciousness, so that once she stops being a prostitute, she quite seamlessly starts being a "prostitute." It is important for the narrative and for Minpei that the "misunderstanding" not lead to a new, different understanding of her as not a prostitute, but rather to a new, different understanding of her as a metaphorical prostitute. Not being a prostitute frees her all the more to be a "prostitute."

The woman plays the role of "prostitute" in Minpei's version of her history. He would probably not have come into class consciousness if he had not coded what he saw as a prostitute, simply because he probably would not have stayed long enough to reconsider his views. Minpei is able to feel morally superior for not having consumed her services only so long as he still thinks she is a prostitute. That is, once he recognizes that she is in fact not a prostitute but rather a freak show, he will be forced to realize that he has already consumed her – he got what he paid for – by being a willing audience member and looking at her. In all of these senses, it is necessary to the narrative that the woman be a prostitute, at least in Minpei's recognition of her.

In fact, that the "prostitute" of the story is not actually a prostitute could easily slip by the reader because the ending pushes the trope of the prostitute to its full signifying potential in the narrative. The woman, if not an actual prostitute, is still seen as metaphorically prostituting herself just as the proletariat metaphorically prostitutes him/herself for wages. It is in this sense that Minpei sees "a martyr instead of a prostitute" as he recognizes that she has sacrificed her life. However, the moment that he sees her as a symbol is predicated on understanding that the woman is not alone, that in fact, all of them are sick and dying. "Prostitution" is therefore first and foremost metaphorical as it stands in for the exploitation of an entire class of people.

As in so much of Hayama's fiction, the trope of the prostitute is so powerful that it may overwhelm the rest of the narrative, causing us, in fact, to forget or not notice that the woman is not a prostitute. Throughout this story the image of the prostitute has been used as a trope for the oppressed class with little consideration for the status of actual prostitutes. That is, seeing her as a symbol relieves the reader of the burden not only of her subjectivity, but also of rethinking women, sex labour, and labour politics.

Sex/gender and labour politics

The figure of the prostitute is implicated in sex/gender politics, and in fact, it gains much of its symbolic power by virtue of those politics. The sex worker occupies a complicated labourer-subject position that distinguishes her from the female factory worker precisely because what she is selling, sex, is understood within a system of sexual desire rather than paid labour. The prostitute in Japanese literature at this time could be seen in terms of sexual desire or class consciousness but not both. Nakano Shigeharu's "New Woman" (Nakano 1928) for example, raises the issue when the narrator makes a special plea for including café waitresses – women who relied on their sexual allure for tips – among those "we" call comrade. What is left implicit in the story is why such women are not already considered potential comrades. Is it because they do not labour in factories or heavy industry? Is it because their labour is hidden behind a professional veneer of pleasure and seduction? Or is it because their labour is "unproductive" as Alexandra Kollontai argued in Soviet Russia? (Kollontai 1977: 267)

Or is it because they are part of a sex industry, which *a priori* excludes them from thoughts of labour? It is no accident that when sexually active women appear in proletarian literature, they appear in the form of the decadent "modern girl" whose sexuality exemplifies everything that is wrong with the petit-bourgeoisie and their self-indulgent consumerist lifestyle. For example, the impoverished Tokyo woman turned film actress Yoshikawa Shinako in Kishi Yamaji's *Go, Stop* (Gō, Sutoppu, 1928–29) (who is the mistress of the capitalist, thus betraying her true class allegiance) is criticized for failing to be satisfied with her 500 yen a month salary. Looked at in the context of the market in which she labours, Yoshikawa wants half of what her male acting partner, who pockets 2,500 yen a month, receives. Nevertheless, the chapter is titled "The Petit-Bourgeoisie are the Parasites of Society," and the reader is left to make the connection between the title and all that Shinako represents.

Hayama tropes the prostitute not once but twice in his early stories, and this suggests that the prostitute functions effectively as a trope in the literature of men coming into class consciousness. In addition to "The Prostitute," Hayama's short story "A Harbour Town Woman" (Minato-machi no onna, 1926a) about a sailor spending the night in a port in Hokkaido also features a prostitute whose insights provide the spark of consciousness for the sailor. The prostitute in "A Harbour Town Woman" is indeed a prostitute, and we can see that Hayama showed a tendency to put difficult proletarian truths into the mouths of prostitute-women: the prostitute's speech becomes increasingly lyrical and then hysterical, and she ends up enigmatically saying that the male customer is her father. But on the way there, she offers a simple proletarian perspective on morality and class. The sailor-customer, Ogura, thinks himself superior because he studies, hoping to better himself, but the prostitute tells him that he can only better himself by stepping on others, by oppressing others. Ogura's success will be at the expense of the proletariat. In addition to being published separately as a short story, "A Harbour Town Woman" is also incorporated into *Life on the Sea* (Umi ni ikuru hitobito, 1926d), one of the most celebrated proletarian novels, as chapters nineteen through twenty-three. In the context of *Life on the Sea*, this incident spurs Ogura to participate in a strike aboard his ship. In contrast, the woman in "The Prostitute" is finally relegated to a metaphorical, or at best an enigmatic, position in the narrative, while the prostitute in "A Harbor Town Woman" has the ability to impact the protagonist's actions.

The influence of Dostoevsky on Japanese proletarian literature is evident, and like Dostoevsky, Hayama uses the figure of the enlightened sex worker to present a truth not otherwise accessible. The main difference between the troping of the two prostitutes in his stories is that, while Ogura's prostitute may speak enigmatically, her message is clear; in contrast, Minpei's prostitute delivers a truth that cannot quite be deciphered. Ogura's prostitute has a profound impact on the way Ogura comports himself and on his decision to join in the strike as a leader (in *Life on the Sea*), while Minpei's prostitute has been filed away under the unbelievable but true. The truth that the eponymous "prostitute" speaks is lost in this mysterious, strange tale, and we do not know whether her words have any impact on Minpei. We do not know if he is able to comprehend her words and actions in any way other than as a symbol for the oppressed class.

Why is it that "The Prostitute" was able to appeal to diverse literary critics even while other overtly political, proletarian pieces repelled them? In a sense, despite the obviousness of the metaphor of the oppressed class as prostitute, the story resounded with ambiguities, even for the core of the proletarian literature movement. In *Bungei sensen*, the most important journal on proletarian literature at the time, a round-table discussion focusing on Hayama in December 1926 discussed how "The Prostitute" presented a challenge to interpret: Was it condescending to the weak? Was it humanitarian? Was it proletarian? Was it all three? Maedakō Hiroichirō said that until the last eight lines, the story is humanitarian, so the question is, which is stronger, most of the story or the last eight lines? Maedakō answers that it is the last eight lines, and by "humanitarianism," he said that he means the "feeling of superiority toward the female protagonist" and the "resultant emotion of pity toward the woman that comes from encountering someone weak" (Hayashi *et al.* 1926: 25). When Maedakō says that the story is humanitarian until the last eight lines, he is referring to the moment when the young narrator sees a martyr instead of a prostitute, someone who "represented the entire fate of the oppressed class." In other words, it is humanitarian until the moment when the prostitute stops being a prostitute and starts being a symbol.

What is not mentioned by the male critics – either in the Shinkankaku-ha, the *bundan*, or the proletarian core – is the question of what all of this means for female sex workers. As we have already noted, sex/gender were being harnessed to make visible class relations in labour literature around the world. Vera Mackie points out specifically that in Japan, "Prostitution, in socialist writing, served as a metaphor for the exploitation and degradation suffered by workers under the capitalist system, but these workers [prostitutes] did not become obvious targets for the attention of labour organizations" (Mackie 1997: 101). While prostitution was discussed from a variety of viewpoints by male and female socialists, anarchists, Bolsheviks, and bourgeois feminists, it seems to have been most useful to them as a political metaphor rather than understood as part of a capitalist labour market.

How did women, particularly women affiliated with the proletarian literature movement, receive this story? Hirabayashi Taiko, one of the foremost female radicals at the time, remembers Hayama in terms that shed a different political light on the trope of the prostitute. Before affirming that Hayama was a genius and that the tragedy of his life was "the tragedy of a genius living under capitalism," she casts considerable aspersions on his character (Hirabayashi 1967: 379–83). Her criticisms are thorough and "The Prostitute" does not escape without its share of damage. She emphasizes Hayama's roguish character as if to suggest that a reader should be wary about reading a saintly author in the background of the text. She relates a couple of incidents in which Hayama displayed familiarity with prostitutes and concludes that Hayama's standards with women were quite low, in fact "so long as they were women" was about the only standard he set (Hirabayashi 1967: 381). Her jabs seem to make a mockery of anyone who would see "The Prostitute" as an allegory of class consciousness; after all, the author's character is only thinly veiled in the character of Minpei and most contemporary readers would have recognized Hayama's sailor experience.

For Hirabayashi, Hayama was only writing about what he knew well: prostitutes, pimps, and johns. Unlike the male critics cited, she does not glorify Hayama for the story; rather she dismisses the story as mere evidence of the writer's whore-mongering experience. While she does not criticize "The Prostitute" or Hayama's writing on explicitly feminist grounds, she does point to a concern that the male writers do not address: that the male narrator of "The Prostitute" (or Hayama himself) had access to the world of prostitutes as a working-class consumer.

While the metaphor of the proletariat qua prostitute is effective because it high-lights the exploitation and degradation of an individual, this metaphor is able to function in this way because of heterosexual male privilege. In 1926, Sasaki Takamaru, translator of Lenin, remarked that "it was effective" that Hayama "depicted not the prostitute that usually comes to mind, but an extreme one" (Hayashi *et al.* 1926: 26). Indeed, the naked and dying "prostitute" of Hayama's story is far removed from the ladies of the pleasure quarters that inhabit Japanese fiction. The radicals gathered together to discuss Hayama's works all agreed: this "prostitute" is, indeed, extreme. And perhaps it is the extreme circumstances that lead the reader to agree with Minpei that she is best seen as a trope. Does this mean that a "regular" prostitute would not be recognizable as a labourer or as a trope for the oppressed?

The woman in the story serves as a trope for the entire exploited class, men and women. And yet, in actuality, as a prostitute she would have been servicing those from the working class such as Minpei. The woman's misery is used to represent the misery of an entire class, but such a rhetorical move suppresses the sex/gender politics that in fact subordinate her to her potential male customers. In this sense, the very same dynamics of sex/gender hierarchy that allow class to be rendered visible through sexualization are in effect suppressed.

The metaphor of the proletariat qua prostitute implies that the proletariat's chas-tity or purity is being bought and consumed by the bourgeoisie. However, unlike the working class as a whole, or individual workers for that matter, this prosti-tute's labour would not actually have been exploited by the bourgeoisie, but by her fellow proletarians. As labour-conscious revolutionaries, neither Hayama nor his male contemporaries who lauded the story for its class consciousness would have liked to think of themselves as consumers of a prostitute's labour. More likely, if they did visit a prostitute, it would have been more comfortable to recognize the situation in the terms of sexual desire. Ironically, seeing her as a trope for the oppressed class obscures the sex/gender politics that subordinate her to even poor sailors like Minpei.

Conclusion

"The Prostitute" is typical of a dominant, although certainly not exclusive, mas-culinist proletarian literary imagination in which the exploitation of women is a tremendous rallying force for male protagonists who are able to see in gen-der exploitation a metaphor for class exploitation. Not every work that sees the exploitation of women and children as a metaphor for class exploitation would be masculinist – indeed some affirm the abilities of women and children to become their own revolutionary forces – but in "The Prostitute," only the male protagonist is put in the position of would-be saviour. The "kind of fun" offered to the young, humanistic Minpei turns out to be not prostitution, but the masculinist fun of imagining himself to be the woman's saviour.

The story of "The Prostitute" is an interesting dramatization of the conflict between heterosexual desire and class consciousness on the one hand, and of the displacement of sex/gender differences by the sexualizing of class on the other hand. Rendering class visible through sex/gender means that either sexual desire or class consciousness is visible at any one given time. So long as the woman was a potential object of his desire, Minpei could not come into class consciousness. Just as sex/gender politics are suppressed by the sexualization of class, sexual desire is also a casualty of the sexualization of class.

What is exceptional about this instance of the troping of a woman's body, however, is the way that the text simultaneously posits an alternative reading in which the woman resists being troped. She resists allowing her body to be used allegorically even while she does not resist its being used physically. In the narrative, the woman asserts her subjectivity and the truth of her experience, although it may be unintelligible to the narrator and perhaps to the reader as well. As for the narrator, he comes into consciousness when he recognizes the woman's "prostitution" as a symbol of an oppressed class. The narrator leaves the reader with this heavy symbolism at the end of the story, and since it is the last and perhaps strongest idea, it becomes the dominant meaning of the story. Nevertheless, throughout the story the woman repeatedly demonstrates that the protagonist's understanding is flawed and partial, thus undermining not only the ending, but the narration of the entire story. The text in effect offers two competing narratives: one in which a man overcomes sexual desire and comes to see a "prostitute" as a symbol of the oppressed class, and one in which a woman affirms her subjectivity and defies her would-be savior because he has completely misrecognized her reality. It is the gap between the two versions that produces a haunting and irreconcilable story about class consciousness and sexual desire. The complexity of the story mirrors the complexity of gender and sex in the socialist movement, almost as though the story stood as yet another allegory.

Notes

1   Translations of "The Prostitute" are mine, based on the first version published in *Bungei sensen* (Literary Front), in November 1925. A very fine English translation by Lawrence Rogers can be found in a forthcoming anthology of Japanese proletarian literature edited by Norma Field and Heather Bowen-Struyk (University of Chicago Press), as well as *Critical Asian Studies* (2004), 35: 1, pp. 143–56.

References

Akagi, K. (December 1925) "Romanchikku bundan no shokō" [A ray of light in the romantic *bundan*], in *Bungei jidai*.

ECD, Kurumisawa, K., Honda, Y. (July 2007) "Puroretarian bungaku no gyakusei" [The counter-attack of proletarian literature], in *Subaru*.

Faison, E. (2007) *Managing Women: Disciplining Labor in Modern Japan*, Berkeley: University of California Press.

Field, N. and Bowen-Struyk, H. (eds) (forthcoming) *For Dignity, Justice, and Revolution: An Anthology of Japanese Proletarian Literature*, Chicago: University of Chicago Press.

Frederick, S. (2006) *Turning Pages: Reading and Writing Women's Magazines in Interwar Japan*, Honolulu: University of Hawai'i Press.

Garon, S. (1987) *The State and Labor in Modern Japan*, Berkeley: University of California Press.

Hayama, Y. (November 1925) "Inbaifu" [The prostitute], in *Bungei sensen*.

——. (January 1926a) "Semento-daru no naka no tegami" [Letter in a cement barrel], in *Bungei sensen*.

——. (August 1926b) "Minato machi no onna" [Harbour town woman], in *Bungei shunjū*; later included in the collection of short stories called *Inbaifu* [The Prostitute] as well as incorporated into *Umi ni ikuru hitobito* [Life on the Sea].

——. (1926c) *Inbaifu* [The prostitute], Tokyo: Shunyōdō.

——. (1926d) *Umi ni ikuru hitobito* [Life on the Sea], Tokyo: Kaizōsha.

——. (1933) *Hayama Yoshiki zenshū* [The complete works of Hayama Yoshiki], Tokyo: Kaizōsha.

——. (1962) "Letter in a Cement Barrel," in I. Morris (ed., trans.), *Modern Japanese Stories: An Anthology*, North Clarendon, VT: Tuttle.

——. (1967) *Umi ni ikuru hitobito* [Life on the Sea], in Takenouchi S. (ed.) *Hayama Yoshiki, Kuroshima Denji, Hirabayashi Taiko shū*. Vol. 56 of *Gendai Nihon bungaku taikei*, Tokyo: Chikuma shōbo.

——. (1976) *Hayama Yoshiki zenshū* [The complete works of Hayama Yoshiki], Tokyo: Chikuma shobō.

——. (2004) "The Prostitute," L. Rogers (trans.), in *Critical Asian Studies* 36: 1.

Hayashi, F., Kobori, J., Maedakō, H., Kaneko, Y., Sano, S., Nakano, S., Kaji, W., Sasaki, T., Yamada, S. (December 1926) "Hayama Yoshiki-ron: sayoku bundan shinsakka-ron 3" [Hayama Yoshiki discussion: discussions of new authors by the leftwing *bundan* 3], in *Bungei sensen*.

Hirabayashi, T. (1967) "Hayama Yoshiki no omoide" [Reminiscences of Hayama Yoshiki], in Takenouchi S. (ed.), *Hayama Yoshiki, Kuroshima Denji, Hirabayashi Taiko shū*, Vol. 56 of *Gendai Nihon bungaku taikei*, Tokyo: Chikuma shobō.

Kishi, Y. (1928–29) *Go, Stop* (Gō, Sutoppu), serialized in *Tokyo Maiyū Shinbun*, republished as a book by Chūō Kōron in 1930.

Kollontai, A. (1977) "Prostitution and Ways of Fighting It," Speech to the third all-Russian conference of heads of the Regional Women's Departments, 1921. *Selected Writings of Alexandra Kollontai*, Allison & Busby, 1977; Translated by Alix Holt. http://www.marxists.org/archive/kollonta/works/1921/prostitution.htm.

Kume, M. *et al.* (March 1926) "*Shinchō* gappyōkai" [*Shinchō* literary discussion], in *Shinchō*.

Mackie, V. (1997) *Creating Socialist Women in Japan: Gender, Labour and Activism, 1900–1937*, Cambridge: Cambridge University Press.

Montefiore, J. (1996) *Men and Women Writers of the 1930s: The Dangerous Flood of History*, London: Routledge.

Nakano, S. (1928) "New Woman" [Atarashii onna], in *Shinchō*, republished in *Puroretaria bungakushū*, Kaizōsha: 1931.

Rabinowitz, P. (1991) *Labor and Desire: Women's Revolutionary Fiction in Depression America*, Chapel Hill, NC: University of North Carolina Press.

Sata, I. (1987) "Crimson," in Y. Tanaka (ed. and trans.), *To Live and To Write*, Washington, DC: The Seal Press.

Shea, G. T. (1964) *Leftwing Literature in Japan: A Brief History of the Proletarian Literary Movement*, Tokyo: Hōsei University Press.

Spivak, G. (1988) "Can the Subaltern Speak?" in C. Nelson and L. Grossberg (eds), *Marxism and the Interpretation of Culture*, Urbana, IL: University of Illinois Press.

Tamanoi, M. A. (1999) "Japanese Nationalism and the Female Body: A Critical Reassessment of the Discourse of Social Reformers of Factory Women," *Women and Class in Japanese History*, H. Tonomura, A. Walthall, and H. Wakita (eds), Ann Arbor, MI: Center for Japanese Studies.

Tokunaga, S. (1929) *The Sunless Street* [Taiyō no nai machi].

Uranishi, K. (1973) *Hayama Yoshiki, kindai bungaku shiryō* 6 [Hayama Yoshiki, modern literature resources], Tokyo: Shashoku sōgō kikaku.

——. 1988 *"Umi ni ikuru hitobito* to *Kani kōsen."* (*Life on the Sea* and *The Factory Ship*). *Nihon bungaku kōza 6: kindai shōsetsu.* Tokyo: Taishūkan shoten.

——. 1994 *Hayama Yoshiki: kōshō to shiryō* (Hayama Yoshiki: investigations and resources). Kokubungaku kenkyū sōsho. Tokyo: Meiji Shoin.

Yamada, S. 1954 *Puroretaria bungakushi – fūsetsu no jidai (gekan)* (The history of proletarian literature: the stormy period, vol. 2). Tokyo: Rironsha.

3 Gender and Korean labour in wartime Japan

Elyssa Faison

The subject of Korean labour in wartime Japan has garnered increased attention since the early 1990s when movements for redress from the Japanese government began to gain momentum. Colonized by the Japanese state from 1910 until 1945, Korea was subject to the most thoroughgoing application of colonial administration and cultural assimilation policies among the various territories that made up the Japanese empire. The demands for redress have come from different segments of Japan's former colonial population who were subject to coerced forms of labour by and for the imperial state. Korean groups have been the most vocal in calling for reparations and formal apologies from the Japanese government, which has steadfastly refused all demands for monetary compensation and official apology. The Korean military sexual slaves ("comfort women," who are discussed in Chunghee Sarah Soh's essay in this volume) drafted to serve the Japanese Imperial Army on the continent and throughout Japan's occupied territories in Asia have gained the most international attention for their efforts to publicize the continuing plight of women whose lives have been shattered by their wartime experience. Lawsuits against the Japanese government have also been filed on behalf of a smaller number of Korean women drafted during the last years of the war to work in Japanese textile factories.[1] Korean men forced to work in Japanese coal mines made up another significant population of labour coerced by the imperial state, and lawsuits demanding apology and reparation for workers in mines run by Mitsui and other companies have similarly gained international attention.[2] In addition to the drafting of Koreans for sexual and industrial labour, the Japanese state also conscripted Koreans into the Japanese Imperial Army by the last years of the war. Although these various forms of state-led forced conscription began in earnest in 1939, the roots of such systems stretch further back into a much longer history of Korean out-migration to the metropole and other areas of the expanding Japanese imperium beginning at the time of the peninsula's formal annexation in 1910.[3]

Instances of women's forced sexual labour and the forced recruitment of men for industrial labour have received the most attention from scholars and the general public in recent years, but the less-remarked-upon recruitment of Korean women and girls for factory work offers another aspect of Japan's military and industrial mobilization for total war. This essay draws on an increasingly large body of literature on Japanese colonialism and on wartime labour mobilization of Koreans to examine policies of women's education and assimilation in Korea, the reliance on a middle-class ideal of womanhood that required such education, and the application of this gendered and class-based ideology to policies of wartime labour mobilization. I argue that gender and class determined to a large degree the political relationship of colonial subjects to the imperial state. Moreover, these relationships were central to the state's methods of recruiting labour for total war mobilization by the time hostilities broke out with China in 1937. Class and educational background had much to do with whether a young Korean woman would be recruited into factory work, or as a military sexual slave.

Beginning in the Meiji period (1868–1912), the state's recognition of Japanese male citizenship focused on men's rights and obligations as household heads, rights of political participation including voting, and military conscription. Japanese women had none of these rights, but were instead recognized by the state according to their ability and willingness to comply with the ideal of good wife and wise mother, a decidedly middle-class notion of feminine roles. This ideal required supporting a husband in his role as household head and in his military and civic duties to the state, and in raising children to be educated and obedient imperial subjects capable of reproducing the gendered norms into which they were raised. In order to promote stability and acquiescence to Japanese rule within colonized Korea, colonial administrators and the Japanese government applied versions of these norms of male and female citizenship in their promotion of cultural assimilation. The precise nature of what they deemed appropriate Korean manhood and womanhood was negotiated according to the state's need for labour and for avoiding social unrest in the colony.

The Japanese state, unlike Western imperialist powers of the time, legitimized its colonial rule of Korea by arguing for "oneness." The slogan "*naisen ittai*," or "Japan and Korea as one," encapsulated this demand for unity just as a host of other concepts (*dōbun dōshū* or "same script, same race"; *isshi dōjin* or "impartiality and universal benevolence"; and *kazoku kokka* or "family state") emphasized cultural and familial bonds between the two peoples (Meyers 1984: 97). But by the late 1930s the ideological use of these calls for oneness sometimes clashed with the military and economic realities of a country engaged in total war. This dissonance between the legitimating rhetoric of a colonial power and the practical necessities of mobilizing labour and populations limited the possibilities of integrating Koreans into Japan's labour force. In some cases, as with the conscription of Korean men for military service, the rhetoric dovetailed with state needs and allowed a colonized population to be mobilized as patriotic subjects. That is, ideals of male citizenship included the right and obligation of military service, making military conscription for Korean men consonant with the aims of assimilation. In other cases, like the attempts to recruit Korean women to work in Japanese factories, long-term indoctrination into the ideology of "good wife, wise mother" ultimately hampered Japanese efforts to mobilize a population taught that domestic work was the only appropriate option. Only the small minority of Korean women and girls who received an education in Japanese-run "national schools" (*kokumin gakkō*) were seen as having the qualifications for work in factories in Japan, and it was simultaneously only these girls who could be considered potential "good wives and wise mothers." In contrast, Korean women from poor families with little education (and usually even less Japanese acculturation) found themselves outside the scope of any prevailing definitions of "womanhood" in both Korean and Japanese societies. This marginalized (but numerically large) group was the most likely to be forced to work as military sex slaves in comfort stations, as the possibility of factory work in Japan was not open to them.

Prewar Korean labour and labour mobilization in Japan

Taiwan and Korea became Japan's first colonial possessions in 1895 and 1910 respectively, and remained the centerpieces of Japanese colonial administration until the end of the war in 1945. Because of its geographical proximity to the Japanese islands, the perception of a shared history and culture with Japan (see Oguma 1995), and its agricultural and labour resources, Korea emerged by 1920 as the most important and visible part of the Japanese empire, both domestically and to foreign observers. The slogan *gozoku kyōwa*, or "harmony of the five races," gave Koreans the privilege of second place in the empire's racial hierarchy after the Japanese (followed by Chinese, Manchurians, and Mongolians). But despite this status among Japan's colonial territories, growing poverty in colonized Korea – especially among the tenant farmer class – led to steady increases in out-migration, with Japan receiving the largest number of Korean immigrants. In 1925 Japan's Korean population was in the vicinity of 150,000. In 1936, on the eve of war with China, that number had increased to around 800,000. By the time the war ended in 1945, continued financial desperation coupled with Japanese state policies of forced labour recruitment for the purpose of increasing war production resulted in Japan's resident Korean population booming to well over two million (Weiner 1994: 122, 198). Most of these immigrants were men, and until the last years of the war, labour recruitment of Koreans to Japan was voluntary, at least in the sense that there was no draft or legal requisitioning of workers.

A 1936 survey of Koreans living in the greater Tokyo metropolitan area found that most of the nearly 3,700 respondents (out of a total population of almost 40,000 Koreans living in the region) indicated that they found working in Japan preferable to staying in Korea, primarily because of the greater ease of finding jobs and the higher wages paid in Japan compared to back home (Nakagawa 1994: 182–83). Colonial agricultural policies had resulted in such dire conditions for rural families in Korea's southern provinces that immigration continued to be seen as a viable option through the early 1940s. In fact, a Japanese recruiter looking to hire 200 Korean men in 1942 found twice as many applicants for positions in the hard-hit regions of Chŏllanam and Kyŏngsangbuk provinces, where farming families suffered under rice requisition policies that forced them to give up even the agricultural products needed to sustain their families. Likewise, recruiters for Yawata Steel Works in Fukuoka prefecture in Japan easily recruited 130 men from the 180 applications they received from Kyŏngsangnam province. In a survey of some of the applicants, many said they wanted to work in Japan even though they realized there would be little food even there, because they believed that at least there would be *some* distribution of food, which would be better than staying in Korea and starving. Still other applicants observed that since they could not sustain their household economy as things were, they were willing to try going anywhere to see if things might be better (Yamada *et al.* 2005: 141). These motivations for "voluntarily" taking work in Japan indicate that the real choices for Koreans were limited, and that family survival often dictated decisions involving emigration.

While Korean immigration to Japan still made up only a small fraction of the country's total population, Japan's domestic population increased by more than 13 per cent between 1930 and 1940 from over 64 million to over 73 million largely due to government-led efforts to increase birth rates for the sake of expanding the labour pool. In terms of the workforce, those same years saw an explosion of nearly 600 per cent in the size of the military (for a total of just under 1.7 million in the armed forces), and substantial increases in the numbers of workers involved in heavy industries and war-related industries such as mining (89.2 per cent) and manufacturing and construction (38.4 per cent) – all male-dominated jobs. In contrast, the total number of workers engaged in agriculture, fishing, and domestic service declined (by 2 per cent, 4.4 per cent, and 11.6 per cent respectively). It is likely that many of the men in these occupations moved into industrial and military service, and many of the women engaged in domestic service left those jobs to fill the gap left by men in agriculture. Many women engaged in agriculture only on a part-time basis, and their numbers were not large enough to offset the losses by men who left the fields for other types of work (United States Strategic Bombing Survey 1947: 48–49).

A similar pattern emerged in Korea, where the Government General (the Japanese colonial administration in the colony) encouraged and facilitated the use of cooperative childcare facilities so that women could take over the agricultural work of men whose labour had been requisitioned for war production (Higuchi 2005: 58). As with Japanese women, Korean women's mobilization was predicated on a middle-class notion of womanhood based on the ideal of "good wife, wise mother" promoted by the state. This set of ideas about the proper roles of women within the family also suggested that women could best serve the state in the domestic sphere. This does not mean that the state believed that most women would fall into this category of women competent to manage households configured as nuclear families with a male bread-winner cum household head; however, the policies regarding women's labour were predicated on this ideal. Promotion of these ideas prevented more aggressive labour mobilization of women who had the educational background to potentially fulfil the ideal of domestic womanhood.

Korean education and labour mobilization

Mobilizing women in Korea – as workers and as loyal imperial subjects – was a much more fraught and contradictory process for the Japanese state than was the mobilization of Korean men. This is not to say that the mobilization of Korean men took place with ease or without an abundance of complex negotiations over the meanings, rights, and obligations of subjecthood for men – as became particularly apparent when a shortage of manpower in the armed forces made it both possible and necessary for Koreans to be first admitted voluntarily and later conscripted for service in the Japanese Imperial Army. But men were expected to hold jobs outside the domestic realm. For men, there was no contradiction between fulfilling their social role as household head and serving the state. For women, on the other hand, a complex calculus that considered age, marital status, and educational level determined how, when, whether, and what kind of labour mobilization the Japanese state might impose. This calculus did not preclude the state from recruiting women of all classes and educational backgrounds as comfort women, but it did define the requirements for recruitment into factory labour within the main Japanese islands.

While violent coercion was certainly used in the mobilization of both male and female labour, especially and overwhelmingly during the final years of the war, no colonial power, including Japan, has ever mobilized its subject peoples exclusively through violence. Indeed, the Japanese imperial state marshalled a vast array of ideological tools with which to foster cooperation among all its colonized populations. Central to this ideological mobilization, in Japan as well as in Korea, were educational institutions. Education played a critical role not only in attempts to inculcate patriotism and loyalty, but also in shaping and at times circumscribing the possibilities of legal and forced capitulation to the needs of the state. In Korea, state-sponsored education was based on the strategy of *kōminka*, or "making imperial subjects." *Kōminka* efforts in Korea intensified beginning in 1937 after the outbreak of war with China, and included efforts as diverse as religious reform aimed at involving Koreans in Shinto practices and emperor worship; the "national language" movement, which culminated in the complete removal of Korean language study from school curricula in 1941 in favour of all-Japanese language instruction; and changes in the family registration system beginning in 1940 that promoted the adoption of Japanese names by Koreans (Chou 1996).

The policy of *kōminka* began officially in October of 1937, when the Korean Government General required the recitation of the "Oath of Imperial Subjects" at all public gatherings in Korea (Chou 1996: 43). This made the oath part of the daily activities of schools, and for Korean schoolchildren pledging the oath was roughly analogous to the daily recitation of the Imperial Rescript on Education by schoolchildren in Japan. But where the Rescript asked Japanese children to remember that the "Imperial Ancestors have founded Our Empire on a basis broad and everlasting," and that it was their duty to "render illustrious the best traditions of your forefathers" (translated in Lu 1997: 343), Koreans were admonished in the much shorter Oath (which was written in two versions: one for adults, and a simpler text for children) to remember their duties as imperial subjects – a status the Government General rightly feared might be forgotten, ignored, or rejected without constant indoctrination. The Oath of Imperial Subjects read in its entirety:

1   We are the subjects of the imperial state; we will repay the emperor and the country with loyalty.

2   We, the subjects of the imperial state, will love each other and work together in order to strengthen our unity.
3   We, the subjects of the imperial state, will cultivate stoicism, discipline, and strength so that we may exalt the imperial way.[4]

Among the Korean population, children who attended school on a regular basis would have the most exposure to the oath, as well as many other aspects of *kōminka's* assimilationist programs like the teaching and use of the "national language" (Japanese).

In the early years of colonization, the Government General took a heavy-handed approach to reforming the Korean school system, creating in 1911 a classification of common, industrial, and specialized schools, and mandating four years of elementary education and then four years of higher school for boys and three for girls. Large numbers of Christian mission schools, which had done so much to promote female education in the late nineteenth and early twentieth centuries, shut their doors or scaled back their operations in the wake of ordinances standardizing a rigid curriculum and restricting religious education. With the closure of many of these mission schools, the dearth of other Korean-run schools, and the inability or lack of will on the part of the Government General to open more than a small number of public secondary schools, not even 4 per cent of Korean school-aged children attended public school in 1919. Even after more rigorous efforts to reform education policies were put in place following the failed 1919 Korean independence movement, literacy rates, especially for women, remained extremely low (Yoo 2008: 61–64). In 1942 school attendance rates for Korean girls hovered around 33 per cent, and despite much-publicized policies to enforce Japanese-language education and usage, only 8 per cent of Korean women had even a rudimentary ability in Japanese by the end of 1941 (Higuchi 2005: 56).

Weak and underdeveloped though these assimilationist education policies may have been, they were mirrored by labour mobilization policies that took into consideration – especially in the period before total war mobilization began – the national and gender ideologies that *kōminka* espoused. The modernizing reforms the Japanese state had put into place itself, and then first promoted and later demanded for Korea, included new visions of womanhood that placed women squarely in the domestic realm, charging them with the maintenance of the household, while making the household the basic unit of state control. The good wife, wise mother ideology was new in the way it demanded women be educated in order to manage household finances and to raise children loyal and obedient to both the family patriarch and the imperial state embodied by the emperor. But unlike the New Woman of the post World War I-era who flaunted conventions, practiced free love, wore Western styles, aspired to occupations other than wife and mother, and refused to conform to state demands for legible and stable family units (Silverberg 1991, Sato 2003), the image of the good wife and wise mother contained elements that could be linked to less Western and more "traditional" ideas about womanhood and family.

Some male Korean intellectuals, in fact, eventually found this more conservative aspect of the state-sponsored good wife, wise mother ideology useful in trying to assert a true "Korean" womanhood. They saw authentic Korean womanhood as under assault by Western and Japanese colonialist policies as well as by the new women and modern girls who had become conspicuous on city streets and in the press by the 1920s. As Insook Kwon has explained, "Under colonialism, male nationalists thought that the New Women's direct denial of existing patriarchy and sexual morality might cause the collapse of Korean tradition and solidarity" (Kwon 1998: 395). Other male Korean intellectuals such as Cho Kakuchu, who had earlier extolled the virtues of plain-spoken Korean women as compared to their indecisive Japanese counterparts, in the 1940s rushed to praise the demure and loyal good wife of Japan, and hoped Korean women could become more like her (Fujitani, forthcoming).

This turn by Korean male intellectuals away from alliances with Korean women (as Koreans) and towards ideological alliances with Japanese male colonizers (as men) by the 1940s had the effect of binding colonial policy even more firmly to conservative visions of womanhood and the family – visions that not only offered a strategy for fostering loyalty and control through the family unit, but now also promised support from Korean male elites. The result was that during wartime the Japanese state could only mobilize women's labour within the parameters of the gender ideology they had so carefully promoted.

National mobilization and forced recruitment

Within Japan, the National General Mobilization Law (*Kokka sōdōin hō*) of 1939 ushered in a series of ordinances aimed at restricting labour mobility and allowing the state and industry to more directly regulate placement through a worker registration system (Gordon 1985: 266–72). The ability of the state to mobilize Japanese women for labour purposes was limited by the same rhetoric that had helped mobilize them for patriotic duty to the state as wives and mothers, and by a pronatalist agenda spurred by labour shortages. Although the Citizen's Labour Patriotic Cooperation Order of 1941 required thirty days of labour service per year from unmarried women aged fourteen to twenty-five, enforcement of this provision was lax. State officials worried more about how to protect women's "special characteristics" (as future mothers) than about resolving the immediate labour shortages by staffing factories with women (Faison 2007: 142–45).

The Korean Government General had similar difficulties mobilizing Korean women's labour, precisely because these same gendered ideologies about women's place in the family disallowed a reading of women as "labour." But as the war dragged on and Japan's manpower and material resources reached a breaking point, the state issued the Girls' Service Voluntary Labour Act (*Joshi Kinrō Teishin Kinrō Rei*) in August 1944, thus systematizing a series of smaller ordinances from 1943 and 1944 that had sought to mobilize unmarried elementary school graduates of at least fourteen years of age, whose labour was not necessary for their family's household economy. The Girls' Service Voluntary Labour Act went into effect in Korea at the same time as Japan (Yamada *et al.* 2005: 148–49). Regional organization of Girls' Labour Volunteer Corps took place across Korea. Even though the Korean Government General undertook surveys identifying "surplus" labour among Korea's smallholding farm families whose production levels were low, it did not make great efforts to mobilize female surplus labour outside of the agricultural contexts in which the women already lived. Thus, Korean women under wartime mobilization rules, like their Japanese counterparts, were more often used to replace conscripted male agricultural labour in their home areas. The historian Higuchi Yūichi, who has conducted some of the most detailed studies of Korean wartime labour mobilization, gives six main reasons for the Government General's reticence in aggressively conscripting female Korean labour (Higuchi 2005: 64–65):

1   There were few factories that could employ women in the southern Korean provinces in which the majority of the "surplus" labour existed.
2   Most of the rural women identified as surplus were married and had households, and thus could not be separated from those households to be sent to far-off factories.
3   Because most of these women had not received formal schooling or worker training, they could not easily transition into an efficient wartime labour force.
4   Most of these rural women had extremely limited Japanese language abilities.
5   Both men and women would resist the idea of women's labour outside of the context of household or agricultural labour, in large part because of strong Confucian traditions of women being in the home.
6   The types of labour that were most needed by the wartime state included mining, construction, and factory workers, and other kinds of heavy labour that were deemed unsuitable for women.

Thus, Korean women did not fit neatly into the patterns of forced labour recruitment from the peninsula that began in 1939 with the application to Korea of the National General Labour Mobilization Law.

The patterns of this wartime forced labour recruitment have been well documented. The Japanese state articulated three consecutive systems of labour conscription beginning with a policy of recruitment (*boshū*), which lasted from 1939 to 1942. This first stage of recruitment involved representatives from private Japanese companies travelling to areas in Korea designated by the Korean Government General to recruit workers for mining and construction from among the economically desperate populations of regions hardest hit by Japan's colonial agricultural policies. The next stage of "official mediation" (*kan assen*) replaced the "voluntary recruitment" strategy early in 1942 and lasted until 1944. In this second phase, the Korean Labour Association (*Chōsen Rōmu Kyōkai*), a state-supported organization operated by Koreans but sponsored by the Government General, undertook the recruitment, organization, and placement of workers from Korea who would be sent to companies in Japan. The final stage, in place from

September 1944 until the end of the war, consisted of a labour draft (*chōyō*), which extended the application of the National Conscription Law from only those workers in war-related industries, to workers in all industries (Weiner 1994: 196, Naitou 2005: 93, Matsumura 2007: 73–93).

While these labour mobilization policies affected mostly men, nearly half of whom were drafted in the final years of the war and ended up working in Japanese coal mines, the Girls' Service Voluntary Labour Act did result in some notable recruitment of groups of educated, unmarried girls for work in Japanese factories. Among the larger mobilizations of the Girls' Labour Volunteer Corps was a contingent of 150 girls gathered in Korea's Kyŏnggi Province (which included the provincial capital of Seoul) who set out for work at Japan's Fujikoshi Company in early 1945. The Fujikoshi Company of Toyama Prefecture specialized in machine tools, and became a significant supplier for Japan's military efforts in the 1930s. Founded in 1928, the company employed a mere 166 workers in 1933, thirty of whom were women. By 1935 Fujikoshi had experienced enough growth to expand and specialize its operations, and it pioneered the use of a specialized division of female workers. These women workers, Fujikoshi found, were extremely adept at product inspection, metal tempering, and thread cutting (of screws). As the company grew, particularly with government support during the war, the number of factory workers it employed grew exponentially, and women made up an increasingly large proportion of those workers. In 1941 Fujikoshi employed 11,523 workers, 26 per cent of whom were women, and by 1945 the number of employees reached 31,245 with women comprising 36 per cent of this total (Fujikoshi Kōzai Kabushiki Kaisha 1953: 194–96; see also Kim 2007: 93–95).

When the group of 150 members of the Korean Girls' Labour Volunteer Corps arrived in Toyama, they were placed in a six-month training course in which they were to learn about "the spirit of Japan and Korea as one"; "the spirit of imperial women's labour service"; and "the spirit of Fujikoshi work." After the first month of group training sessions that focused on "the woman of the imperial nation," the recruits had instruction on "daily life" along with technical work training (Yamada *et al.* 2005: 165–66). The company expressed delight that the work of these Korean Girls' Labour Volunteer Corps members was equal to that of Japanese girls, and that many of them finished their six-month training course in little more than three months. But at the same time it acknowledged that immediately upon the group's arrival in Toyama, three of the girls ran away and deserted (Fujikoshi Kōzai Kabushiki Kaisha 1953: 201). While Fujikoshi officials were quick to point out that soon after the desertion labour-relations involving the Korean recruits reached a "harmonious" equilibrium, the escape signals the coerced nature of the Girls' Labour Volunteer Corps.

From testimony gathered from former Korean female labour recruits at Fujikoshi, a number of whom brought a lawsuit against the company for employing them as forced labour and failing to pay wages (the lawsuit was dismissed due to a statute of limitations technicality and finally settled out of court in 2000), we have some indication of the conditions under which these girls were recruited. The historians Yamada Shōji, Higuchi Yūichi, and Koshō Tadashi have compiled data gathered from interviews, court proceedings, and secondary literature on thirty-seven Korean girls recruited into the Girls' Labour Volunteer Corps between February 1943 and March 1945 for whom detailed information about age, region, place and method of recruitment, and eventual place of work exists. Six of these recruits went to work for the Tokyo Asaito Textile Company, twenty-two were employed by Fujikoshi in Toyama, eight worked for the Mitsubishi Heavy Industries Nagoya Airplane Factory, and one was sent to the Kanegafuchi Spinning textile company. The recruits ranged in age from twelve to sixteen, though most were thirteen, fourteen or fifteen at the time of mobilization (Yamada *et al.* 2005: 179–80).

The girls in these studies reported various reasons for going to work in factories in Japan. A teacher or other school official recruited 75 per cent of the girls, while a government official, a representative of the National General Labour Mobilization Korean League, or a company representative recruited the rest. The vast majority of women in this sample (nearly 84 per cent) were convinced to go because of promises or threats. These included promises of abundant food, opportunities for continued education and the chance to make good wages; threats that if they did not volunteer some other family member would be drafted in their place; and appeals to their sense of national duty. Only two girls in this sample actually received call-up orders from the Government General (Yamada *et al.* 2005: 149–59). A fear of reprisals from teachers mixed with the promise of continuing their studies made these forms of coercion appear voluntary in some aspects, but the intense pressure put on school teachers to force girls to volunteer, coupled with their young age, made any claims of voluntarism or agency on the part of recruits no more than rhetorical.

The girls recruited into the Girls' Labour Volunteer Corps had been studying in "national schools" and learning the Japanese language. They received this education at a time when 92 per cent of Korean women remained unable to use Japanese, and most did not or had not attended school. This suggests that only a minority of Korean girls, probably from middle-class families, were qualified according to the needs of Japanese industries to become recruits. It was also only girls and women from families with such educational opportunities that could hope to live up to the Japanese and Korean nationalist-supported ideal of good wife, wise mother. This made large numbers of women and girls from poorer families subject to different modalities of mobilization, making many of them vulnerable to recruitment as comfort women.

The policies of the imperial state defined national belonging in Korea according to degree of assimilation – a measure already determined by gender and by class. That is, imperial subjecthood meant for all Koreans by 1940 the ability to speak Japanese and to have a Japanese name, even though the majority of Koreans did not meet this standard even by the end of the war. For women it additionally meant inculcation in the ideals of good wife, wise mother, which in turn required the proper education to manage a household and raise the next generation as loyal imperial subjects. For men, it meant loyalty to the state and to the emperor in the form of labour service, and after 1938, military service. Examining the recruitment of Korean comfort women and Korean imperial soldiers allows us to see more clearly how these issues of class and gender determined Koreans' relationship to the state, and thus the types of violence, coercion and labour to which they might be subject.

Comfort women and Korean imperial soldiers

The first "comfort stations" – brothels set up for the sexual gratification of Japanese imperial soldiers and sailors – were opened in 1932 following the expansion of Japanese military activity on mainland China following the Manchurian Incident (1931) and the subsequent fighting between Japanese and Chinese forces in Shanghai that came to be known as the First Shanghai Incident. Early women recruits in these comfort stations came from Japan and included Koreans resident in Japan. But after the violence that followed Japan's 1937 military takeover of the Chinese Nationalist capital of Nanjing, known as the Nanjing Massacre or the Rape of Nanjing because of the hundreds of thousands reported butchered or raped by invading Japanese forces, the number of comfort stations throughout China increased dramatically and their establishment became more systematized. For the Japanese military, it was believed that the system of comfort stations might prevent the rape of local civilian populations, stem the spread of venereal disease among soldiers, and thwart the spying efforts of Chinese guerillas seeking to gain access to military information through the unregulated liaisons of Japanese soldiers and Chinese women (Tanaka 2002, Yoshimi 2000).

By the end of the war the comfort woman system had grown to include between 200,000 and 300,000 women, most of them Koreans brought to China for the front line troops. Recruitment of comfort women was coercive, often involving lies by labour brokers who would promise young women and girls high-wage jobs in Japan before taking them to comfort stations in China, Singapore or Borneo. Comfort women were not prostitutes because they did not enter into sex work voluntarily, and they very rarely received wages other than the worthless tickets that soldiers would hand to them as "payment" for services rendered.

The promise of factory jobs offered as part of mobilization into the Girls' Labour Volunteer Corps also became one of the recruitment tactics of labour brokers sent to Korea to procure comfort women for the troops. The complexities of the class dynamics at play in the recruitment of Korean girls and women as comfort women, and as members of the Girls' Labour Volunteer Corps, becomes clear in this passage from the historian Yuki Tanaka:

> It was shortly after August 1944, when the Women's Voluntary Labour Service Law was enacted, that a rumour spread in Korea that all unmarried girls over fourteen years old would be forced to become comfort women. Many middle-class and upper-class Korean families withdrew their daughters from women's colleges and hurriedly arranged marriages for them to avoid their being drafted. However, some families from the lower strata felt trapped. For example, in September 1944, a girl called Kim T'aeson, who was then nineteen years old and living with her uncle, was hiding in an attic of his

house. One day when she came out of the attic and was having a meal down-stairs, a Japanese man with a Korean partner visited the house, and offered her a "job" in Japan. Thinking that work in Japan would be a far better option than becoming a comfort woman, she accepted their offer. She ended up in a comfort station in Burma.

(Tanaka 2002: 41–42)

We do not know from this passage what kind of education Kim T'aeson had before her recruitment, or how well she met the criteria of potential good wife, wise mother and ideal female imperial subject. But what seems clear from her story and from what we have learned of the girls who were ultimately recruited for factory jobs in Japan is that education and evidence of assimilation that could only be attained by middle- and upper-class Koreans were required for recruitment into such factory work. This qualification, however, might not necessarily preclude one from being drafted as a comfort woman.

While for Korean women national belonging as national service was measured by an ability to play the role of good wife and wise mother, for Korean men a key measure of belonging was the ability and willingness to render military service – even though such service did not become possible for them until 1938. Military conscription for Japanese men began in 1872, and was central to the government's efforts to define an official version of manhood, "in which a soldier was part of a military institution created by and embodying the state, at the command of the emperor" (Cook 2005: 271–72). After the passage of the Universal Suffrage Law in 1925, the rights and duties of Japanese men included heading a household and participating in the parliamentary process by voting in national and local elections, in addition to military service. (Despite the term "universal" in the name of the law, women did not get the vote in Japan until after the war.) Belying the rhetoric of oneness embodied in the slogan *naisen ittai*, Korean men had none of these rights and duties except that of heading a household. The same suffrage law that allowed most Japanese men to vote had also nominally enfranchised Korean men living in Japan, but residency and other requirements meant that few Koreans in the metropole could qualify to exercise this right, and Koreans living on the peninsula had no voting rights or representation in the Imperial Diet at all.

Projecting increased needs for military personnel after the war with China began, the Japanese state allowed Koreans to enlist in the army voluntarily beginning in 1938. As in the case of mobilized women workers, Japanese authorities hoped to attract military volunteers who had received sufficient *kōminka* education to be able to speak and understand the Japanese language, work in a majority Japanese context, and demonstrate loyalty to the emperor and the imperial state. Beginning in August 1943, the intensification of the war and Japan's desperate need for soldiers as well as labourers resulted in the promulgation of the Military Service Law, which extended military conscription to Korean men. By the end of the war over 200,000 Koreans had served in the Japanese imperial armed forces, the vast majority of them as conscripts (Fujitani 2007: 17), and a number of them were ultimately tried as war criminals by the Allies because of their involvement in running POW camps

(Utsumi 2001). Unlike minority soldiers and sailors in the American armed forces during World War II, Korean soldiers were not segregated into separate units, but rather were dispersed throughout majority Japanese units. While racism existed in both contexts, the United States government had no formal policy or even state discourse of equality regarding Japanese Americans, thousands of whom were relocated from the West Coast to detention camps by government decree after the attack on Pearl Harbor, as part of state and popular paranoia that all Japanese residents and their American-born children were or could be activated as agents of the enemy Japanese Empire. Many of the soldiers who made up the segregated Japanese American units came from these camps, either as volunteers or as conscripts. In contrast, the Japanese state had long promoted a rhetoric of assimilation, asserting that while Koreans might not be equal to Japanese, they were still full-fledged imperial subjects. This acceptance of Koreans as imperial subjects may account for the lack of segregated units in the Imperial Army. Still, racism and discrimination against Koreans in the military were manifest in other ways. Military authorities stipulated that up to 80 per cent of Koreans could serve in rear support units such as field hospitals and facilities set up for the internment of prisoners, while only 20 per cent could hold front-line combat duties (Utsumi 2005: 81).

Military service thus followed in pattern if not in exact chronology the stages of labour recruitment for Koreans in other forms of work; namely, a period of less coercive "voluntary" service (though none of the periods under discussion involved only uncoerced, truly voluntary recruitment), followed by more formal systems of conscription. It also relied, especially in the earlier phase, on appeals to a sense of belonging in the nation, and a sense of loyalty to the emperor and the state. As historian Takashi Fujitani has trenchantly observed, "the more the Japanese empire came to depend upon the Korean population for soldiers and sailors, the more difficult it became to exclude them from the nation" (Fujitani 2007: 17). It became so difficult, Fujitani notes, that in April 1945 the national Diet passed a law allowing "male imperial subjects residing in Korea and Taiwan, twenty-five years of age and older, and who also paid a minimum of fifteen yen in direct national taxes, [to] vote in elections for representatives to the Diet's Lower House" (Fujitani 2007: 19). Although the war came to an end before this law could go into effect, it indicates the way a gendered notion of male imperial subjecthood created powerful rhetorics of inclusion in the colonies as well. This idea of male imperial subjecthood was formulated by the state with metropolitan (Japanese) men in mind, assuming a male subject with the attendant rights and duties of household headship, political participation and representation, and military service. Labour conscription and military conscription in Korea could not be put into effect or understood outside the context of the gendered and classed ideas of imperial subjecthood promoted through *kōminka* education.

Conclusion

Total war mobilization involved not so much new strategies for labour recruitment, but an intensification of recruitment patterns that had been used since the early years of Korean colonization. Approximately 670,000 Koreans were mobilized to work in Japan during the period from 1939 to 1945 in which the National Mobilization Law was in effect (Yamada *et al.* 2005: 69–71, 266). This number does not include the 200,000–300,000 Korean women drafted as comfort women, or the over 200,000 Korean men who served in the Japanese military. Many of the jobs in Japanese factories required workers who understood enough Japanese to be managed by Japanese supervisors, and who had been instilled with enough of the *kōminka* ideology at least to understand (if not accept) the arguments that all subjects of the imperial Japanese state should work for its benefit for the greater glory of the emperor, and should understand the Japanese to be liberators of Asia from the yoke of Western imperialist tyranny. Those who did not have such education were more likely to end up working in a military brothel or underground in the deplorable conditions of Japan's coalmines.

Education was also central to an ideology of womanhood that promoted a home-centered ideal emphasizing household management skills and the raising of children loyal to the imperial state. This ideal limited the ways the state could mobilize female labour in the wake of the acute labour shortages of the early 1940s. By promoting a domestic ideal for women in Korea – an ideal supported by conservative male Korean intellectuals – the Japanese state could only explicitly recruit young unmarried girls who, it was argued, would only be doing temporary work for the good of the nation and who would later be able to return to domestic life, marriage, and household management.[5] Thus, girls from middle-class families who had some education and who could potentially fulfil the goals of good wife, wise mother after their labour service had ended were the only ones eligible for recruitment into factory work in Japan. This was often coercive and unremunerated work, but it was work unavailable to many poorer, uneducated Korean girls and women who were more likely to be recruited as comfort women for the imperial armed forces.

The language used to speak of women and girls drafted for sexual labour and for industrial labour had by the 1940s converged, such that the term *chŏngsindae* (*teishintai* in Japanese), meaning "voluntary labour corps," was used to refer to both kinds of service, though when applied to recruitment as a military comfort woman, the term was used as a euphemism.[6] Such euphemistic usage continues and has in fact intensified in recent years, with *chŏngsindae* generally used in Korean media and scholarship to refer to former military comfort women, thus erasing the experience of mobilized factory work. Of course the term "comfort woman" (*wianbu* in Korean, *ianfu* in Japanese) is also a euphemism, but one that is still used today in Korea (though no longer in Japan) to refer to women currently engaged in military sexual labour. Since the 1950s such labour has serviced US military personnel in the camp towns around American bases in South Korea rather than Japanese forces. This continued use of "comfort woman" to designate a contemporary manifestation of military sex work required that a different term be used to refer to the forced military sexual labour organized by the Japanese during the Asia–Pacific War.[7] The use of *chŏngsindae* in this way points to the long history of the interplay between industrial work and sex work for women in

Korea and Japan, both in real terms and in the popular imagination. But it also erases the experience of wartime female factory conscripts in favour of a narrative that more viscerally points to the victimization of the Korean people at the hands of Japanese imperialists.

Examining the Japanese state's recruitment policies for female industrial workers from Korea in the context of other forms of wartime labour mobilization suggests that gendered notions of belonging to the imperial state framed the possibilities for such recruitment. The ideologies of assimilation and of ideal domestic womanhood combined to inhibit the state's ability to recruit large numbers of women for factory work, even as the demands of total war required a larger industrial workforce.

Notes

1   A useful website hosted by George Washington University lists the status of lawsuits brought against the Japanese government on behalf of women and men from Korea and China who have alleged coercion and non-payment of wages related to their work for the Japanese state and Japanese companies during the war. The site also lists various suits brought on behalf of comfort women. See *Memory and Reconciliation in the Asia-Pacific*, http://www.gwu.edu/~memory/data/judicial/index.html (accessed September 9, 2008).
2   Korean women laboured underground alongside men (often their husbands) during the early period of Korean labour recruitment in Japanese coal mines, but six years prior to the forced recruitment of Korean mine workers that began in 1939, women miners had been legally banned from underground work. See Smith (1999: Ch. 3).
3   Out-migration from Korea to the Japanese metropole increased steadily from the time of annexation until the late 1920s, at which time Japanese restrictions on immigration to the home islands shifted the flow of Korean workers to Manchuria (Brooks 1998).
4   This is the adult version of the oath, as translated by the author.
5   Janice Kim (2007) has suggested that women drafted into the Girls' Labour Volunteer Corps for factory work in Japan may have been more likely to break with gender norms by continuing to work in wage-paying jobs after the war.
6   Indeed, the word "voluntary" was also used euphemistically whether applied to industrial or sexual labour service. Janice Kim (2007) emphasizes that originally the term *chŏngsindae* was only meant to apply to women mobilized under the Girls' Service Voluntary Labour Act for factory work.
7   Both Hyunah Yang (1998) and Chunghee Sarah Soh (in her essay in this volume) make this point.

References

Brooks, B.J. (1998) "Peopling the Japanese Empire: The Koreans in Manchuria and the Rhetoric of Inclusion," in S.A. Minichiello (ed.) *Competing Japanese Modernities*. Honolulu: University of Hawai'i Press, pp. 25–44.

Chou, W.Y. (1996) "The Kominka Movement in Taiwan and Korea: Comparisons and Interpretations," in P. Duus, R. H. Myers and M. R. Peattie (eds) *The Japanese Wartime Empire, 1931–1945*, Princeton, NJ: Princeton University Press, pp. 40–68.

Cook, T.F. (2005) "Making 'Soldiers': The Imperial Army and the Japanese Man in Meiji Society and State," in B. Molony and K. Uno (eds) *Gendering Modern Japanese History*, Cambridge, MA: Harvard University Asia Center, pp. 259–94.

Faison, E. (2007) *Managing Women: Disciplining Labor in Modern Japan*, Berkeley: University of California Press.

Fujikoshi Kōzai Kabushiki Kaisha (1953). *Fujikoshi nijūgonen* [The twenty-five year history of Fujikoshi], Tōyama: Fujikoshi Kōzai Kabushiki Kaisha.

Fujitani, T. (2007) "Right to Kill, Right to Make Live: Koreans as Japanese and Japanese as Americans During WWII," *Representations* 99 (Summer): 13–39.

—— (forthcoming) *Racism under Fire: Koreans as Japanese and Japanese as Americans in WWII* (tentative title).

Gordon, A. (1985) *The Evolution of Labor Relations in Japan: Heavy Industry, 1853–1955*, Cambridge, MA: Harvard Council on East Asian Studies.

Higuchi, Y. (2005) "Senjika Chōsen ni okeru josei dōin" [The mobilization of women in wartime Korea] in Hayakawa N. (ed.) *Shokuminchi to sensō sekinin* [The colonies and war responsibility], Tokyo: Yoshikawa Kōbunkan.

—— (2001) *Senjika Chōsen no minshū to chōhei* [The masses and conscription in wartime Korea], Tokyo: Sōwasha.

Kim, J.C.H. (2007) "The Pacific War and Working Women in Late Colonial Korea," in *Signs* 33, 1: 81–103.

Kwon, I. (1998) "'The New Women's Movement' in 1920s Korea: Rethinking the Relationship Between Imperialism and Women," in *Gender and History* 10 (November 1998) 3: 381–405.

Lu, D.J. (1997) *Japan: A Documentary History*, Armonk, NY: M.E. Sharpe.

Matsumura T. (2007) *Nihon teikoku shugika no shokuminchi rōdōshi* [A history of colonial labour in imperial Japan], Tokyo: Fuji shuppan.

Memory and Reconciliation in the Asia-Pacific, http://www.gwu.edu/~memory/data/judicial/index.html (accessed September 9, 2008).

Meyers, R. (1984) "Japanese Attitudes Towards Colonialism, 1895–1945," in R. Myers and M. Peattie (eds) *The Japanese Colonial Empire, 1895–1945*, Princeton, NJ: Princeton University Press.

Naitou H. (2005) "Korean Forced Labor in Japan's Wartime Empire," in P. H. Kratoska (ed.) *Asian Labor in the Wartime Japanese Empire: Unknown Histories*, Armonk, NY: M.E. Sharpe.

Nakagawa K. (ed.) (1994) *Rōdōsha seikatsu chōsa shiryō shūsei I: Jōyō rōdōsha* [Collected documents on the daily life of workers I: daily labourers], Tokyo: Seishisha.

Oguma, E. (1995) *Tan'itsu minzoku shinwa no kigen: "Nihonjin" no jigazō no keifu = The myth of the homogeneous nation*, Tokyo: Shinyōsha.

Sato, B.H. (2003) *The New Japanese Woman: Modernity, Media, and Women in Interwar Japan*, Durham, NC: Duke University Press.

Silverberg, M. (1991) "The Modern Girl as Militant," in G.L. Bernstein (ed.) *Recreating Japanese Women*, Berkeley: University of California Press, pp. 239–66.

Smith III, W.D. (1999) "Ethnicity, Class and Gender in the Mines: Korean Workers in Japan's Chikuhō Coal Field, 1917–45," University of Washington, Ph.D. dissertation.

Tanaka, Y. (2002) *Japan's Comfort Women: Sexual Slavery and Prostitution During World War II and the US Occupation*, New York: Routledge.

United States Strategic Bombing Survey (1947) *The Japanese wartime standard of living and the utilization of manpower*, Washington, DC: Manpower, Food and Civilian Supplies Division.

Utsumi A. (2001) "Korean 'Imperial Soldiers': Remembering Colonialism and Crimes Against Allied POWs," in T. Fujitani, G.M. White, and L. Yoneyama (eds) *Perilous Memories: The Asia-Pacific War(s)*, Durham, NC: Duke University Press.

Utsumi, A. (2005) "Japan's Korean Soldiers in the Pacific War," in P.H. Kratoska (ed.) *Asian Labor in the Wartime Japanese Empire: Unknown Histories*, Armonk, NY: M.E. Sharpe.

Weiner, M. (1994) *Race and Migration in Imperial Japan*, New York: Routledge.

Yamada S., Higuchi Y. and Koshō T. (2005) *Chōsenjin senji rōdō dōin* [Wartime labour mobilization of Koreans], Tokyo: Iwanami shoten.

Yang, H. (1998) "Remembering the Korean Military Comfort Women: Nationalism, Sexuality, and Silence," in E.H. Kim and C. Choi (eds) *Dangerous Women: Gender and Korean Nationalism*, New York: Routledge.

Yoo, T.J. (2008) *The Politics of Gender in Colonial Korea: Education, Labor and Health, 1910–1945*, Berkeley: University of California Press.

Yoshimi, Y. (2000) *Comfort Women*, S. O'Brien (trans.), New York: Columbia University Press.

4 Military prostitution and women's sexual labour in Japan and Korea

Chunghee Sarah Soh

For centuries in Japan and Korea the state regulated prostitution. Access to women's public sexual labour constituted a core element of what might be called "the law of male sex-right" (Rich 1980: 645). Although licensed prostitution was officially abolished in southern Korea in November 1947 under the United States of America Military Government in Korea, a private system of women's public sexual labour euphemistically referred to as "customary business" (*p'ungsokŏp*) continued to prosper in a variety of manners and places in Korea. In fact, since 1945 the United States military in postwar Japan and postcolonial Korea has had easy access to the sexual services of "comfort women" in numerous local camp towns in the two countries, despite the Japanese and Korean laws against prostitution legislated since then. The historical euphemism "comfort women" initially referred to tens of thousands of women who were subjected to forced prostitution and sexual slavery for the Japanese military during the Asia–Pacific War (1931–45).[1] However, the term was also used in both postwar Japan and postcolonial Korea to refer to women sex workers servicing the military.

This chapter examines historical legacies of the customary practice and political economic policy dimension of prostitution as women's sexual labour in the (hetero) sexual landscapes of Japan and Korea. In particular, it focuses on women's sexual labour for national militaries and highlights the historical role of the "state as pimp" (to borrow John Lie's phrase) (Lie 1997). It shows how both Japan and South Korea instituted and sanctioned military prostitution for foreign forces stationed in postwar Japan and postliberation Korea respectively, as well as the South Korean Army's own "special" "comfort women" system enacted during the Korean War (1950–53).

A primary purpose of this discussion is to explain the societal neglect of Japan's wartime "comfort women" survivors for nearly half a century after the end of the Asia-Pacific War. I do so by exposing the social and political economic history of a culturally rooted indifference to the circumstances of women labouring in the sex industry owing to the prevailing masculinist attitude toward prostitution as a stigmatized yet "customary business" where women labour for men's naturalized sexual desires and "needs."

Stigmatized yet "customary": Korean women's sexual labour

Women's sexual labour in South Korea and Japan's capitalist consumer cultures today is offered as part of a wide variety of commodified services – erotic dancing, bar hostessing, and barbershop massage, not to mention outright prostitution. As such, it deserves more scholarly attention as quintessentially gendered customary care labour in the masculinist sexual culture. Its economic contribution to the gross domestic product has yet to be comprehensively acknowledged in accounts of the proverbial "economic miracles" of postwar Japan and postliberation Korea. It is remarkable that scholarly works on the relationship between gender and work in East Asian economic development – including those written by female researchers (such as Brinton 1993) – have routinely ignored the contribution of women's public sexual labour to these countries' economies.

Given the centuries-old negative attitude toward women's sexual labour for pay, as well as women's marginalization in the conventional labour market, it is hardly surprising that most Koreans and Japanese in postwar years have not considered the personal ordeals of surviving "comfort women" worthy of public debate or a campaign for social justice. As a matter of fact, Korean government officials – whose perspectives on gender relations are steeped in the masculinist sexual culture – did not consider the "comfort women" issue worth broaching during the fourteen years (1951–65) of bilateral negotiation to normalize diplomatic relations between Korea and Japan: they saw it primarily as a militarized form of prostitution or stigmatized sexual labour.

Furthermore, after the signing of the bilateral treaty with Japan in 1965, Korean society condoned sex tourism – euphemistically dubbed as *kisaeng* (professional entertainer) tourism – for Japanese men. When the number of Japanese visitors to Korea rapidly increased after 1965, *kisaeng* tourism became enormously popular among predominantly male Japanese visitors to Korea in the late 1960s (KCWU 1983, JAPA 1995). In an effort to earn foreign currency, the Korean government condoned the commodification of public sexual labour for its former colonizer offered by young Korean women billed as *kisaeng*, even though the traditional *kisaeng* system no longer existed as a formal institution. By the end of the 1960s, the state began to see foreign-currency-earning prostitutes as an important human resource in its national economic development. The administration of the Prostitution Prevention Law no longer applied to prostitutes serving foreign visitors in specially designated tourist hotels, nor to prostitutes serving American servicemen in the camp towns called *kijich'on* (Pyŏn and Hwang 1998: 44). In the 1970s Korean women who wished to work formally for foreign tourists at the specified hotels had to acquire a license certifying their health status and the completion of required orientation lectures given by male professors who emphasized the importance of their "patriotic" work of helping earn precious foreign currency for the nation's economic development (KCWU 1983: 24).

The commercially organized *kisaeng* tours became ready sources of income for many young Korean women. The majority of Japanese men who visited Korea to attend *kisaeng* parties came from the lower classes to enjoy sexual entertainment at one-fifth of the cost of comparable services in Japan (KCWU 1983). The euphemistic term "*kisaeng* party" masked "mass prostitution." Typically, planeloads of men were transported in buses to special *kisaeng* houses/restaurants called *yojŏng* (*ryōtei* in Japanese) set in the grand traditional Korean-style architecture. There, the "tourists" were fed and entertained by attentive *kisaeng*, in imitation of the way wealthy business people and powerful officials used to hold their exclusive parties in the colonial period. Clad in traditional garments of *ch'ima* (long skirt) and *chŏgori* (short jacket) and sitting next to a sex tourist, a *kisaeng* would feed the tourist with chopsticks and fill his glass with beer or other alcoholic drinks. At the end of such parties almost all men took their partners along to the hotel for sexual intercourse (KCWU 1983: 19).

Ironically, it was the very phenomenon of Japanese men's *kisaeng* tourism in Korea that gave rise to the Korean and Japanese women's alliance to campaign against sex tourism. As I have discussed elsewhere (Soh 1996), this joint campaign would lay the foundation for Korean women's organizations to refocus their activism from the late 1980s on the historical exploitation of military "comfort women" during imperial Japan's war of aggression.

Here we must consider the issue of unequal power relations between nation-states as a critical factor in the long history of Korean women pressed into performing stigmatized sexual labour for men of other states (beginning with China's Yuan dynasty in the thirteenth century).[2] In other words, the issue of redressing Korean "comfort women" survivors' personal ordeals goes beyond the usual class-based exploitation of women in the sex industry and into the political history of international power relations between Japan and Korea as colonizer and colonized.

Nevertheless, the institutional roots of Japan's wartime military "comfort women" system must be located in the early modern system of licensed prostitution in feudal Japan (see Fujime 1997) as well as the Japanese and Korean traditions of professional entertainers, the *geisha* and *kisaeng*, who trained formally in the arts of literature, music, and dance to entertain male clients. The boundary between "entertainment" and "prostitution" could get rather fuzzy in the lives of traditional *geisha* and *kisaeng*. Moreover, Korean *kisaeng* would become essentially synonymous with prostitutes after the Japanese licensed prostitution system was transplanted to colonial Korea (1910–45) (Kim et al. 1972: 522–23, Yim 2004: 27).

The question to ask at this point is: did the end of the Asia-Pacific War bring about the end of military prostitution and sexual slavery for working-class women in vanquished Japan and liberated Korea? The answer, unfortunately, is a resounding "no." Both Japan and Korea condoned the continued exploitation of women's public sexual labour for the "comfort" of soldiers, especially foreign troops, for the more than half a century since the end of the war in 1945. To be sure, forcible recruitment by state agents no longer prevailed, and there existed no colonial subjects to be exploited. However, pimps and other sex trade entrepreneurs continued their fraudulent and coercive methods to recruit impoverished young women. Published materials have also shown that some surviving wartime "comfort women" – both Japanese and Korean – found themselves selling sex to the foreign soldiers that landed in defeated Japan and liberated Korea.[3]

"National policy comfort women" in occupied Japan

In defeated Japan women and women's bodies became a critical concern in the days immediately after its unconditional surrender. To protect the nation's female population, Japan's fearful officials took the initiative to establish "special comfort facilities" for the Allied forces that were to occupy the country for seven years (1945–52) (see Duus 1979, Dower 1999). That there existed real danger of sex crimes against ordinary women in occupied Japan is undisputed. From the first day of the occupation, sexual and other crimes by US soldiers were "rampant."[4] Given the widespread panic and masculinist cultural assumptions about human sexual behavior it is understandable that the Japanese government would issue an order to establish "special comfort facilities" for fear of violent sexual attack by US soldiers. The officials emphasized the need to make the people understand that the purpose of this order was to "protect Japanese women," that is, "respectable" (middle-class) Japanese women (Duus 1979: 21–29, Shiga-Fujime 1993). Building comfort stations for the occupying forces – as a sort of preemptive "gift" from the vanquished to the victors – was done out of fear of the demonized Other, not a matter of making money. The "national policy on comfort women" project could not be left to brothel owners alone, and the government was willing to spend up to 100 million yen to get the project started. Officials believed that this was a cheap price to pay for "the purpose of preserving the pure blood of the Japanese nation" (Duus 1979: 41).

Further, the government directive indicated that women who worked at these facilities as "gifts" or sanctioned "booty" for the victorious warriors should be recruited from among the *geisha*, already licensed or private prostitutes, waitresses, and habitual sex criminals (Duus 1979: 27). Japanese police officers appealed to former prostitutes "to work again for the sake of the nation and for the [safety] of the Japanese people" (Tanaka 2002: 135). The message was loud and clear: women who engaged in public sexual labour would merit no protection by the government. Public announcements that appealed to women's patriotism like the one below drew destitute women into the comfort facilities:

> We are looking for women of the New Japan who will do their part in rebuilding our nation by doing the important deed of providing comfort for the American forces stationed in Japan. From ages 18 to 25. Shelter, food, and clothing provided.
>
> (Shiga-Fujime 1993: 7)

When the Allied Forces – composed of mainly American soldiers – landed in Japan, the Japanese government was ready to offer these women as "gifts of the vanquished." The Special Comfort Facilities Association was formed on 23 August 1945 and was officially recognized five days later; it was renamed the Recreation and Amusement Association (RAA) about a month after that. The RAA guidance committee was composed of representatives from such agencies as the Departments of Internal Affairs, Foreign Affairs, Finance, and Transportation as well as Tokyo Prefecture and the police (Duus 1979: 40–41). "Comfort facilities," including houses of prostitution, cabarets, and dance halls, spread quickly to some twenty other cities (Dower 1999: 130). The association ran twenty-one comfort stations for the Allied Forces, whose basic structures and the way they were operated closely resembled wartime comfort stations run for the Japanese military.

The treatment of the Japanese postwar "comfort women" by the state contrasts sharply with the experience of their Korean counterparts. The paternalistic Japanese bureaucracy took care to monitor the material welfare of Japanese nationals labouring as "comfort women" for occupying foreign forces. The government provided remuneration for their sex work, which included double the usual monetary reward – 50 per cent of the fee – as well as high-quality daily necessities, such as free meals, a decent kimono, and a good supply of cosmetic products from the renowned Shiseidō corporation.

By December 1945, however, American officials of the Supreme Command for the Allied Powers (SCAP) concluded that Japan's licensed prostitution system amounted to human trafficking and should be abolished. The Japanese Police Office then issued on 12 January 1946 a notice regarding the abolition of licensed prostitution, expressing its regret over the "recent social situation" that forced the closure of a system that had exercised a "considerable effect" on public (sexual) morality. The notice also assured licensed brothel owners that they would be allowed to operate as private entertainment businesses. The practice of advance payment (*maegari*) was now forbidden since that could be interpreted as human trafficking. That same day four Japanese NGOs, including the Japan Woman's Christian Temperance Union, submitted a joint petition to abolish all licensed prostitution. The timing of the petition is reported to have been tied up with the American intention that the abolition not be seen a matter of one-sided moral pressure. The 300-year history of the licensed prostitution system came to an end on 20 February 1946, as a result of the SCAP directive. Among the nearly 2,000 prostitutes working in Tokyo, about 400 were affected by the closure ordinance. By changing their working title from *kōshō* (licensed prostitute) to *settaifu* (hostess), however, they were able to continue labouring as private prostitutes (Duus 1979: 161–68).

Soon, over 500 "national policy 'comfort women'" lost their jobs when the facilities of the RAA were closed at the end of March 1946, several weeks before the Tokyo War Crimes Tribunal began. These facilities had been beleaguered by the rampant spread of venereal diseases. But sexual and romantic contact between Japanese women and foreign men continued in the SCAP offices, dance halls, beer halls, and the streets of occupied Japan throughout the period of the Tokyo Tribunal and beyond (Duus 1979; Dower 1999).[5] Some Japanese women became "war brides" who married men of the Allied forces and emigrated to their husbands' home countries.[6] In Japan as well as the Allied nations where these women would make their new homes, many would face social attitudes that conflated "war bride" with "war booty" or prostitute.

Japanese women and the Korean War

During the Korean War (1950–53), occupied Japan turned into a "sexual 'comfort' camp" for the US military. American soldiers fighting in Korea were flown to Japan to spend their "R & R" (rest and recuperation) leave of five days for every six weeks of combat duty. It is said that R & R was referred to as "I & I" among the soldiers, meaning intercourse and intoxication (Duus 1979: 291). Not surprisingly, the peak year for military prostitution in postwar Japan was 1952. In that year, about 13,000 cases of trafficking were investigated by Japanese police, and more than 70,000 women worked as prostitutes serving US soldiers (Duus 1979: 292–93, Shiga-Fujime 1993: 7). In the military camp town of Yokosuka alone the foreign currency these women earned for the year amounted to between 200 and 300 million yen (Duus 1979: 292).

At the same time that the sex trade was booming, many Japanese women suffered individual and gang rape by US soldiers (Dower 1999, Tanaka 2002). Some women working on US military bases were forcibly taken to Korea and made to serve as "comfort women" there; some of them were even killed.[7] Eight of fifteen Japanese nurses who were flown in from the Yokota Air Force base hospital to Korea on 27 July 1950 were gang raped by US soldiers after they had finished taking care of the wounded at the front line just outside Pusan (I. Kim 1976: 267–68).

Post-occupation Japan enacted the Prostitution Prevention Law in 1956. The law went into effect in 1957, except for the penal provisions that were enforced in 1958 (Shiga-Fujime 1993, Garon 1997: 202). In the case of Okinawa, however, the law was not enforced until 1972, the year in which the American-occupied islands were finally returned to Japan (Tomimura 1982: 188). Even so, this law was meant only to curb rather than prohibit prostitution, as leaders of the Japan Woman's Christian Temperance Union lamented (Garon 1997: 202).

Today, many women from developing countries migrate to Japan to work in the adult entertainment industry. They are referred to as *Japayuki-san*,[8] or young migrant women from developing countries traveling to Japan for work, which is a play on the term *Karayuki-san* (overseas prostitute) from prewar Japan. Many in Japan now avoid use of the term, preferring to use such terms as "immigrant workers." In the 1980s the majority of *Japayuki-san* came from the Philippines and Taiwan, while in the 1990s women from Thailand became the latest arrivals to the multi-ethnic sex industry in Japan (Constantine 1993).

"Camp town 'comfort women'" in Korea

After its liberation from Japanese rule in August 1945, the Korean peninsula was divided into two: Soviet troops occupied the northern half and the US military the southern half. The ongoing US military presence in South Korea led to the formation and maintenance of "camp towns" (*kijich'on*, in Korean) around the military bases, a development that has had a striking social impact on Korean communities.[9] *Kijich'on* (literally, base or camp [*kiji*] village [*ch'on*]) refers to the civilian world of commercial establishments and residential buildings that have sprung up around the US military bases and cater to the needs of the American GIs. It is "a place where Koreans and Americans – mostly male military personnel – meet in an economic and emotional marriage of convenience" (Fulton 1998: 200). As of the end of 1996, 37,000 American troops supported the economies of ninety-six *kijich'on*. The estimated number of *kijich'on* prostitutes over the first four decades of the American presence ranges between 250,000 and 300,000 (H. Kim 1997: 14).[10]

Kijich'on prostitution has evolved through four distinct phases. During the first phase (1945–48) the American military government's elimination of licensed prostitution led to privatization of the sex trade. In the postliberation political uncertainty and economic destitution, many people, including prostitutes from the now-closed brothels and "comfort women" returnees like Pak Sun-i (b.1930; pseudonym) gathered near the American military bases. Koreans coined new terms such as *yang-galbo* (Western whore), or more euphemistically *yang-gongju* (Western princess), to refer to compatriot women who did sex work for the American military. Notably, until the early 1990s the South Korean media routinely used the term *wianbu* ("comfort women") to refer to prostitutes for the American troops.

The *kijich'on* sex trade consolidated and expanded during the second phase, which began with the Korean War. In her testimony, Pak Sun-i who had laboured at three different comfort stations in Japan from 1944 to the end of the war, recalled:

> At twenty-seven years of age, I was having a hard time making ends meet in Tongduch'ŏn (the largest *kijich'on* just outside Seoul).[11] I ended up cohabiting with a staff sergeant of the US Army for about two years. ... One of my friends from the days at a comfort station in Japan also worked as *yang-gongju*, but she passed away.[12]

An American veteran who served in Korea in the 1950s after the end of the Korean War recounted that on Friday nights half-ton trucks would bring into the base a few hundred women to stay the night or the weekend with the soldiers (Cumings 1992: 171). In 1958, five years after the armistice, the majority of about 300,000 prostitutes in Korea reportedly served American soldiers.[13] Some of them, like their earlier Japanese counterparts, married and emigrated to the United States as wives of servicemen.[14]

The third phase of *kijich'on* prostitution started in 1971 as a result of two important events that brought to a head underlying tensions between the Korean and US governments. Katharine Moon (1997) has discussed this in detail in her study of the role military prostitution played in the strategic relationship between the two states in the 1970s. First, the 24 July 1969 announcement of the Nixon Doctrine concerning the withdrawal of American troops resulted in the pullout of 20,000 troops from Korea by the end of 1971 (H. Kim 1997, Moon 1997: 58–59). Second, a series of fights between black and white soldiers broke out in the summer of 1971 over racial discrimination practiced at local bars (Moon 1997). Soldiers also complained about "unhygienic *kijich'on* women" and demanded that soldiers be treated better as "VIPs who came to rescue Korea" (H. Kim 1997: 15). The Korean government, under the general-turned-president Park Chung Hee, wished to prevent further withdrawals of US troops and responded quickly and positively to the demands of the American military. To deal with the complaint of unhygienic conditions in the *kijich'on* sex industry, the Korean government started a clean-up campaign that included infrastructure improvements and enforced regular medical examinations of prostitutes; infected women were to be detained at special centers (Moon 1997). The government thus began active engagement in the surveillance and control of prostitutes servicing the US military. *Kijich'on* prostitution, for all practical purposes, had taken on the characteristics of licensed prostitution.

In the 1980s, when Korean and US troops regularly conducted major joint military exercises called "Team Spirit," *kijich'on* sex workers were moved around by brothel owners as mobile brothels, "just like the Japanese military 'comfort women,'" to serve the American soldiers (H. Kim 1997: 22). Encouraged by brothel owners who promised good money, and sarcastically referring to themselves as the "blanket squad" (*tamnyo pudae*), they followed the soldiers during the exercises (H. Kim 1997: 23). Each would engage in sexual labour with twenty to thirty soldiers a day on those occasions. In the 1990s these annual exercises were curtailed to several small-scale joint exercises in such port cities as Pusan, P'ohang, and Chinhae. Each time an exercise took place, *kijich'on* women moved to the respective port, prompting an activist to refer to them as "*che2ŭi chŏngsindae*," or the second [generation] comfort women (H. Kim 1997: 24).

In the fourth phase, since the late 1980s, the *kijich'on* sex industry has been reshaped by the development of "industry-style prostitution" in the broader society. That is, the growth of the adult entertainment industry has created a host of new types of sexual labour that offer prostitution as a byproduct of legal personal care services at such places as massage parlors, bathhouses, and barbershops. These new types of sexual labour have spread to the *kijich'on* as well. Women in these businesses sometimes turn to the *kijich'on* on weekends to earn extra money or to meet prospective husbands among the American soldiers. In addition, some teenagers and college students visit the *kijich'on* looking for opportunities to practice their English and make friends with American servicemen. Some of these "wanderers" turn into *kijich'on* sex workers (H. Kim 1997: 19).

A notable feature of the internationalization of the sex trade in South Korea since the 1990s is an influx of foreign women from "third world" countries. Korea's economic success and the consequent enrichment of the domestic economy have made *kijich'on* sex work for US servicemen comparatively less attractive for young Korean women. These women have found that with a weakening US dollar they can earn more money in the domestic sex industry where their clients are likely to be high-earning South Korean men. To fill the shortage of *kijich'on* workers, foreign women, mostly from the Philippines, have been brought in to work at the nightclubs (Cheng 2007). Since the collapse of the Soviet Union, thousands of Russian women have also migrated to Korea to work as entertainers singing and dancing at nightclubs, but some of them have been forced into prostitution, not only for American soldiers but also for Korean civilian men.[15] The Korean public television station, KBS, reported on 29 May 2001 that about 4,000 Russian women worked in the Korean adult entertainment industry, and some of them were suffering financial exploitation and even human rights abuses.

A 2003 research report found that foreign women now outnumber Korean women in the *kijich'on* clubs for the American military in northern Kyŏnggi Province: Filipina women were the most numerous, with Russian women taking second place.[16] The Filipinas are generally very young and able to speak English. Some have been "imported" as entertainers by Korean entrepreneurs and others are illegal migrant workers. These foreign women are more easily controlled than Korean workers, since some Korean sex workers have taken collective action to safeguard their livelihood, which they felt was threatened by competition from migrant women. Korean women criticize the business owners for the "unpatriotic" hiring of Filipina women, who they believe rob Korean sex workers of the opportunity to "help the national economy by earning foreign currency" (Chŏng 1999: 352). It is ironic that the rhetoric of patriotism started by male government officials has thus come full circle: now it is the sex workers themselves who resort to patriotic language to rally nationalist support against their foreign competitors.

Despite the end of the Cold War in Europe, some 100,000 American troops continued to be stationed in Japan and Korea at the end of the twentieth century (Johnson 1999: 109). Since the division of the Korean peninsula has yet to be resolved, the continued presence of the American military in East Asia – as a stabilizing "guarantor" of regional security – is expected until at least the year 2015 (Johnson 1999: 121). Japanese, Korean, and foreign women will continue to engage in sexual labour in camp towns in the foreseeable future. The atrocities that Japan's imperial army committed against women have been amply aired in recent years, but few people outside of South Korea are aware of heinous sexual crimes committed by American military men, most of which go unpunished due to the unequal Status of Forces Agreement (SOFA) between the superpower US and Korea. One particularly gruesome case involving the murder of a Korean prostitute (Yun Kŭm-i) by an American soldier (Kenneth Markle) prompted an unprecedented mass demonstration of 3,000 people in a *kijich'on* called Tongduch'ŏn in 1992.[17] The cruelty of the crime mobilized enraged residents to stage a series of demonstrations that eventually led to the formation of an NGO, the National Campaign for Eradication of Crime by US Troops in Korea, in 1993. According to statistics compiled by this NGO, an average of two crimes per day were committed by US troops from January 1993 to June 1996, and on average the Korean government exercised jurisdiction in 0.7 per cent of cases. The Yun Kŭm-i murder case is one of the very few that resulted in the criminal serving his sentence in a Korean prison.

"Special comfort women" for the Korean army

The fact that the Korean military also availed themselves of the "special comfort unit" during the Korean War has received little public attention even after the Korean women's movement in support of the "comfort women" began in the 1990s. Only piecemeal anecdotal materials on it had come to light from memoirs written by retired generals and the testimony of soldiers who fought in the war. Retired General Kim Hǔi-o, for example, describes an instance of using prostitutes as "comfort" in his 2000 memoir, *In'gan ǔi hyanggi* (The Aroma of Humanity). As his company was preparing for nighttime combat training, he received instructions regarding the "fifth supplies" of six "comfort women."[18] According to his recollection, they were brought in from Chong-Sam, the then famed red-light district in Seoul. The women were sent to his company to be employed for eight hours during the day. General Kim remembers his ambivalence about the arrangement that led to soldiers forming long queues in front of the tented barracks. Two women were allocated to his platoon and one of them was first sent to him as the platoon leader. He wrote that after exchanging small talk with the woman, he gave her a bundle of ration biscuits he had accumulated and handed her over to a first sergeant (H. Kim 2000: 70–80, quoted in K. Kim 2002: 77–78).

It was not until February 2002, however, that the first scholarly work presented the embarrassing truth that the Korean military also created and operated its own "comfort women" system. Notably, the presentation of this research took place in Japan.[19] Korean sociologist Kim Kwi-ok presented her paper focusing on military "comfort women" and military comfort stations during the Korean War. It is based on her study of the official record of the military, *Hubang Chǒnsa* (War History on the Home Front), published by the Korean Army in 1956, as well as the memoirs of retired generals and testimonial narratives of those who had been involved in the system in one way or another.

It is still not clear exactly when the special comfort units were established. Kim estimates that they began in 1951. The closing date, by contrast, is specified as March 1954 in the army document that pointed out that the cessation of warfare eliminated their necessity. She argues that the Korean military ran its system through three types of "comfort" operations. First, they ran "special comfort units" called *T'ǔksu Wiandae* in seven locations – three in Seoul and four in Kangwǒn Province, including Ch'unch'ǒn. It is not clear how many women were kept at these stations, but using partial figures disclosed in *Hubang Chǒnsa*, Kim surmises the number of "comfort women" to be about 120.[20] Second, the military also operated mobile units that visited the barracks; and third, they hired women working in private brothels to service the soldiers.

While the recruitment process for women in the South is not very clear, during the Korean War South Korean agents kidnapped some women from the North (K. Kim 2002: 71). Thus the general operational methods for the South Korean army comfort system are strongly reminiscent of the Japanese system. All the Korean War comfort women had to undergo regular medical examinations by army doctors to combat STDs. The similar pattern of operations included the women being classified according to the ranks of the men they served, soldiers lining up in front of their tents, and a hierarchical order of access to their sexual service. Nearly identical pictures emerge of wartime military sexual behaviors for both Japanese soldiers and their postcolonial Korean counterparts. Given the much shorter period of warfare, however, the number of women used by the Korean military is much smaller compared to the Japanese. Another difference that is of political significance for the Koreans is that the men and women were of the same nationality. Despite the generalized underlying assumption that soldiers need to have access to sex (customarily offered by lower-class women), however, when Japanese soldiers used women of colonial Korea (1910–45) for their sexual recreation, many Koreans felt deeply humiliated for their lack of political economic power to prohibit such exploitation. Now that the post-Cold War transnational women's human rights movement has helped produce an international discourse of the wartime Japanese military comfort system as sexual slavery and a war crime, it is easier for Korean society today to denounce the Japanese, who were colonial oppressors and wartime aggressors, for crimes against Korean women than it is to criticize the Korean state, the Korean military, and Korean men for similar crimes against women of their own ethnicity and nation that occurred during the Korean War and into the present.

Characterizing the Korean military comfort system as an "unfortunate offspring" of the Japanese colonial legacy, Kim Kwi-ok called for victimized women, civic organizations, and scholars to come together and confront the unresolved issues of this historical injustice. The media reports of Kim's work, however, have generated little response. There has been no public outcry regarding the Korean military's use of "comfort women" during the Korean War or its violation of women's human rights. Korean silence over these issues is reminiscent of earlier societal indifference toward survivors of imperial Japan's comfort system. It mirrors the reticence of many Japanese to come to terms with the history of their country's wartime comfort system. As in the case of Japan, many in Korea, including retired military leaders, apparently regard the women's sexual labour simply as the performance of gendered *customary sex labour* in order to meet the needs of fighting men. It is noteworthy that military authorities have acknowledged that the system of special comfort units contradicts the national policy of banning licensed prostitution. Nonetheless, they have insisted that the special units were created to fulfill an important strategic end.

In light of the long history of similar masculinist sexual mores, it is both significant and unsurprising that the rationale cited by the Korean army for establishing comfort units should mirror that of Japan's imperial forces in the 1940s. As in the Japanese case, the Korean military argued that these units were critical to raising morale and preventing servicemen from forcing unwanted sex on the civilian population. In other words, the Korean military regarded its comfort system as a kind of "necessary social evil." This very masculinist perspective, in fact, had also been argued by high officials in defense of the *kisaeng* system of the Chosŏn dynasty (1392–1910) (Yi 1992 [1927]). It is clear that both the imperial Japanese military and the postcolonial Korean army leadership shared the belief in men's uncontrollable need for, and therefore right to, women's bodies, whether in war or peace. While the fact that Korea's army leadership had been trained with imperial Japanese forces may also be a factor that contributed to the creation of the "special comfort units," the South Korean "comfort women" system was fundamentally rooted in this long cultural history of the *kisaeng* system and later colonial licensed prostitution whose legacy lived on in South Korea.

Conclusion

The deep-rooted historical masculinist legacy of treating women's sexual labour as stigmatized yet customary underlies the socio-cultural and political economic dimensions of both Japanese and Korean society's indifference to the suffering of numerous women pressured into performing sexual labour for the military during and after the Asia–Pacific War. The societal silence and indifference to the comfort women in postliberation Korea until the 1990s (when the comfort women redress movement began [see Soh 1996]) must be understood in terms of not only interstate power relations but also prevailing masculinist sexual mores. On the personal level the surviving victims' silence was partly due to the fact that, as a group, they hailed from lower-class families and lacked the political power to press for justice. However, the masculinist sexual culture, which stigmatized women victims of sexual violence – not to mention sex workers – and the women's own enculturation in such a culture would have meant that initiating social or legal action was simply out of the question: their action, they believed, would only bring further shame not only to themselves but also to their families. Their one recourse was to do everything in their power not to have their past disclosed. Testimonials of Korean survivors reveal their acute shame of having lost their virginity and having performed sexual acts for many men. Most thought they had forfeited their future marriage eligibility.[21]

Not surprisingly, from 1948 to 1989 the male-dominated Korean National Assembly concurred with the state's political economic position regarding Korean women's sexual labour at the camp towns and at urban tourist hotels – it was necessary and positive for the promotion of national security and economic growth (Cho and Chang 1990). Every single day during my research trip to Korea in January 2000, I observed couples: middle-aged Japanese men accompanied by young Korean women, eating breakfast together at a downtown hotel restaurant in Seoul. More than a quarter of a century after women in Korea and Japan began fighting against sex tourism in the 1970s, Japanese sex tours to Korea continue, albeit less conspicuously, in smaller groups and without using the term *kisaeng*.[22] Prosperous middle-class Korean men, meanwhile, have embarked on their own international quest for sexual adventure. This has been dubbed "Don't-Ask Tourism" (*mutchima kwankwang*) and takes them to the less developed countries of Southeast Asia.

However, when it comes to the issue of Japan's wartime "comfort women" system, which has been redefined by the international community as a prominent case of violence against women in armed conflict, no social critic or public intellectual in Korea would dare to take the customary masculinist position that such a system benefits the economy or promotes national security. This is because the comfort women issue has been redefined as military sexual slavery and a war crime by the international community owing largely to women's collaborative movement for redress in Japan and Korea.

Still, little critical public discourse has occurred on the legacies of that historical institution or the social structural dimension of Korea's comfort women tragedy.

Few are willing to consider the unsavoury fact that, accustomed to indigenous public institutions that have granted customary sex rights to men, and licensed by the colonial government, many Koreans did not hesitate to collaborate in recruiting and running comfort stations by trafficking in girls and young women.[23] Rather than deal with the messy and unpleasant complications of the historical record, Korean public discourse has simplistically elevated the survivors to heroic symbols of national suffering under Japanese colonialism and its imperialist war of aggression.

By contrast, Japan, which is unavoidably seen as the perpetrator nation, has been in turmoil over contested representations of the comfort women phenomenon and its responsibility in the matter. Meanwhile, the international – as well as domestic – trade in public sex prospers in the capitalist economies of Japan and Korea despite endless incidents of criminal abuse of women so employed by both foreigners and compatriots. The social historical legacies of masculinist sexual culture and political economic realities in the two countries continue to help construct women's sexual labour as stigmatized yet customary care labour for masculine "needs."

Notes

Acknowledgments: This chapter is drawn from my book *The Comfort Women* © 2008 by The University of Chicago. All rights reserved. I have conducted ethnographic field research on the topic in Korea, Japan, the United States, and the Netherlands since 1995. I am grateful for the financial support this research received from the Association for Asian Studies Northeast Asia Council, the Japan Foundation, the John D. and Catherine T. MacArthur Foundation, San Francisco State University, and the University of Leiden International Institute for Asian Studies.

1 For a recent study of the subject, see Tanaka (2002).
2 For a historical overview of the role of the state in Korean women's sexual labour, see Soh (2004a).
3 See, for example, Kawata (1992/1987) and Shirota (1971) for postwar experiences of public sexual labour of Korean and Japanese comfort women survivors, respectively.
4 For a discussion of such crimes and official reports on sexual violence committed by the occupation forces against Japanese women, see Tanaka (2002: ch. 5).
5 Vera Mackie (private communication, July 2006) notes that different groups within the Allied Occupation acted slightly differently. The forces in southern Japan, part of BCOF, but largely Australian, for example, carried out medical inspections and tacitly recognized their soldiers' use of brothels for a time, until this became a controversy in the Australian media and parliament.
6 See Nitta (1997) for stereotypes about war brides in Japan and the United States. See also Yuh (2002) for similar prejudices against Korean "military brides."
7 For shocking, but little known, stories of Japanese women's suffering of sexual violence and war crimes committed by American troops in the battlefields in Korea during the Korean War, see Fujime (1999).
8 See Usuki (1983) for stories of Korean women as *Japayuki-san*. For an analysis of Southeast Asian women's experiences, see Mackie (1998).
9 For an analysis of Korean fictional writing on *kijich'on*, see Fulton (1998).
10 For life histories of sex workers for the US military in Korea, Japan, and the Philippines, see Sturdevant and Stoltzfus (1992).

11 For a description of the bar system in Tongduch'on in the late 1980s, see Sturdevant and Stoltzfus (1992: 176–79).
12 For her life story, see Hangak Chŏngsindae-munje Taech'aek Hyŏpŭihoe (HCTH) 1997: 225–36. Quotation from pp. 233, 235.
13 *Kyŏnghyang Sinmun* (August 11, 1958) reported the figure to be 59.1 per cent; the reliability of these statistics, which were quoted in Chŏng Hi-jin (1999: 300), is not clear.
14 For more information on Korean war brides, see Soh (1995).
15 Korean men reportedly find Russian women exotic and having sex with them is referred to in their slang as riding on a "white horse" (*paengma*).
16 The research conducted by Durebang, an NGO for women's human rights, was reported in *The Internet Hankyoreh* (http://www.hani.co.kr/, accessed December 19, 2003).
17 Kenneth Markle (twenty years old at the time of the crime), a private of the US Army stationed in South Korea, murdered Yun Kŭm-i, a 26-year-old sex worker, by battering her with a Coke bottle and stuffing it into her womb. He also shoved an umbrella into the anus of the bleeding, dying woman and stuffed matches into her mouth. He then sprinkled soap powder over her body, apparently to eliminate evidence of the murder. (The National Campaign for Eradication of Crime by US Troops in Korea, n.d.)
18 It is notable that Korean records refer to the women as the "fifth category supplies" – an addition to the four normal supply categories, which is reminiscent of the Japanese classification of comfort women as "military supplies" (see Asō 1993).
19 It was given at the Fifth International Symposium on Peace and Human Rights in East Asia held at Ritsumeikan University in Kyoto, Japan, February 22–25, 2002. A special report on it was published in the Internet newspaper *Ohmynews* (http://www. ohmynews.com/, accessed February 22, 2002).
20 According to the memoir of Retired General Ch'ae Myŏng-sin, the South Korean Army ran three or four "comfort units" (*wianbudae*), each composed of about sixty women (Ch'ae 1994: 267, quoted in K. Kim 2002: 76).
21 For testimonials of Korean survivors, see the multi-volume publications put out by HCTH since 1993.
22 I learned during my field research that the Japanese slang term *tachi* (a suffix that indicates the plurality of the noun), as in *onnatachi* [women], has replaced the term *kisaeng*.
23 A notable exception is the case of Rhee Younghoon (Yi Yŏnghun), professor of Korean economic history, whose public statement on the comfort women issue generated a fierce controversy in September 2004. See, for example, the September 3, 2004 issue of *Donga Ilbo*. For an analysis of personal stories of Korean comfort women survivors who were deceived by such collaborators, see Soh (2004b).

References

Asō, T. (1993) *Shanghai yori Shanghai e* [From Shanghai to Shanghai], Fukuoka: Sekifūsha.
Brinton, M.C. (1993) *Women and the Economic Miracle: Gender and Work in Postwar Japan*, Berkeley: University of California Press.
Ch'ae, M.S. (1994) *Sasŏn ŭl nŏmkonŏmŏ* [Traversing the death lines], Seoul: Maeilkyŏngje Sinmunsa.
Cheng, S.L. (2007) "Romancing the Clubs: Filipina Entertainers in US Military Camp Towns in South Korea," in M. Padilla, R. Parker, and R. Sembert (eds) *Love and Globalization*, Nashville, TN: Vanderbilt University Press, pp. 226–51.
Cho, H. and Chang, P.W. (1990) "Perspectives on Prostitution in the Korean Legislature, 1948–89," in *Yŏsŏnghak nonjip* [Journal of Women's Studies] 7: 109–11.

Chŏng, H.J. (1999) *Chugŏya sanŭn yŏsŏngdŭr-ŭi inkwŏn* [Women's human rights come alive upon death], Han'guk Yŏsŏngŭi Chŏnhwa Yŏnhap [Korean Women's Telephone Association] (ed.), Seoul: Hanul, pp. 300–358.

Constantine, P. (1993) *Japan's Sex Trade: A Journey through Japan's Erotic Subcultures* Tokyo: Yenbooks.

Cumings, B. (1992) "Silent but Deadly: Sexual Subordination in the US-Korean Relationship," in S.P. Sturdevant and B. Stoltzfus, (eds) *Let the Good Times Roll: Prostitution and the US Military in Asia*, New York: The New Press, pp. 169–75.

Dower, J.W. (1999) *Embracing Defeat: Japan in the Wake of World War II*, New York: W.W. Norton.

Duus, M. (1979) *Haisha no okurimono* [Gifts of the vanquished], Tokyo: Kōdansha.

England, P. (2005) "Emerging Theories of Care Work," in *Annual Review of Sociology* 31: 381–99.

Fujime, Y. (1997) "The Licensed Prostitution System and the Prostitution Abolition Movement in Modern Japan," in *positions: east asia cultures critique* 5, 1: 135–70.

——. (1999) "Reisen taisei keiseiki no beigun to seibōryoku [The US Military and its sexual violence during the formational period of the Cold War system]," in *Josei, Sensō, Jinken*, 2. Tokyo: Kōrosha.

Fulton, B. (1998) "*Kijich'on* Fiction," in H.I. Pai, and T.R. Tangherlini (eds) *Nationalism and the Construction of Korean Identity,* Berkeley: Institute of East Asian Studies, University of California, Berkeley, pp. 198–213.

Garon, S. (1997) *Molding Japanese Minds: The State in Everyday Life,* Princeton, NJ: Princeton University Press.

Han'guk Chŏngsindae-munje Taech'aek Hyŏpŭihoe [HCTH] and Chŏngsindae Yŏn'guhoe, (eds). (1993) *Chŭngŏnjip I: Kangje-ro kkŭllyŏgan Chosŏnin kunwianpudŭl* [Collection of testimonies I: Forcibly recruited Korean military comfort women], Seoul: Hanul.

Han'guk Chŏngsindae-munje Taech'aek Hyŏpŭihoe [HCTH] and Han'guk Chŏngsindae Yŏn'guhoe (eds) (1997) *Chŭngŏnjip: Kangje-ro kkŭllyŏgan Chosŏnin kunwianpudŭl 2.* [Collection of testimonies: Forcibly recruited Korean military comfort women 2], Seoul: Hanul.

Japan Anti-Prostitution Association [JAPA] (1995) *Against Prostitution and Sexual Exploitation in Japan*, Tokyo: JAPA.

Johnson, C. (ed.). (1999) *Okinawa: Cold War Island*, Cardiff, CA: Japan Policy Research Institute.

Kawata, F. (1992/1987) *Ppalgan kiwajip: Chosŏn esŏ on chonggunwianbu iyagi* [The house with a red-tile roof: The story of a Korean military comfort woman], Han U-chŏng (trans.), Seoul: Maeilkyŏngje Sinmunsa.

Kim, H.O. (2000) *In'gan ŭi hyanggi: Chayuminju/taegongt'ujaeng kwa hamkkehan insaengyŏkchŏng* [The aroma of humanity: Life trajectory that accompanied the liberal democracy/anti-communism struggle], Seoul: Wŏnmin.

Kim, H.S. (1997) *Kijich'on, kijich'on yŏsŏng, honhyŏradong: Silt'ae wa sarye* [Camp town, camp town women, mixed-blood children: Reality and cases], Tongduch'ŏn, Kyŏnggi Province, ROK: Saeumt'ŏ.

Kim, I.M. (1976) *Tenno no guntai to Chōsenjin ianfu* [The emperor's forces and Korean comfort women], Tokyo: San'ichi shobō.

Kim, K.I. (2002) "Han'guk Chŏnjaeng kwa Yŏsŏng: Kunwianbu wa Kunwianso rŭl Chungsimŭro" [The Korean War and Women: With a Focus on Military Comfort Women and Military Comfort Stations]. Paper presented at the Fifth International Symposium on Peace and Human Rights in East Asia, February 22–25. The Japan Conference Proceedings. Kyoto: Ritsumeikan University, 68–82.

Kim, O.G. *et al.* (1972) *Han'guk yŏsŏngsa* [History of Korean women], Seoul: Ewha Womans University Press.

Korean Church Women United [KCWU] (1983) *Kisaeng kwankwang* [Kisaeng tourism], KCWU Charyo [Material] No. 1, Seoul: Han'guk Kyohoe Yŏsŏng Yŏnhaphoe [KCWU].

Lie, J. (1997) "The State As Pimp: Prostitution and the Patriarchal State in Japan in the 1940s," in *The Sociological Quarterly* 38, 2: 251–63.

Mackie, V. (1998) "Japayuki Cinderella Girl: Containing the Immigrant Other," in *Japanese Studies* 18, 1: 45–63.

Moon, K.H.S. (1997) *Sex Among Allies: Military Prostitution in US-Korea Relations.* New York: Columbia University Press.

National Campaign for Eradication of Crime by US Troops in Korea (n.d.) *Cases of Crimes Committed by US Military Men*, Seoul: Unpublished document.

Nitta, F. (1997) "Japanese Women Who Crossed the Oceans: War Brides Reconsidered," *Journal of Kibi International University* 7: 165–75.

Pyŏn, H. S. and Hwang, C.I., (1998) *Sanŏphyŏng maemaech'un e kwanhan yŏn'gu* [A study of industrial type prostitution], Seoul: Han'guk Yŏsŏng Kaebalwŏn.

Rich, A. (1980) "Compulsory Heterosexuality and Lesbian Existence," in *Signs* 5, 4: 631–60.

Shiga-Fujime, Y. (July 1993) "The Prostitutes' Union and the Impact of the 1956 Anti-Prostitution Law in Japan," in *US–Japan Women's Journal English Supplement* 5: 3–27.

Shirota, S. (1971) *Maria no sanka* (Maria's song of praise), Tokyo: Nihon kirisuto kyōdan shuppankyoku.

Soh, C.S. (1995) "Korean War Brides," in F. Ng (ed.) *The Asian American Encyclopedia*, North Bellmore, NY: Marshall Cavendish, pp. 934–36

——. (1996) "Korean 'comfort women': Movement for Redress," in *Asian Survey* 36, 12: 1227–40.

——. (2004a) "Women's Sexual Labor and the State in Korean History," in *Journal of Women's History* 15, 4: 170–77.

——. (2004b) "Aspiring to Craft Modern Gendered Selves: 'Comfort Women' and Chŏngsindae in Late Colonial Korea," in *Critical Asian Studies* 36, 2: 175–98.

Sturdevant, S.P. and Stoltzfus, B. (1992) *Let the Good Times Roll: Prostitution and the US Military in Asia*, New York: The New Press.

Tanaka, Y. (2002) *Japan's Comfort Women: Sexual Slavery and Prostitution during World War II and the US Occupation*, London and New York: Routledge.

Tomimura, J. (1982) *Mō hitotsu no Himeyuri butai* [One more Himeyuri unit], Tokyo: JCA shuppan.

Usuki, K. (1983) *Gendai no ianfutachi: Guntai ianfu kara Japayuki-san made* [Modern comfort women: From military comfort women to *Japayuki-san*], Tokyo: Gendaishi shuppankai.

Yi, N.H. (1992 [1927]) *Chosŏn haeŏhwasa* [The History of Chosŏn Kisaeng], Seoul: Tongmunsŏn.

Yim, C.G. (2004) *Pam ŭi Ilche ch'imnyaksa* [Nightly history of imperial Japan's invasion], Seoul: Hanpitmunhwasa.

Yuh, J.Y. (2002) *Beyond the Shadow of Camptown: Korean Military Brides in America*, New York: New York University Press.

5 Slum romance in Korean factory girl literature*

Ruth Barraclough

I heard a shocking thing today. I had stepped off the bus and was making my way home when I heard "Hey! *Kongsuni*[1] [Factory Girl]!" A group of male students were slouching nearby.

"Hey *kongsuni*! What are you gazing at? You worthless bitch."

There was no way I would take that so I replied, "So I'm a *kongsuni*. So what have you got to be proud of? Just because you scraped into school, does that make you scholars? What a load of crap. You should improve your minds, you losers."

But they kept going with their drivel.

"You ignorant bitch, what do you know? This ignorant bitch, how dare she. ..."

I swallowed down the abuse I wanted to give them, and went on my way. As soon as I got home I burst into tears I was so outraged. Why do we have to hear such things? Why do we get called this *kongsuni*?"

From Na Po-sun, *Even Though We Have So Little: Workers' Collected Writings* (1983)

You'll never know how many things are hidden from a woman in good clothes. The bold free look of a man at a woman he believes to be destitute – you must *feel* that look on you before you can understand – a good half of history.

Elizabeth Robins, *The Convert* (1907)

From the 1960s through to the 1980s Seoul busied itself in becoming a showpiece of industrial luxury to outshine that rival city to the north: Pyongyang. In these decades hundreds of thousands of country girls flooded into Seoul's back streets, carrying within them dreams of what they might find in the newly constructed boulevards and skyscrapers of the capital. As the lynchpin of South Korea's first stage of export-oriented industrialization, factory girls have been simultaneously thanked and dismissed, elevated and patronized as symbols of a patriotic and self-less devotion to national/family prosperity. Not only did the political suppression of factory girls in all-male unions and their economic marginalization in dead-end jobs obscure the significance of their role in late industrializing South Korea, but they were also central to the rapid development project in so many ways that seemed to efface them – as low-paid, diligent workers; as financial supporters of rural households; as young females slotted in at the bottom of the factory's gen-der hierarchy in ways that provided continuity with older patriarchal hierarchies.

When they asserted themselves as workers, and exposed the contradictions in their society that effaced them at the same time that it leaned upon them so heavily, they provoked the wrath of their employers, of the police, and sometimes of fellow male workers. The dissident labour movement responded to their endeavours for democratic relations in the workplace and in wider society by sentimentalizing them and fitting them into the "feminized position of victim" (Johnson 2001: 149). It is for these reasons that the writings of working-class women themselves are crucial to understanding their lives and times in these years. Marginal to the meta-narratives of national development and of class struggle, factory girls created their own narratives and in so doing wrote searing commentaries on Korea's industrialization experience.

This chapter takes as its archive the autobiographical literature of South Korean working-class women to examine the intimate effects of rapid industrialization. In particular I focus upon two recurring dilemmas for these authors: their precarious standing in South Korea's literary world, and their struggle to articulate a "working-class femininity." The authors endeavoured to construct a literature of agency in a literary and social world that barely acknowledged the interior world of lower-class women. They shared intimate truths with a society that was highly exploitative of the provincial girls come to work in Seoul's factories. Even as they ventured into literature these authors struggled with the persona of "factory girl": an identity loaded with contradictory subtext about poverty, sexual availability and labour movement heroism. I argue that these autobiographies, which at the time were read as straight accounts of working-class female suffering in a repressive state, question deeply held assumptions about culture and the feminine in South Korea's industrializing milieu.

These autobiographies were written in a maelstrom of economic, social and sexual upheaval, at a time when there was no clear language to describe ubiquitous occurrences like sexual harassment or sexual assault.[2] Rather than focusing upon the widespread sexual violence, or the threat of predatory behavior that overshadowed South Korea's military-run society, these writings instead adopt a defensive tone to expound upon factory girl virtue. They wrestle with the paradox of being condemned as unfeminine by manual labour, while at the same time their economic vulnerability overdetermines their sexuality. It is when we examine the problem of romance in factory girl writings that the sexual politics of poverty come clearly into view. Here we see as it was experienced the dangers of looking for love in a society that codes you as a "huntable creature."[3]

Becoming a writer

Before going on to examine the extraordinary place of these books in South Korean society in the 1980s and discuss excerpts from them, I want to stay with this moment of working-class women writing. And I should state from the outset that I am not describing some representative woman writer, but two quite distinct authors who read each other's work and published around the same time, in the late 1970s and early 1980s in South Korea. The authors are Chang Nam-su, who

published *The Lost Workplace* (*Ppaeatkin illt'ŏ*) in 1984 with the prominent literary publisher Ch'angjakkwa pip'yŏngsa, and Sŏk Chŏng-nam who wrote *Factory
Lights* (*Kongjang-ŭi pulpit*), also published in 1984. These two books would make
famous the world of Seoul's factory districts in the 1970s in tales of strikes and
slum romance, and they found a ready readership.[4] But rather than arguing that
they be awarded a place in the Korean literary canon as minority voices or anything else, I will attempt to show how powerfully these works stand as they are, at
the intersection of working-class politics and literary movements.

The central role of working-class women in South Korea's rapid industrialization over the 1960s, 1970s and 1980s has been obscured by their marginalization
in poorly paid, self-effacing jobs. The crucial part they played in capital accumulation cannot be divined from the remuneration they received, or in their job security, or in the possibilities for promotion in their workplace. Socially it is hard to
find evidence of their value or significance anywhere – they left school early, their
concerns were largely ignored in the press, and in public culture and "high art"
they appear to be almost completely invisible. Even on their way to work, they tell
us, they were taunted and harassed in the streets for being *kongsuni*, degraded by
their need for money and the manual labour they engaged in.

It was against this obscurity that working women wrote autobiographies. I place
this form of self-construction in the context of South Korea's state-led rapid industrialization that asked young blue-collar men and women to sacrifice themselves
for a future prosperity (Park 1970: 2–3). The contradictions that factory girls were
caught in reinforced their marginalization: they were central to the export market,
and the wages they remitted home helped sustain the rural economy, but they were
never seen as "real workers." They held temporary positions at the bottom rungs of
the factory. When labouring women began to assert themselves as workers in union
campaigns at the Tongil and YH factories and other worksites, the response from
factory owners and the police was ferocious. The suppression of working-class
women was a key feature of South Korea's successful export-led development,
while the opposition strategies the women employed reveal them as both critical of
and enmeshed in the gender and class ideologies that were part of their lives.

Autobiography, as the very symbol of self-representation, was itself a stand
against the social world that had for so long overlooked them. Yet this literature's
counter-hegemonic position is more complex than a simple binary relation to "high
culture" or state censorship in the 1980s.[5] For not only was the state under General
President Chun Doo Hwan (1980–88) itself struggling to attain hegemony in the
years these books were published and distributed but "high culture," or at least one
stream of literary culture, was turning to worker narratives and *minjung misul*, or
people's art movements, as a source of revitalization.[6]

The autobiographies I examine in this essay are representative of the cultural
creativity coming from working-class people throughout the 1980s. Plays, street
theatre, public shaman ceremonies, music troupes, collections of essays, short
stories, poetry anthologies and even a movie, *P'aŏp Chŏnya* (The Night Before
the Strike), were performed or circulated informally as part of a substantial dissident cultural market in South Korea. They were part of a wider *minjung* or

people's movement that in the 1970s and 1980s sought to popularize indigenous, "plebeian" cultural traditions and make them part of everyday life (Choi 1995: 105–18). The two books I discuss were published by "progressive" commercial publishing houses and were sold in the country's largest bookstores – Kyobo mungo and Chongno sŏjŏm.[7]

The literary historian Kwŏn Yŏng-min includes labour literature in a wider category of literature spawned by South Korean industrialization. He writes:

> As we passed through the 1980s, fictional accounts of the situation of the labour problem and the conventional form [of novels themselves] underwent change. With the beginning of the democratization movement and the opening of the political system, [workers' literature] gave a lifelike reflection of the enormous changes brought about by the liquidation of the structure of authoritarian society in the late 1980s. … It is accurate to say that the social problems brought about through the process of industrialization were to make workers' very lives and inequities a matter of concern in literature.[8]

So this factory girl literature was part of a broader "labour literature" while at the same time it addressed concerns and desires particular to working-class women. In this essay I will be drawing from two of these books, Sŏk Chŏng-nam's *Factory Lights* and Chang Nam-su's *The Lost Workplace*, and make reference to several others.

Factory girl heroines

Chang Nam-su begins her autobiography *The Lost Workplace* with a history of her family's circumstances when she was growing up in the countryside in Miryang-gun in South Kyŏngsang province. From the very preface of the book Chang Nam-su writes commandingly. She judges her family relations as "feudal" and when her father is compelled to make the journey to Seoul one lean spring, Chang Nam-su describes it as "the way the first generation of industrial workers began." Her memories of school are vivid and she describes how she discovers the limited horizons of the poor as she and the other school students watch the wealthy daughter win the class prize (even though Nam-su received the highest marks). She writes of her regret at the abrupt end of her school years, and it is a familiar theme in Korea's working-class autobiographies. Throughout these first few pages Chang Nam-su draws upon a broad lexicon. She describes farm life like a farmer, analyzes her circumstances like someone who had spent a long time in movement circles, and yet writes simply and directly to her readers. It is when, in the midst of a rural idyll, Chang Nam-su describes herself sitting up a tree astride a branch reading *Tess* that the first jolt of autobiography hits the reader. Like Chang, the reader too is engrossed in a book with a peasant girl heroine, but in this case the protagonist is the interpreter as well as the central character.

This moment is the reader's first glimpse of Chang Nam-su's skilful repudiation of the received image of working class and peasant girls as voiceless victims, unaware also of their pretty plight in literature. *Tess* is Thomas Hardy's novel *Tess of the D'Urbervilles*, a story about the pitiful lives of peasant girls in England and their ruin at the hands of men and religion. Chang Nam-su's favourite books feature the plucky peasant girl heroine – Katusha in Leo Tolstoy's *Resurrection* and Tess in *Tess of the D'Urbervilles*.

The novel *Tess of the D'Urbervilles* is an interesting touchstone of the movement of literature into the lives and leisure time of maidservants, peasant daughters and factory girls. Published in England in 1891, the book divided public opinion when it first appeared, with many readers unable to countenance a novel whose main character was, amongst other things, an unwed mother. But for many English readers of *Tess*, particularly those of the newer reading public, lower middle-class and working-class females of the late nineteenth and early twentieth centuries, it was a relief to encounter Tess: "a poor working girl with an interesting character, thoughts and personality," writes Edith Hall in her autobiography of servant life in the 1920s. Hall continues:

> This was the first serious novel I had read up to this time in which the heroine had not been of "gentle birth," and the labouring classes as brainless automatons. This book made me feel human and even when my employers talked to me as though I wasn't there, I felt that I could take it; I knew that I could be a person in my own right.[9]

In South Korea also, working-class women reported an ambivalent relationship to literature. When Sŏk Chŏng-nam is introduced to a male poet, her first acquaintance with someone involved in the literary world, he laughs at her taste in poetry – Byron and the German poet Heine – who represented the tastes of educated readers a half century earlier (Sŏk 1984: 54). Sŏk Chŏng-nam initially loves the library for workers at Tongil Textiles because there she can read poetry uninterrupted for a couple of hours at a time and forget about her cramped life and menial job. She is content to exchange her labour on the factory shift for the hours of "dreaming" in the library (Sŏk 1984: 18). Yet the literature she eventually writes is not unconnected with her own lived experience. Rather than reinforce the divisions between labour and literature, between what Raymond Williams calls "the values of literature and the lives of working people" (Williams 1983: 221), Sŏk Chŏng-nam in her own literature renders these divisions ambiguous, in stories that are pitched as much to factory girls as they are to poets and other possible readers.

Like *Tess of the D'Urbervilles*, Chang Nam-su's *The Lost Workplace* is also about a peasant girl who is caught up in some of the great themes of the times – the journey to Seoul, entering the factory economy, and joining the union movement's culture of dissent. But Chang Nam-su writes herself as heroine and reveals her autobiographical world with the confidence of someone aware that they are making history. It is no coincidence that those who directly experienced the strikes and the crackdown at Tongil, Wŏnp'ung and YH factories authored the first labour literature. As these young people were dismissed from their jobs, moved to other areas, changed their names and found temporary employment, and began to write of their experiences, they made visible the social structures that had quashed them for so long. They articulated how they were fighting a social economy that rated their labour and their person "cheap," a political arrangement that demanded their "sacrifice," and a cultural order that aided in the suppression of writing by lower-class females.

It is such a voice that Raymond Williams refers to when he writes of the prevalence of the autobiographical form in the industrial literature of Wales. Of the working-class authors Williams says:

> These writers, after all, although very conscious of their class situations, were at the same time, within it, exceptional men [sic], and there are central formal features of the autobiography which correspond to this situation: at once the representative and the exceptional account.
>
> (Williams 1983: 221)

The coupling of "representative and exceptional," the tension between the individual and collective nature of the working-class autobiography took its toll on the authors. They were engaged in an ambivalent process, to disrupt class lines at the same time that they were memorializing a working-class version of life. Jacques Ranciere, in his book *The Nights of Labour*, deconstructs the relationships between workers and intellectuals in nineteenth-century France and calls attention to the disruptions that occur when workers try to escape to another kind of life through writing, only to become the embodiment of their class as proletarian authors, or proletarian poets. Ranciere poses the question: "How is it that our deserters, yearning to break away from the constraints of proletarian life, circuitously and paradoxically forged the image and discourse of worker identity?" (Ranciere 1989: 64)

It is a salient question for South Korean working-class authors also. Caught in the bind between honouring the experience of working-class life and fleeing from it, they attempted to reconcile these two endeavours through the genre of autobiography, situating their self-portraits within the social structures that impinged upon their lives. Thus, even in the most intimate and personal episodes in their books they make explicit the social causes of their experiences: the influence of poverty on sexuality and of family burdens on the decision to take perilous jobs.[10]

Part of the power and novelty of these autobiographies stemmed from the very suppression of writing by young impoverished females, evidenced by a truncated education and a massive juvenile labour market. The very intimacy of the autobiographical genre gave these authors the space to write revealingly of themselves and their circumstances. Sŏk Chŏng-nam would write about the costs of autobiography, the stigma of revealing one's occupation, and consequently one's poverty and vulnerability, to the public.

Sŏk Chŏng-nam does not reveal the identity of the poet who first read her work and encouraged her to publish her diary. Although she only hints at his full name, she nevertheless gives a revealing sketch of his person and character. When a friend of Sŏk Chŏng-nam persuades her to meet a poet from the Christian Academy, a Christian organization with strong social justice leanings, who expressed an interest in reading her writings, Sŏk fantasizes about what this poet will be like. She imbues her fantasy of him with all the hackneyed, romantic traits of a poet of convention: "I [had] imagined him above all to be a noble individual with long, curly locks cascading down his shoulders and a brilliant light in his haunted eyes" (Sŏk 1984: 54). Instead, she tells us with palpable disappointment, her poet was a chubby chap in his thirties. Sŏk Chŏng-nam is further dismayed when he proceeds to address her in "low" or "informal" language.[11]

Sŏk Chŏng-nam hesitates to give permission to the poet to read her diary, but she cannot explain to him the reasons for her vacillation. She explains them to us:

> More than anything else what shamed me was that this diary would reveal how destitute, how plagued by poverty my life was. Of course as I was a factory girl making my own living people would naturally assume that I was poor, just as the poet had. But if he were to discover just how degrading my life up until now had been. … Even thinking about the exposure brought goosebumps to my flesh. If it is published there would be no escaping the humiliation.
>
> (Sŏk 1984: 55)

In this disclosure Sŏk Chŏng-nam is candid about the personal costs of autobiography, and the convictions that urge her to dare publication of her diary as an autobiography. In entrusting her book to a literary world that had rarely before done justice to representations of working-class women, Sŏk Chŏng-nam was facing a dilemma. Added to that was the fact that her first piece, *Pult'anŭn nunmul* (*Burning Tears*), an account of the Tongil dispute, was published while she was still working at Tongil Textiles.

At first, people above her in the factory took pride in the fact that one of their employees was to be a published writer, and a female guard sought out Chŏng-nam and said "I heard that you have a talent for writing, keep it up," and stroked her hair (Sŏk 1984: 55). But once the piece appeared, the atmosphere quickly changed to one of cool animosity. Sŏk Chŏng-nam was called in to meet the labour manager who told her she had created "vile propaganda" against Tongil and had been used by the magazine, which only wanted a shocking story to sell its product (Sŏk 1984: 55). She was warned, but not dismissed, and meantime readers of *Wŏlgan Taehwa* (*Monthly Dialogue*), a literary magazine, were in 1976 reading one of the first pieces of what would become a revitalized proletarian or labour literature (*nodong munhak*) movement.

Some of the most avid readers of the new labour literature were university students, who found themselves portrayed in this literature as markers of the divisions between people from different classes. Nowhere were these divisions depicted more forcefully than in the intimate tales of class romance.

In these tales Chang Nam-su illustrates the fragile relations between young people working in factories and people studying at universities. Here young female workers reveal how thin-skinned they are about all the things that define them in the abstract – status, employment, poverty and lack of education. Throughout the 1970s and early 1980s young, unmarried, curious youth had flooded into the capital looking for work. In 1983, 72 per cent of women in the manufacturing sector were aged between 18 and 24 (Moon 2005: 77). Many of them had come alone to Seoul, and sent wages home to their families in the provinces.

Class romance

Episodes of romance in working-class literature are pervaded by a sense of the dangers of romance for factory girls, shadowed by the romance economy of the streets. The proximity of red light districts, the financial and glamorous appeal of employment there, and the many attractive guises of the pimp added up to make falling in love a potentially perilous business. Working-class women, and all women close to poverty, were haunted by prostitution, part of the shadow economy of South Korea's economic boom and the hunting ground for Korea's oversized military class. The extensive prostitution industry described in Chunghee Sarah Soh's chapter in this volume spilled over into working-class districts as well as middle-class suburbs of Seoul. Shop windows displaying women could be found tucked beneath overpasses, prominent in university districts, as well as close by all the large railway stations. "The Love Story of Unhŭi," a cautionary tale of class romance from Chang Nam-su's *The Lost Workplace*, exemplifies the hazards of falling in love outside of one's class.

Unhŭi is a country girl living and working in Seoul. She is from Chŏlla Province in the southwest of Korea and works at a factory that makes dolls' clothes. On a rare day off Unhŭi goes with friends to visit the palaces of Seoul she has always dreamed of seeing, and at the museum at Kyŏngbok Palace she meets the affable, attractive university student Sŏngho. They strike up a friendship that soon becomes intense and despite the warnings of friends Unhŭi devotes herself to Sŏngho – tidying his lodgings and even lending him money for his school fees and expenses. One evening after her shift Unhŭi is waylaid by Sŏngho who begs her for a favour – can she lend him the 200,000 won he needs urgently for a purpose he asks to remain secret? Unhŭi hesitates, then says yes, without knowing how she will get such a large sum of money. They spend that night together in a hotel and sexually consummate their relationship.

The next morning Unhŭi rises early and goes to the lodgings of her friend Mihwa, who has saved 300,000 won to send to her parents to pay off the family's debts. But Mihwa is not home and the landlady lets Unhŭi inside to wait. In her great haste Unhŭi yields to temptation and takes the money, thinking to explain all to Mihwa later.

Unhŭi goes straight to Sŏngho's lodgings, but this time the spell between them is broken. There is a new coldness between them, and after giving Sŏngho the money Unhŭi is leaving when she sees another woman – well-dressed and beautifully made up – walk up Sŏngho's lane. This, it seems, is Sŏngho's real girlfriend – a woman of his own class. Sŏngho cannot hide his discomfiture and Unhŭi, overcome with distress, dashes away and reaches home only to find a plain-clothes policeman waiting for her. Unhŭi and Chang Nam-su are in prison together when Unhŭi tells her story.

Unhŭi's story of infatuation, theft and incarceration displays the principle that someone must pay the price for the privilege exercised by a higher class to loaf through an industrial revolution.[12] Factory women like Unhŭi could find themselves bankrupted by this romance economy that paid them for their labour while charging them exorbitantly for their credulity, boredom and loneliness, and consequent craving for leisure and romance.

Strictly speaking Unhŭi is not in the employ of Sŏngho, and hands money over to him because he asks for it and not because she has earned it for him. But their economic and erotic transaction that exposes her while it enriches him is close enough to the conventional relationship of prostitute and pimp to serve as a warning to all of Chang Nam-su's working class female readers.

In a nuanced account of her own class romance, Chang Nam-su explores the possibilities of an equal relationship. The historian Chŏng Hyŏn-baek was the first to point out what an intricate picture we can form of South Korean society in the 1970s by following the course of the romance between Chang Nam-su and the university student Hyun-u, "a relationship formed through shared interests and wide reading" (Chŏng 1985: 126). A love affair culminating in marriage into a higher class was one of the few ways that factory girls could escape the dormitories or tiny slum-lodgings, and the private degradations of poverty.

The year is 1977 and the author, Chang Nam-su, was nineteen, and had just started work at the prestigious Wŏnp'ung Mobang textile factory in Seoul.[13] Chang Nam-su had gone home to South Kyŏngsang province in the southeastern part of Korea to renew her identity papers. She has just said farewell to her grandmother on the station platform and boarded the local train for a slow ride back to Seoul, when she was drawn into a conversation:

> The young man in the next seat addressed me.
> "Miss, where are you going?"
> "I go as far as Yŏngdŭngp'o, and where are you going?"[14]
> "That's lucky, I'm going to Yongsan. Shall we talk a little?"
> I smiled as I nodded my head. He was a second-year student at K University and his name was Hyŏn-u. I told him I was working but I also wanted to study more and for the moment was studying [part-time] at a night school.
> (Chang 1984: 35)

The night school Chang Nam-su was attending at this time, Hallim Hagwon, was not part of the political "night school movement" – a joint venture between radical students and workers – but an ordinary evening class where factory workers could study for their middle school certificate. Yet this exchange illustrates how education was a flash point for factory girls who had left school unwillingly to earn money or make way for a sibling. To labour by day and study by night as Chang Nam-su was doing at this time was to cram two lives into one and put an almost intolerable strain upon one's body.

While she never reveals how hard-won is her learning, the flow of knowledge between "worker" and "intellectual" is shown as very much two-way in this exchange:

> "Let's be friends, and lower our language."
>
> Even though I assented to this I could change my language only after he pointed out to me again and again [that I was using high form]. As we talked I felt that our ideas were similar and I chattered away without resting. We discussed Tolstoy's *Resurrection* and *Demian* by Herman Hesse.
>
> (Chang 1984: 35)

The novels discussed by Nam-su and Hyŏn-u are revealing. *Resurrection* by Leo Tolstoy is the story of the spiritual redemption of the dissolute Prince Nekhlyudov who forgoes his early promise when he seduces and then abandons his family's treasured servant, Katusha. Besides being a tale of spiritual atonement, *Resurrection* is also a class love story. *Demian* also relates a spiritual journey, where the impressionable author, a schoolboy, meets the enlightened and charismatic Demian at school and falls under the influence of his doctrine – that organized religion and public morality are cant. We can appreciate that Hyŏn-u is not shamming but has really read both books as he knows not to offer himself as the rake Prince Nekhlyudov but rather proposes to play-act the magnetic, svengali-like Demian:

> "Nam-su, was Demian fantastic?"
>
> "Yeah, just great."
>
> "Really? Then, can't I be Demian for you?"[15]
>
> "Psh … Hyŏn-u, no way."
>
> "Why? Why 'no way'?"
>
> I was bursting with laughter.
>
> He was laughing too. I showed him *Monthly Dialogue*,[16] and told him to read the article in it called "Human Market."
>
> "What's it about? Nam-su, you tell me."
>
> So I went into a full explanation for him. Before we knew it the train was passing Anyang.
>
> "Look, that looks like a business; why does it have its lights on at night?"
>
> "Because they're working," I retorted brusquely.
>
> "What! They're working at night? They really keep working at night too?"
>
> I was struck dumb. How can this person not know that? What kind of a person is he? This "friend" asking if people work into the night? A great gust of loneliness squeezed my heart and made me miserable. Ah, how can this person be so content knowing so little about the world? Are all university students like this?
>
> He saw my expression. "I really didn't know. That people keep working into the night, I mean. It must be because I have passed life so ignorantly. But poverty also has its happiness, doesn't it? I'm convinced that the poor are happier than the rich."
>
> "Ah, so Hyŏn-u took the bumpkin train so he could taste a little of that 'poverty'? What a treat! Do you know a little about real poverty?"

At my sharp retort he bowed his head.

He didn't go to Yongsan but got off with me at Yŏngdŭngp'o.

"We can't part like this. Shall we have something to eat?"

"No thanks, I'm off."

"Well then give me your address. I'll send you a letter."

"No. See you Hyŏn-u."

As I turned away he put out his arms like a child and blocked my way, he wouldn't let me pass.

"OK then Hyŏn-u, you write down your address for me. I'll send you a letter. That's alright isn't it?"

He had no choice but to take out some paper and write down his address.

"Aiyu, how can your handwriting be this bad?"

But he didn't answer me and just kept writing.

"I shall write," I promised myself.

I waved to him from the bus but he just stood there looking after me. In that empty dawn bus I said to myself, "All right, let's write. And I'll tell you a little more about the world," and soon after that I did write. His reply came immediately …

(Chang 1984: 35–36)

Chang Nam-su and her new friend Hyŏn-u deepen their acquaintance through correspondence, and make a plan to meet:

I picked a day and a place that suited me and sent him the letter. On the day of our meeting I arrived at the rendezvous place exactly on time, but he didn't come. I waited for ages and only when my pride was thoroughly bruised did I get on a bus, alighting at the terminal, Suyuri. The April Uprising memorial is nearby. He had talked about the April Uprising. … The memorial's white pillars drew my eye. I walked through the graveyard then sat on the lawn and passed several hours just thinking. He had stood me up. I could not bear that on our very first date he had stood me up.

(Chang 1984: 35–37)

The April Uprising memorial in northern Seoul that Chang Nam-su wanders into is the memorial to students who died in the April Revolution of 1960. Fired on by troops on the orders of President Syngman Rhee as they led demonstrations in Seoul to protest election rigging, political corruption and police violence, the demonstrators soon gained control of the streets and within days brought down the government. The April Uprising memorial has been an important symbol for students of their painful and exemplary past in leading the attack against corrupt regimes. However this memorial holds little consolation for Chang Nam-su, whose own political acuteness seems so much greater than that of the student Hyŏn-u.

I had been dreaming of him as a possible boyfriend. What a fool I was. He is a university student. He's not someone who has the time to sit and listen to a *kongsuni* like me musing about the world.[17] … Two days later a letter arrived.

"I am truly sorry for not keeping our appointment on Saturday. Conscript duties prevented me. I had no opportunity even to contact you. ..."

I knew as soon as I read those words that he couldn't have helped what happened. ... His voice asking me "Do people work at night?" swirled around in my head. I am a worker in a textile factory and he is a university student. ... How much I had learned in the space of a few days.

If he had not been a university student I cannot say if my pride would have been so wounded, or if I would have understood his missing our appointment, or if I would be meeting him still. The Saturday evening he had asked me to telephone I spent deep in thought, then suddenly I had the urge to see my night-school friend Song-ja ...

(Chang 1984: 37)

It is during her walk around the fruit gardens at Oryu-dong with Song-ja the next morning that Nam-su reveals the depth of her resentment. Nam-su and Song-ja stumble across an enclosure of dogs that will be used to make soup. Song-ja explains to Nam-su that the dogs have been drugged so that their bark does not carry and disturb the neighbourhood, and Nam-su stands and listens, transfixed by the dogs' hoarse voices and bulging eyes. This is her moment to reflect, which she does ruthlessly:

As I got closer I saw that the dogs were all barking in unison but no sound came from them. It is a dog's instinct to bark and yet here they had been muffled while they strained to bark in the most agonizing way. ... I too felt my throat constrict and something seemed to grip my chest.

(Chang 1984: 38)

Chang Nam-su recognizes herself in the trapped, gasping dogs. She describes the feeling of not only being trapped by class – by poverty, by lack of education, by one's sensitivity to slight – but above all knowing better than anybody exactly how trapped and voiceless you are. It is such a voice that Raymond Williams describes when he writes of:

[T]hat deep ambiguity of a subordinated people, a subordinated class, whose visions are larger not only than those of the alien system by which they are dominated but larger also than is tolerable, when you are that far down and still seeing that far up.

(Williams 1983: 228)

Chang Nam-su is compelled to reflect on the social contradictions that have thwarted her desires:

The love stories that have come down to us from olden times were of a king and a country maiden, a princess and a woodcutter. But in this society it is university student and university student, the boss's daughter and the son of an elite government bureaucrat, the worker with other workers, and so it all seems to fit into a tidy cliché. It is not people meeting each other with the deep sense of [sharing something as] human beings, but name goes with name, prestige goes with prestige, and so it goes on. ... When we who work in factories fall in love, we're called sluts. If a university student gets into a scrape it's viewed indulgently, but if a worker makes a mistake everyone is disgusted.

(Chang 1984: 100)

Chŏng Hyŏn-baek interprets Chang Nam-su's relationship with Hyŏn-u as an opportunity to escape her working life and rise in class status through love and marriage:

As they become closer we can sense [Chang Nam-su's] intellectual curiosity, and the student's attraction to her intelligent attitude. With the deepening of the relationship she falls into a profound internal conflict. She ends up deciding that he cannot suit her on the understanding that they are both people of their class. In so doing she throws away this opportunity given to her [to rise in class status] and reveals her resentment.

(Chŏng 1985: 126)

The implication is that Chang Nam-su is refusing the transformation from Factory Girl to Lady. She will not cross classes, and by this stage the reader can recognize the principle she is struggling for – the utopian vision of a different society – where people can meet and fall in love, not as "factory girl" and "university student," but free of the constraints of a class society. In fact, for Chang Nam-su love exposes more directly than any possible argument why love cannot solve all, why politics and society and money must intrude.

Factory girl virtue

Chang Nam-su's love tales tell us not only about the social world of factory girls, but about their morality also. The labour of factory girls that degraded them in the eyes of a patriarchal and class-conscious society also brought them into social proximity with women who laboured in brothels in the booming informal economy of the 1970s and 1980s. The reticence of factory girls on the subject of prostitution is striking.[18] Chang Nam-su's *The Lost Workplace* is a book determinedly about factory girl virtue.

It is clear that factory girls who struggled to convince the public that they were respectable could not afford to compare themselves to women who worked in the red-light districts. As Elaine Kim has noted, the "traditional [upper-class] Korean view that women's labour outside the home degrades the family" meant that when women from the poorer classes entered employment in the new social space of the factory they were conspicuous as an affront to femininity (E. Kim 1998: 142). Yet this focus on a lack of femininity is in many ways a mystification that distracts us from the extreme sexualization of lower-class women that went hand in hand with their economic vulnerability. How else could it be that these "unfeminine" factory girls are the same huntable creatures of Seoul's evening streets, crowded buses, palaces and factory districts? Here the gap between femininity and sexuality is bridged by sexual harassment that becomes a form of sexual discipline to make "unfeminine" women more sexually docile.

Because womanhood was defined by attributes that were out of reach for the poorer classes of women, working women came to be seen as tainted by an unfeminine need for money. The received image of working-class women as tainted by economic need affected factory women acutely. Femininity, beauty and grace were "class properties" in South Korea, unattainable for factory women.[19] Chang Nam-su explains:

> People say that women's voices should not go over the wall; women should be modest, talk in a cultured manner, and behave gently. ... Then what are we? If we measure ourselves in those terms, we are nothing. We have to be loud in order to communicate on the shop floor; we have to wear uniforms and rush between the machines; naturally our movements are coarse. If the only price we get paid for our endless working for our country's industrial development and economic growth is the contemptuous name of *kongsuni*, and the deprivation of our femininity, then, what are we? For whom are we working, and for what are we living?[20]

> (Chang 1984: 42–43)

But while their femininity was in question, working-class women's sexual availability became overdetermined in this particular type of "law and order" society that barely acknowledged sexual assault as a crime. This is the surplus message of factory girl autobiographies, a context that the labour movement itself could not acknowledge. As Kim Won has shown, factory girls were constructed as either "sexless" or "productive labour" by the labour movement that had no capacity to critique the breach of both Confucian norms and middle-class morality that labouring women appeared to represent (W. Kim 2004: 45–46). In this way these authors had much more at stake and addressed a far deeper set of problems than the labour movement was able to encompass. The authors tell us how nerve-racking, thrilling and fraught it was to look for love in a social world that read your class background at a glance and made its own assumptions.

Conclusion: but is it literature?

It is important to note that prior to the publication of these works, autobiography by working-class women was not part of any recognizable literary tradition in Korean society. Indeed when they first appeared, these books opened up the whole question of the production of cultural authority. The authors make explicit the connections between the conditions of literary production, the emancipatory role literature can play both personally and socially, the joys of writing, and the gruelling schedule a working woman must obey if she wants to publish anything.

They remind us how ill-equipped they are to join the canon, membership in which is conditional on one's prose being swept clean of the writer's sweat and other evidence of exertion.

That being said, these works by Sŏk and Chang do not stand outside the literary market that published and received them. Indeed it is interesting to note that the most popular factory girl autobiography of this period, Song Hyo-soon's *The Road to Seoul*, relays a sensibility of Christian meekness and feminine suffering, a kind of "working-class weepy," that makes it more dated than the works by Chang and Sŏk I have discussed here. More than the autobiographies by Chang and Sŏk, *The Road to Seoul* fitted into already established conventions of the portrayal of working-class women as sentimental figures, in literature as well as in the labour movement. By contrast, Sŏk Chŏng-nam and Chang Nam-su present themselves as literary and social subjects in ways that implicate the middle class in their experience of degradation. They illustrate the slippage between the poverty of their working life and the richness of their interior worlds, and Chang Nam-su in particular clearly names the sexual politics of poverty.

Yet these two authors remain ambiguous presences in South Korea's literary circles in the 1980s. We need only turn to Chang Nam-su's introduction to her autobiography to observe how difficult it is for her to place herself: "I am no famous politician, no celebrity, no artist. … Like most workers I am only the unwanted daughter of a poor farming family who became a factory girl" (Chang 1984: 3). Here she is longing for a secure place in the cultural and social hierarchy, while at the same time deriding that hierarchy. Perhaps one of the most striking innovations shared by these two autobiographies was to tie political and literary representation together, in works that are framed as a challenge both to literature and to society, foreshadowing a new kind of world where working-class women might be central protagonists.

It is no coincidence that the 1970s and 1980s should have produced our richest sources on the lives of female textile workers in South Korea. These were the years when women workers fought for and gained the attention of their society through a militant union movement, and created a space for themselves in literature. For Chang Nam-su and other factory women, fighting low wages was also about fighting the repression of desire. These works show how difficult it was to be sexually curious on small wages, how gender discipline encompassed by the word "femininity" worked to control factory girls, and how class and sexuality were intextricably intertwined. Despite these restrictions, Chang Nam-su writes that one might reject low wages and degrading conditions and all the determinism of poverty and believe in the possibility of other kinds of relationships, glimpsed one night on a slow train to Seoul.

Notes

* An earlier version of this chapter was published as 'When Korean Working-Class Women Began to Write' in Ch'angjakkwa Bip'yŏng [Creation and Criticism] Vol 127, Spring 2005. I would like to thank the editors of Ch'angjakkwa Bip'yŏng,

especially Paek Nak-chung, for kindly permitting me to republish portions of that article here.

1 *Kongsuni* is a derogatory term that roughly translates as "factory girl."
2 The term "sexual harassment" (*song hŭirong*) first appeared in public parlance in South Korea in the early 1990s, and sexual harassment only became a legal offence in 1998. I am grateful to Yi Eun-sang of the Korea Sexual Violence Relief Centre for this information. See Shim (2004: 312–14) for more details.
3 The term is J.M. Coetzee's (1996: 82).
4 Other autobiographical works from this period include Yu Dong-wu's *Ŏnŭ Dolmaengi-ŭi Oech'im* (The Cry of One Stone), published in 1984; Pak Yŏng-gŭn's edited collection of workers' writings *Kongjang Oksang-e Olla* (To The Factory Roof), also published in 1984; an edited collection by Kim Kyŏng-sŭk, *Kŭrŏna Urinŭn Ŏje-ŭi Uriga Anida* (But We Are Not Yesterday's We), published in 1986; and *Uridŭl Kajin Kŏt Pirok Chŏgŏdo – Kŭllojadŭl-ŭi Kŭlmoŭm 1* (Even Though We Don't Have Much: Workers' Collected Writings 1), published in 1983. In addition, unpublished collections of stories and autobiographical writings also circulated in factories, night schools and literary circles throughout the 1980s. Kim Pyŏng-ik discusses this process in P.I. Kim (1989: 12–13).
5 An example of this literary censorship is the ban on the re-printing of Korean proletarian literature published in the 1920s and 1930s. This ban was lifted in 1987.
6 For a discussion of the decisive role of the middle class in the unravelling of the Chun Doo Hwan regime see Jang Jip Choi (1993).
7 Although I do not have definite sales figures, the books were all available in mainstream bookstores by the late 1980s.
8 Kwon Yŏng-min is here referring to a wider body of literature than this study can consider. For more on 'industrial literature' see Kwon (1985: 318, *passim*).
9 From Elizabeth Hall (1977: 39–40), quoted in Rose (2001: 275).
10 See, for example, Chang Nam-su's discussion of her friend Nam-ok's decision to go to Iran for work that would be "well paid but hellish," and her death there in a road accident one month later (Chang 1984: 56–58).
11 The use of honorific address forms in Korean is a defining marker of status. Thus the poet, who is older than Sŏk Chŏng-nam, is a well-educated man and of a higher social status than she, has a wide linguistic choice. He can address her using a variety of honorific forms, or he can drop the honorifics altogether. That he chooses to do the latter shocks Chŏng-nam, who does not have the wide linguistic choice that the poet in his social status enjoys, and must address him with honorifics attached, despite the fact that he shows no such delicacy towards her. It is a suggestive choice, but the poet's option of address cannot be called incorrect. Rather, he might be said to have misjudged their social distance, a view that Sŏk Chŏng-nam appears to hold as she subtly upbraids him in her book. She says of him "this man I was meeting for the first time addressed me as though he were an old friend who had known me since I was a small child" (Sŏk 1984: 54). That the (mis)use of honorific and informal address forms was a significant issue for many working-class women can be judged by the frequency with which the issue appears in their writings. For a rare example of equal address forms despite unequal class relations see the section later in this chapter on class romance. In making this argument I am indebted to the research of Gi-Hyun Shin (1999).
12 I borrow this turn of phrase from Michael Sprinker who wrote, "Someone must ultimately pay the price for the privilege exercised by the ruling classes not to engage in productive labour" (Sprinker 1998: 185).
13 Wonp'ung Mobang would become famous as the centre of one of the fiercest labour disputes of the 1970s. For more information see Han'guk Kidokkyo Kyohoe Hyŏbuihoe (1984: 403–8).

14 Yŏngdŭngp'o is an industrial suburb of Seoul that would become a center for labour protest in the 1980s.
15 "Demian" the character appears in several different guises in Hesse's novel, beginning with the schoolboy Demian, but also appearing as a portrait painting, as Frau Eva, and as the author himself; and his image becomes symbolic of spiritual self-awakening.
16 *Wolgan Taehwa*, or Monthly Dialogue, is the magazine where Sŏk Chŏng-nam made her literary debut.
17 Here Chang Nam-su uses the derogatory term *kongsuni* to refer to herself as something shabby and insignificant.
18 While men frequently drew parallels between working-class women and prostitutes, factory girls rarely did. One exception is Kim Kyŏng-suk who wrote about prostitutes and factory girls: "You and I are from the same lot, all thrown out by this society. But is it right to live like this without making any protest against the world which treats us like worms?" From K.S. Kim (1986: 106), quoted in Koo (2001: 137).
19 I borrow this term from Patricia Johnson (2001: 34).
20 Translation by S.K. Kim (1997: 172).

References

Chang, N.S. (1984). *Ppaeatkin Ilt'ŏ* [*The Lost Workplace*], Seoul: Ch'angjakkwa Bip'yŏngsa.

Choi, C. (1995) "The Minjung Culture Movement and the Construction of Popular Culture in Korea," in K.Wells (ed.) *South Korea's Minjung Movement: The Culture and Politics of Dissidence*, Honolulu: University of Hawai'i Press.

Choi, J.J. (1993) "Political Cleavages in South Korea," in H. Koo (ed.), *State and Society in Contemporary Korea*, Ithaca, NY: Cornell University Press, pp. 13–50.

Chŏng, H.B. (1985) "Yŏsŏng Nodongja-ŭi ŭisik kwa Nodong Sekye: Nodongja Suki Punsŏkŭl Chunsimŭro" [Women Workers' Consciousness and the World of Work: Analyzing Workers' Writings], in *Yŏsŏng* [Women], 1: 116–62.

Chŏng, M.S. (1993) "70 Nyŏndae Yŏsŏng Nodong Undong-ŭi Hwalsŏng-e Kwanhan Kyŏnghŏm Sekyejok Yŏngu" [A Study on the Women's Labour Movement in the 1970s], Masters Thesis, Ewha Women's University.

Christian Conference of Asia's Urban Rural Mission (eds.) (1982). *From the Womb of Han: Stories of Korean Women Workers*, Hong Kong: Christian Conference of Asia's Urban Rural Mission.

Coetzee, J.M. (1996) *Giving Offense: Essays on Censorship*, Chicago, IL: University of Chicago Press.

Hall, E. (1977) *Canary Girls and Stockpots*, London: Luton.

Han'guk Kidokkyo Kyohoe Hyŏbuihoe [National Council of Churches in Korea] (1984) *Nodong Hyonjang kwa Chungon* [*The Scene and Testimony of Labour*], Seoul: P'ulbbit.

Johnson, P. (2001) *Hidden Hands: Working-Class Women and Victorian Social Problem Fiction*, Athens, OH: Ohio University Press.

Kim, E. (1998) "Men's Talk," in E. Kim and C. Choi (eds.), *Dangerous Women: Gender and Korean Nationalism*, London: Routledge, pp. 67–117.

Kim, K.S. (1986) *Kŭrŏna Urinŭn ŏje-ŭi uriga Anida* [But We Are Not Yesterday's We], Seoul: Tolbegae.

Kim, P.I. (1989) "Recent Korean Labour Novels: 'Labor' Literature vs. Labor 'Literature,'" in *Korea Journal* 29, 3: 12–22.

Kim, S.K. (1997) *Class Struggle or Family Struggle: The Lives of Women Factory Workers in South Korea*, Cambridge: Cambridge University Press.

Kim, W. (2004) "The True Character and Desires of Factory Girls: A Critical Study of 1970s 'Factory Girl Discourse,'" in *Sociology Research* 12, 1: 44–80.

Kim, Y.S. (1987) "Phases of Development of Proletarian Literature in Korea," in *Korea Journal*, 27, 1: 31–45.

Koo, H. (2001) *Korean Workers: The Culture and Politics of Class Formation*, Ithaca, NY: Cornell University Press.

Kwon, Y.M. (1985) *Haebang 40 Nyŏn-ŭi munhak, 1945–1985* [*Korean Literature in the 40 Years Since Liberation, 1945–1985*], Seoul: Minumsa.

Moon, S. (2005) *Militarized Modernity and Gendered Citizenship in South Korea*, Durham, NC: Duke University Press.

Na, P.S. (ed.) (1983) *Uridŭl Kajin kŏt Pirok Chŏgŏdo – Kŭllojadŭl-ŭi kŭlmoŭm 1* [*Even Though We Don't Have Much: Workers' Collected Writings 1*], Seoul: Tolbekae.

Pak, Y.G. (ed.) (1984) *Kongjang Oksang-e Olla* [*To The Factory Roof*], Seoul: P'ulbitt.

Park, C.H. (1970) *Our Nation's Path*, Seoul: Hollym.

Ranciere, J. (1989) *The Nights of Labour: The Workers' Dream in Nineteenth-Century France*, Philadelphia, PA: Temple University Press.

Robins, E. (1907) *The Convert*, London: Methuen.

Rose, J. (2001) *The Intellectual Life of the British Working Classes*, New Haven, NC: Yale University Press.

Shim, Y.H. (2004). *Sexual Violence and Feminism in Korea*, Seoul: Hanyang University Press.

Shin, G.H. (1999) "Politeness and Deference in Korean: A Case Study of Pragmatic Dynamics," PhD dissertation, Monash University.

Sŏk, C.N. (1984) *Kongjang-ŭi Pulbitt* [*Factory Lights*], Seoul: Ilwŏl Sogak.

Song, H.S. (1982) *Sŏulro Kanŭnkil* [*The Road to Seoul*], Seoul: Hyŏngsŏngsa.

Sprinker, M. (1987) *Imaginary Relations: Aesthetics and Ideology in the Theory of Historical Materialism*, London: Verso.

Williams, R. (1983) *Problems in Materialism and Culture*, London: Verso.

Yu, D.W. (1984) *Onŭ Dolmaengi-ŭi Oech'im* [*The Cry of One Stone*], Seoul: Ch'ŏngnyŏnsa.

6 Shipyard women and the politics of gender

A case study of the KSEC yard in South Korea

Hwasook Nam

One cold day in February 1986 at the Korea Shipbuilding and Engineering Corporation (KSEC) shipyard in Pusan, South Korea, a group of middle-aged male skilled workers, who were deep in discussion, called out to a young worker passing by. They were all colleagues of the same shop, Slip Assembly (*sŏndae chorip*), which put together large steel blocks to form the body of ships.[1] The older workers asked the young welder, "Why don't you try it [i.e., running in the upcoming union representatives election]?" Without waiting for a reply, the older workers happily clapped their hands, saying, "That concludes the matter!" (C. Kim 2006a).

On the surface, the brief exchange looked like shopfloor politics as usual during election time. The election, which would choose three representatives for the shop of 144 people, was held every year. This year's election had stimulated more interest among workers than usual, however. This was the year union representatives would elect a new union president for a three-year term at the annual Assembly of Union Representatives meeting. The KSEC union presidency was a much-coveted position and competition for it was keen. The presidency brought power and prestige. In addition, the company, one of the biggest employers in the Pusan region, had a cozy relationship with the union at the time and supported union leaders in various ways, including financial ones. The KSEC union presidency also could serve as a stepping stone to even more lucrative and powerful positions in national-level union organizations.[2] As a result, during election times campaign money flowed like water in and around the yard, and workers joked that in Yŏngdo, where the yard was located, "even dogs run around with cash in their mouths" (C. Kim 2006a). As we shall see, however, the seemingly innocuous move by older colleagues to encourage a young worker to run for election turned out to be a radical and subversive action that challenged the power structure on the shop floor and in the yard.

Looking back, this moment marked the small beginning of a fast-unfolding chain of events that culminated in the democratization of the KSEC union a few years later. The KSEC (Hanjin Heavy Industries since 1989) workers had once boasted a powerful democratic union, possibly the strongest local union in South Korea during the 1960s.[3] In the fall of 1969, the Park Chung Hee (Pak Chŏnghŭi) government stepped in to crush this militant union, which had been waging a series of legal and illegal sit-ins and strikes for over a year. A new pro-company leadership led by P'aeng Chongch'ul was installed by the end of the year, and began to cooperate with management, police, and the KCIA (Korean Central Intelligence Agency) to control the once volatile workforce at the yard and to mobilize them for the national goals of labour peace and productivity gains. In stark contrast to the practices of the union in the 1960s, the KSEC union after 1970 showed little enthusiasm for upholding democratic principles in union affairs. Union offices were monopolized by foremen, who, together with the section chiefs (*kwajang*), held absolute power over the critical decisions concerning workers' livelihood, including hiring, work evaluations, promotion, the distribution of overtime, and efficiency pay rates. In the Slip Assembly Shop, three of the seven foremen were expected to run for the representatives positions and nobody else. Now a group of senior workers was asking a young worker to stand up against the power and authority of their foremen. More extraordinary and unsettling was the fact that the young welder chosen for this intimidating task was a woman, named Kim Chinsuk, one of the few women welders at the yard. Apparently, the senior workers, who were in their forties and fifties and whom Kim prefers to call "*ajŏssi(dŭl)*," a term of endearment toward older men, had confidence and trust in her.

The choice of a young woman as a union delegate at a male-dominated workplace like the KSEC shipyard and the steadfast support given her by her male colleagues in the ensuing years, recounted in detail below, force us to rethink the received wisdom on hierarchical gender relations in South Korean industry and society. How was the formation of cross-gender solidarity possible at this shipyard? What kind of changes in the gendered division of labour in the industry lay behind this development? Studies of the particular patterns of labour market segregation by gender and the gendered division of labour in South Korean industries have shown us that young women workers, as in many other industrialized countries, have been channeled into certain sectors that pay relatively lower wages, including textiles, shoe, and electronics industries.[4] Even in female-dominated industries, a rigid gender hierarchy puts male workers in higher and supervisory positions above female workers. Sociologist Seungsook Moon points out at the macroscopic level the link between this pattern of sexual division of labour in the economy and the gendered nature of the nation-building strategy of the Park Chung Hee regime during the 1960s and 1970s (Moon 2005).

Moon's work represents a promising start in the exploration of the role gender played in shaping South Korean development, but we need concrete and local-level studies to corroborate and complicate her thesis of the gender-specific mobilization paths constructed by the Park regime. For example, we do not know much about the changing patterns of gendered division of labour in male-dominated industries such as automobile or shipbuilding in South Korea, even though women workers were also mobilized into those industries, albeit in small numbers. There is a sizable literature on the emergence of a new sexual division of labour in metal and engineering industries in Europe and North America in the twentieth century, especially during World War I and World War II, which opened up certain categories of formerly male jobs for women workers.[5] Was there a comparable development in the South Korean metal industries as they expanded rapidly and began to suffer from a shortage of skilled male workers in the late 1970s and 1980s? Sociologist Young-Hee Shim investigates the limited nature of women's entry into production jobs in heavy and chemical industries under the state-led "Heavy and Chemical Industrialization" (HCI) policy of the 1970s, using statistical and survey data (Shim 1988: 101–54). But this macro-level analysis focuses on why and how women were excluded from "skilled" jobs, and does not address the changing gender dynamics at work following women's entry into male-dominated industries.

My own attempt to explore these issues grows out of my previous work on union activism at the KSEC shipyard. During that research, which focused primarily on male workers, I glimpsed evidence buried in union documents of women production workers at the yard and became aware of the remarkable story of Kim Chinsuk. In the present essay, I focus directly on the female workers at KSEC, utilizing additional documentary and interview sources. I begin by examining the shifting patterns of the gendered division of labour at the KSEC yard and the discourses that justified the structure of inclusion and exclusion of women workers on the shop floor and in the union movement. Workplace and community-level studies of workers' lived experiences reveal in concrete terms the ways in which gender assumptions among state policy makers, managers, workers, and workers' family members shaped the practices of creating and policing hierarchical divisions at work and in society. By following the story of Kim Chinsuk, the essay explores how workers' gender assumptions informed the dynamics of solidarity formation. Furthermore, social relations between male and female workers were shaped not only by an array of gender discourses but also, to a significant degree, by work experiences and the work culture at the yard. Kim Chinsuk's case reveals that the work culture at the KSEC yard in the 1980s was at certain junctures conducive to worker solidarity across the gender line. The story of Kim and her coworkers at the KSEC yard is also worth our attention because it provides a fascinating example of the grassroots activism that predated and fed into the great explosion of labour militancy in South Korea in the summer of 1987, in which heavy-industry workers, including those at the KSEC, played central roles. The KSEC (later, Hanjin Heavy Industries) union that Kim Chinsuk helped democratize continues to be one of the most militant and radical unions in the South Korean labour movement and is known for its strong spirit of solidarity among its members.

A brief history of the union movement at the KSEC yard

The KSEC was established in 1937 by Japanese colonizers as part of the war-time push for heavy-industry building in Korea to serve the needs of the Japanese empire. The company, which went under state management following liberation in 1945, maintained its status as the largest and most advanced shipyard in South Korea until the Hyundai Corporation entered the scene in 1972 with its gigantic shipyard at nearby Ulsan. The KSEC was a leader not only in shipbuilding but also in the production of machines and metal structures in the 1960s, and by the middle of the decade it pioneered the export of ships and ship engines abroad.

A powerful union had emerged at the yard by the mid-1960s, a product of a complex mix of political, economic, and historical factors and circumstances. What is important for our discussion here is that in the second half of the 1960s workers at the KSEC yard participated in a union movement that not only success-fully increased workers' wages and benefits, but also emphasized and practiced democratic principles and procedures in everyday union activities (Nam 2009: chs 4 and 5). In the name of democracy, rank-and-file voices were respected, elec-tions and meetings strictly followed standard democratic rules, the authority of managers and foremen was checked and challenged by the union, and grievances of workers at the lowest rung of the work hierarchy, especially those of temporary workers, occupied a central space in the union agenda (Nam 2003: 312–22; Nam 2009: ch. 6).[6]

As noted above, the democratic leadership of the union was crushed in October 1969 following a long series of strikes, when the Park regime tightened its control over increasingly militant trade unions at the dawn of the authoritarian *Yushin* era. The newly installed leadership of the union enthusiastically embraced the Park regime's call for a spirit of sacrifice and labour peace on behalf of the nation, and restored the power and authority of foremen and managers on the shop floor. During the 1970s and early 1980s, workers at the KSEC yard did not mount overt resistance to the new competition-driven factory regime, in which compliance and consent were rewarded with bigger paychecks and faster promotion.[7] The level of competition among workers was such that a KSEC worker in the late 1980s warned Kim Chinsuk "We'll not be able to achieve anything [in terms of solidar-ity] at the KSEC!" (C. Kim 2006a).[8] Kim recalled that not only men but also women workers at the yard routinely fought amongst themselves over seemingly trivial matters. In her view, the underlying cause of the frequent in-fighting was nothing other than the competition for favours from foremen or managers who determined the amount of overtime and incentive pay (C. Kim 2006a).

The lack of open resistance did not mean that KSEC workers were satisfied with their union or the ever-increasing control over their work by management, how-ever. Grumbling by rank-and-filers sometimes surfaced in the pages of the com-pany journal, *Chogong* (KSEC) (Nam 2003: 457).[9] Resistance was also expressed through the maintenance of a so-called lax work culture, including sleeping, drinking, or lounging around at work, to management's dismay. The KSEC yard was notorious for its loose work culture not just in the 1960s when the union was strong, but even into the 1970s and 1980s (I. Kim 2004).[10] According to labour scholar Jun Kim, when Hyundai began recruiting workers for its new yard, it tried to limit the number of recruits from existing shipyards such as the KSEC because of the concern that recruits from those companies would bring with them the dreaded "loose" work culture of the old shipyards (J. Kim 2004: 32).[11] This meant that despite the competitive work regime, KSEC workers still retained some measure of control over their work life.

In addition to the easygoing work culture, material conditions generated by a rapidly expanding industry – steadily rising wages, fast promotion, ample oppor-tunities to improve one's position by voting with one's feet and moving to another shipyard – help explain why KSEC workers in the 1970s and early 1980s remained silent. By the mid-1980s, however, the workplace politics driven by individualistic concerns was about to change at the KSEC yard as workers once again began to contemplate actions against the union leadership and management.

Masculine subjectivity and women's role in the labour movement: the 1960s

One of the most conspicuous discourses emerging from the KSEC union statements and union meeting minutes of the 1960s is one centered on workers' right to a family living wage (Nam 2009: ch. 5). The family wage ideal is, of course, a familiar one to labour scholars who have shown that industrial workers in many countries built their struggle around it. In South Korea, too, the KSEC unionists anchored their discourse of labour rights in the male breadwinner ideal in the 1960s, and the demand for a family living wage was part and parcel of their call for the recognition of workers' citizenship rights and integral to their historic role as flag bearers in building a new, democratic nation.[12]

Women workers at the yard in the 1960s remained a tiny minority. Statistics that break down the number of workers by gender are limited, but those available show that during the 1960s the number of unionized women workers ranged from 1 to 4.8 per cent of the total union membership.[13] Many of these women workers were clerical workers, typists in particular, but a small number of women production workers did exist in the late 1960s, especially in the hull shop (KSEC Union: 6 September 1967 minutes and 30 September 1968 minutes). These women workers, however, remained almost invisible in the union movement. The union, to its credit, had a "Women's Department" for a brief time from August 1967, but no traces of activities by the department appear in union records (KSEC Union: 9 August and 5 September 1967 minutes).[14]

That does not mean that women were passive bystanders during periods of labour activism. In fact, spirited participation in strikes by women was a conspicuous phenomenon in the life of the KSEC union during the 1960s. Yŏngdo Island, where the yard is located, had been a major industrial site since the colonial period, a place where numerous metal shops and small and large shipyards operated. The majority of workers employed at KSEC in the 1960s came from the city of Pusan and South Kyŏngsang Province, which surrounds Pusan, and most of them lived on Yŏngdo. Since colonial times Yŏngdo developed as a vibrant working-class community, and a thick web of kinship relations, school networks, and neighborhood connections tightly linked workers and their family members to each other.[15] It is thus not surprising that the working-class community of Yŏngdo often rallied for the cause of the KSEC union in times of struggle.

Women's participation in labour struggle reached its peak in the seventeen-day sit-in strike of the union in December 1968, which was provoked by the newly privatized company's sudden dismissal of all 1,200 temporary workers working at the yard. Workers and their families perceived the company's action as an immoral act threatening their livelihood, and women family members spontaneously gathered at the strike scene (Nam 2003: ch. 11; Pak Insang 2004: 41–43; Kwŏn 2006). The way wives of KSEC strikers, by their participation in demonstrations, boosted the legitimacy of their husbands' claims as heads of households under siege appears to be similar to the role of wives in the Daewoo auto workers' struggle over thirty years later, carefully analyzed by Kwon in this volume. Families blocked traffic in the thoroughfare in front of the yard and pleaded with the citizens to listen to work-ers' just demands to get their jobs and livelihood back. In a dramatic moment that shocked everyone, a young mother with a baby strapped on her back threw herself in front of an oncoming bus to prevent it from moving through the demonstra-tors (Kwŏn 2006).[16] Union leaders at the time, according to testimony by one of the four full-time union officials, Kwŏn Odŏk, understood that women's help was crucial to the union's victory. In their estimation, the fear on the part of the KCIA and the police that the sit-in could escalate into a people's riot forced them to pres-sure the company to agree to workers' demands (Kwŏn 2006). At the least, family participation aroused public interest in the strike, and helped mobilize sympathy for the striking workers in the larger society.[17]

Women's contribution to the union victory in the seventeen-day sit-in in 1968 was recognized by the union assembly, convened after the strike victory, when it resolved to deliver a plaque of gratitude to "Granny Hyŏn Puni" (KSEC Union: Assembly minutes, 22 January 1969). Granny Hyŏn, the mother of a KSEC union member, had been involved in the "women's movement" during the post-liberation period, and when women family members gathered in support of the strike, she emerged as a natural leader. Granny Hyŏn made speeches and organized and rallied women throughout the strike. Her leadership and commitment surprised many union men (Kwŏn 2006). Women family members' participation in strikes continued into the following year, which saw a series of massive labour actions. Some women even landed in jail because they hit managers, and union officials' pleas to women to disperse and go home often fell on deaf ears.

Women production workers as family members

KSEC unionists consistently demanded to be compensated with a family living wage, fit for their status as heads of households. How then did male workers make peace with the presence of female production workers at the yard? First of all, "women workers" did not exist as a single category. Prevailing gender discourse at the yard, accepted by men and women, workers and managers alike, distinguished two groups of women workers. One was comprised of unmarried, young women ("*agassi*" or "*ch'ŏnyŏ*," the latter literally meaning a "virgin"), the other of mar-ried, older women ("*ajumma*"). *Agassi* or *ch'ŏnyŏ* workers were supposed to do typing or other clerical work deemed suitable for young women until marriage. Older, married women, on the other hand, were viewed in a very different light and were used as a source of cheap labour for jobs deemed "unskilled" yet not suitable for unmarried women. The main areas of work allowed to these *ajumma* workers were cleaning jobs of various kinds, resonant with the notion of women's domestic duty, and also "unskilled" painting jobs. One particular cleaning task women were extensively used for was the removal of rust from steel plates of ships, using a small, pointed hammer, popularly known for its sound as the "*kkangkkang*" hammer. In the late 1960s the yard employed several dozen of these women *kkang kkang* workers (KSEC Union: 1967 Assembly materials and 6 September 1967 minutes). Rust removal was dirty, monotonous, and arduous work, which was easily defined as "unskilled" work and therefore suitable for low-wage workers, such as these married women (C. Kim 2004b).[18]

A statement made by the union's Welfare Chief at a 1967 meeting provides a clue to who these women workers were and how male workers perceived them. In his understanding, the majority of these women production workers (*yŏgong*) were either family members of the union members who had been killed at work, or those from the families of injured veterans from the military or the police (*kun'gyŏng wŏnho taesangja*). According to Kwŏn Odŏk, in the 1960s almost all *ajumma* workers, which included his own aunt, were housewives who were desperately in need of paid work because their husbands were incapable of providing for the family for one reason or another (Kwŏn 2006; Kwŏn and Chŏng 2006).[19] Hiring of these women workers occurred through personal connections and open recruiting was not done. Evidence is limited, but it seems safe to say that hiring of these *ajumma* workers was viewed and defended by male workers and the union as a solidarity-based act of providing livelihood for families of union members or members of the community, which had lost a functioning breadwinner male head of household. Thus these *ajumma* workers represented an extension of family, rather than an intrusion into male workers' world of women as workers *per se*. The presence of such women workers did not disturb the prevailing notion of male worker-family head, entitled to a family living wage, but rather had the effect of reinforcing it. Witnessing housewives doing dirty and hard work at the shipyard likely reminded workers how important it was for male workers to secure a family wage in order to safeguard the wellbeing and respectability of their family.

In a few cases the union raised gender-specific issues. For example, the Organizing Department in 1968 declared that it would work "to abolish discriminatory treatment toward women vis-à-vis men and to enhance women's rights." In the same year, the union included demands for menstruation leave, maternity leave before and after childbirth, and "equal pay for equal work" in its draft for 1969 contract negotiations (KSEC Union: 1968 "Business Plan" and "Union Draft for the 1969 Contract"). Unlike other issues, which usually went through heated debates at meetings among union officials and representatives from the shop floor, however, gender-specific issues generated little discussion among the unionists. It is not clear why there was a sudden spurt in gender-specific demands in 1968, but it is doubtful that rank-and-file workers engaged in widespread discussion of these women's issues on the shop floor.[20] The prevailing gender assumptions on women production workers highlighted the family welfare aspect of *ajumma* labour. When their presence at the yard was perceived as an aberration from the norm, that is, the idealized working-class family with breadwinner patriarch and stay-home wife and children, it was hard for women's gender-specific grievances as workers to inspire discussion and action from male unionists.

The shifting gendered division of labour and the emergence of welding women

The terrain of the South Korean shipbuilding industry changed dramatically with the entrance of *chaebŏl* (large business conglomerate) corporations, beginning with Hyundai in 1972. As the industry grew rapidly, so did the demand for a skilled shipbuilding workforce. The KSEC, as the most advanced shipyard in the country, became the prime target for recruiting skilled workers by the newly founded shipyards. Samsung's entry into the industry in 1977 and the expansion of the KSEC yard itself in the late 1970s made the skilled worker shortage even more acute. The incredibly rapid expansion of the industry in the 1970s created a need to reconfigure the existing pattern of the division of labour by gender at shipyards. At KSEC, the entry of women into traditionally male jobs like welding and metal cutting began on a small scale sometime before 1977, as the company allowed some women to switch from cleaning or painting work to electrical welding, with successful results (KSEC: July 1977). Encouraged, the company introduced a new program to train "women electrical welding workers" and "gas torch cutting (semi-skilled) workers" at its training institute. The rationale for the hiring of women in men's work, given by the company, was that "safe and easy" jobs became available for women thanks to the technological upgrades and women proved to be more detail-oriented, more adaptable, and obedient workers, who could also "help brighten the work environment" (KSEC: July 1977).

From April of 1977 to February of 1978, two classes of women (a total of 52 in all) finished the program and were hired at the yard (KSEC: February 1980). The qualifications for these semi-skilled jobs, whose training period was shorter (2–3 months) than the usual 6-month or 1-year training term for other skilled jobs, were simple: applicants had to be "healthy women under 40 years of age" (KSEC: February 1980). What is implied in the criteria was "*ajumma* only," but the company did not articulate that. It is likely that nobody expected a *ch'ŏnyŏ* to aspire to do hard, rough, therefore, "unfeminine," work, while it was deemed acceptable for an *ajumma* to do hard physical labour in proximity to men, if necessary for the family. All the women trainees, despite no written prohibition of *ch'ŏnyŏ* workers, were in fact *ajumma*.

This pilot program for training women came to an end when a worldwide downturn in the shipbuilding industry hit South Korean shipyards hard. The program was revived at the KSEC in 1981 after a three-year hiatus, only to permanently close down by the end of that year. The 1981 reopening was precipitated by the entry of another major *chaebŏl*, Daewoo, into shipbuilding, whose new yard on Kŏje Island began to recruit KSEC workers in large numbers (C. Kim 2006b).[21] During 1981, the KSEC training institute accepted women as part of its trainee cohort three times (class 26 through class 28) (C. Kim 2004a).[22] Again the qualifications for the women trainees were vaguely defined: "A healthy woman under 37 years of age" (*Pusan Daily*, 12 January 1981). Electrical welding and metal cutting using machines were newly created jobs at the shipyard as the process of mechanization accelerated in the 1970s. The assumption that developed around these semi-automated jobs was that the machines did the work and the workers' job was to tend the machines. According to Kim Chinsuk, however, in reality electrical welding was difficult work because each worker had to tend several machines at once and move around quickly negotiating piles of heavy steel sheets (C. Kim 2004a and 2006b).[23] Still, the "skills" these mechanized new jobs required were deemed to be at a lower level than traditional cutting and welding skills, the kind of "skill" that was a core component of male workers' work identity and sense of pride at the yard.[24] Even if classified as semiskilled, women's entry into these heavily male trades still had the potential to arouse fear of the dilution of the "skills" of male workers. In the case of the KSEC yard's experimentation with women workers, the small scale of women's entry and the prevailing discourse of *ajumma* labour, which reassured the importance of male breadwinners, seem to have helped soften the anxiety and fear among male skilled workers.

Although the kinds of work women did expanded greatly to include formerly "men's work" like welding and cutting by the late 1970s, the perception of women production workers as a separate class of labour, *ajumma* workers reputed to be "unskilled" or "less skilled," remained stable. Even the association of some level of "skills" with women electrical welders and cutters, expressed in the practice of installing a formal training program for them, was on a shaky ground, since the company often moved women between cleaning or painting jobs and the supposedly skilled jobs of welding and cutting, without first making them go through formal training (Cho 2004). Moreover, the KSEC stopped recruiting women directly after 1981, and turned to subcontracting (*oeju*) firms, which began to supply *ajumma* day labourers for the yard (Cho 2004). The dispatched worker status of these *ajumma* workers made the marginal status of women workers even worse on the shop floor and in union politics. It is also likely that the company strategy of resorting to *oeju* for women's labour had an effect of obscuring the changing sexual division of labour at the yard by conflating women's entry into previously male jobs with the familiar business practice of subcontracting.

Even so, the change was undeniable when men and women found themselves working side by side as welders and metal cutters at the yard. Other shipyards, including Hyundai, also began to utilize women's labour in electrical welding and other more mechanized areas of production work at some point during this time.[25] A new gendered division of labour was quietly taking shape in the South Korean shipbuilding industry, albeit on a much smaller scale and in more of a piecemeal fashion than had happened in European countries and the United States during the wars of the first half of the twentieth century. This change in the division of labour did not generate much resistance by working men or in the society at large. The discourse of *ajumma* labour helped to smooth out the potential tension in the workplace following women's intrusion into the men's world. On the surface, the time-honoured gendered work hierarchy at the yard seemed to have been maintained with only marginal changes. But did the women at the yard accept the discourse on *ajumma* labour?

Subjectivities of welding women

The voices of *ajumma* workers are mute in the available archival sources, and it is difficult to know how they perceived themselves, that is, women doing men's work, and how they constructed the meaning of their work. It is clear, however, that not all *ajumma* workers were destitute housewives, although it seems that the majority of them were indeed breadwinners (Cho 2004; C. Kim 2004a).[26] Of 52 women who finished the aforementioned KSEC training course in 1977 and 1978, at least one welder, Hyŏn Poksun, was not in need of money for family survival. For Hyŏn, the wife of a KSEC worker, the goal was to buy a house, and she succeeded in doing so within a year (KSEC: July 1979).

Interviews with women workers reveal that at least a few viewed welding work in a rather positive light, despite the difficult, dirty, and dangerous working conditions.[27] For example, Cho Ch'unhwa, a female welder I interviewed, explained that she and two friends had learned about the opening at the KSEC in 1981 and decided to take the opportunity because the welding job offered not only much better pay but also much more respectability than domestic (*p'ach'ulbu*) work they were doing at the time (Cho 2004).[28] Kim Chinsuk also remembered listening to women welders proudly talking about their work life on a popular radio talk show, *Im Kukhŭi's Women's Salon* (C. Kim 2004a). The positive impression left by those women welders on the show encouraged her to apply for the KSEC training course. For Kim, Cho, and more than one hundred other women who went through the training program to become welders or cutters, the new positions represented a rare opportunity to move out of low-wage, female jobs.

Women who obtained these better-paying and more respectable positions at the KSEC yard, however, found the work environment difficult in many ways. For Cho Ch'unhwa, the hardest part was moving a piece of heavy welding equipment, called the "holder," to the assigned worksite in the ship (Cho 2004). Male workers did not help out struggling women workers. For Kim Chinsuk, the worst was working in a small, confined space, which workers called the "tank," within which workers welded pieces of large metal blocks together. There was no escape from the heavy haze of fumes and metal dust the work produced (C. Kim 2004a and 2007: 257). Pneumoconiosis and hearing loss were common occupational diseases for welders, which the company ignored, and workers, fearful of dismissal, tended not to report. Welders had to climb up steep ladders, set perpendicular to the ships, and often jumped from one place to another, risking injury or even death. For women workers, not only physically demanding and dangerous working conditions but also frequent sexual harassment by their male coworkers constituted major hardships in work life. Dirty sexual jokes and indecent graffiti on restroom walls made everyday life "almost unbearable" for women. Tales of extramarital affairs or even wife-beating seldom raised eyebrows among male workers (C. Kim 2004b).

By the early 1980s, women came to occupy a significant portion of the yard's workforce. From January 1980 to December 1981, for example, the average ratio of women in the total union membership at the KSEC yard was 8 per cent.[29] But the increase in number did not mean that women as a group became a force to be reckoned with. The factory regime at the KSEC yard in the 1970s and 1980s, discussed earlier, fostered fierce competition rather than cooperation and camaraderie among workers. Structurally, women workers were placed in an even more insecure position than men, and *ajumma* workers often reacted to the competition-inducing labour control system by competing and fighting among themselves. Fights frequently broke out in the female locker room (there was only one locker room for all women production workers), which was a place for them to socialize on a daily basis. The status differences among women between white-collar *agassi* workers and blue-collar *ajumma* workers and between those directly employed by the KSEC and those who worked as dispatched workers also divided women workers.[30] Divided and insecure, women production workers at the KSEC yard failed to generate a unified voice against practices of gender discrimination and sexual harassment. Even so, the work life of *ajumma* workers and the meanings they attached to their breadwinning, skilled work appear to have been much richer and more positive than what the prevailing discourse about *ajumma* labour prescribed them to be.

The odyssey of Kim Chinsuk: from a misfit to a "darn good worker"

Kim Chinsuk, the female welder whose story about running for union office was introduced at the start of this essay, left her home on the Kanghwa Island near Seoul in 1978, and arrived in Pusan with a 5,000-won (about $5) bill that her mother had pressed into her hand at the time of her departure (C. Kim 2006b and 2007: 254–56).[31] With several years of hard work, she believed that she could save enough money to go to college and help out her family. In that regard her story does not deviate much from those we find in memoirs and recollections of other South Korean women production workers. Starting at a sweatshop printing gold and silver patterns on *hanbok* (Korean traditional costumes), she worked at a large garment factory, at a handbag factory, and at a shoe factory. She also tried selling ice cream as a peddler, delivered newspapers and milk, and ended up as a bus girl (*annaeyang*).[32] She quit the nightmarish bus girl job disgusted by the company's action of hiding the news of her mother's death from her out of a concern that a replacement might not be easily found for the day's work. That was when she saw the ad in *Pusan Daily* about the KSEC training program, which included a course for women welders and cutters (C. Kim 2006b and 2007: 255–57). Overjoyed at this opportunity, she did not waste any time in taking her application to the training institute.

What she did not understand at the time was that "a healthy woman under 37 years of age" was a code word for married *ajumma*, not an *agassi* like her. At the institute, an old man behind the reception desk asked whether she had come to submit an application on behalf of her brother. When she said it was for herself, he refused to accept the application form, saying that the work was too hard for a young woman to endure. Back at home, Kim could not give up the hope of becoming a welder, which in her mind would make her dream of saving a lot of money and becoming a college student come true. So she went back to the institute the next day, holding a copy of the *Pusan Daily* ad in hand. But the old man did not budge. When she tried to argue that she was "a healthy woman under 37 years of age," he said that it would be a waste of work clothes that would be issued for her because the work was too hard and she would quit after the first day. Then he volunteered to introduce Kim to "a factory where women work," to which Kim retorted, "I'm coming from a factory where women work!" She returned home but unable to see the chance of a lifetime slip away, she tried one more time. Luckily for her, a young instructor of the institute was manning the reception desk on her third visit, and he accepted Kim's application without asking a question. Her persistence shows the attraction of the woman welder job for a veteran of "feminine" jobs available to young women in South Korea at the time.

Kim Chinsuk's admittance into the training program punctured the seemingly watertight system of utilizing *ajumma* labour in a non-threatening and economical way. Because she was not an *ajumma*, nobody knew exactly how to deal with her. When the training was over, 20–30 women graduates from Class (*ki*) 26 were assigned to various posts. Several women went to work as cleaning workers, despite their training in welding or cutting. A number of women received jobs in automated electrical welding. There were two more unmarried young women other than Kim, but their stay in the training program was a cover for their being hired as office workers through personal connections (C. Kim 2006b).[33] Kim Chinsuk was thus the only *ch'ŏnyŏ* production worker, and the company decided to send her to the Slip Assembly Shop, where male workers did the kind of welding jobs deemed highly skilled, and thus not suitable for women, to say nothing of a *ch'ŏnyŏ*.

The rationale behind this decision to put Kim in an impossible spot, she later learned, was that it was assumed that a *ch'ŏnyŏ* would not be able to endure production work and would soon quit, making it unnecessary to find her a more suitable job. Kim recalled that the shop she reported to did not even have an opening for any worker, male or female, and as soon as she arrived, senior male workers at the shop took away her brand-new hard hat, work shoes, and work clothes (C. Kim 2004a; 2006a; 2006b). It was less a form of hazing than a way of conserving decent work clothes and equipment, which were in short supply; the men acted in the belief that she would not come back to work after the first day. Kim shocked everybody by showing up at work the next day. Several days later male workers returned what they had taken. From then until her dismissal five years later, she never missed a day's work except for the time she was hospitalized with broken legs following an accident on the job.[34]

Once allowed to stay in the shop, Kim faced the challenge of learning the necessary skills. The training she had received at the training institute was woefully inadequate for her assigned job. Skill had been a fiercely guarded asset in the work culture of many South Korean metalworking shops since the colonial period, and even in the 1970s, lacking quality job training or apprenticeship programs, junior workers in South Korean machine-industry companies had to learn skills themselves by observing "over the shoulders" (*ŏkkae nŏmŏro*) the work of senior workers, who were not motivated to share their knowledge with their younger competitors (Sin 2004: 146–48). Kim tackled the problem just like many other young

South Korean workers had. She showed up at work before anybody else, fetched water for senior workers to wash off after work, and never refused overtime work assignments, while constantly expressing her desire to learn. Her dedication and sincerity moved *ajŏssi* workers, who began to help her to gain skill.

After several years of practice and learning, she became an excellent welder with a high reputation for her skill. According to Kim, even twenty years after being fired by the company in July 1986, *ajŏssi* workers at the KSEC still prefaced their reminiscences of her with a statement to the effect that "Chinsuk was a darn good worker." They recalled that, "after she finished a job, there was no need to touch up or fix anything." Kim's admittance as a coworker by male workers hints at aspects of the work culture of shipyard workers, showing that a person's skill level, competency, and the willingness to pull his/her weight were as important as the person's gender in determining the prestige and respectability of a worker.

In fact, she not only broke the barrier to doing a man's job and survived in the harsh, masculine environment of the welding shop, she excelled as a worker, winning a model worker prize. The contradictions inherent in the *ajumma* worker model became apparent in the person of Kim Chinsuk, a young, unmarried woman thriving in tough and difficult men's work. One way to frame and minimize the challenge Kim's case posed to the existing order that arbitrarily differentiated the capacity of men and women and that of *ch'ŏnyŏ* and *ajumma* was to make her an exception that proved the rule. The discourse of the exceptional qualities and capacity of Kim Chinsuk took hold over time. Kim became a celebrity at the yard as the one and only "*ch'ŏnyŏ* welder" in the yard's history. The recognition of her from coworkers and the company as a good worker and an exceptional woman worker began to shape the way Kim saw herself too. Proud to be the only *ch'ŏnyŏ* welder, she wrote an essay for the company journal *Chogong*, glorifying the welding job.[35] Even though the work was so grueling that she recalled she had hated to wake up in the morning, working at the KSEC yard rubbing shoulders with coworkers also filled her life with a satisfying sense of accomplishment and belonging that she had yearned for. Even today, Kim confesses, she misses dearly the relationship with her coworkers. She misses also the hard hat, the ragged work clothes, work shoes, and tools she had to leave inside the company gate.[36]

What motivated her to persist through the arduous journey to gain acceptance and become a skilled worker were the same desires that prompted her to leave home when she was eighteen: making money and going to college. She did not shy away from working long hours, often 7:00 in the morning to 9:30 at night, and lived a frugal life, saving money as much as she could, after sending a portion home.[37] Her "model worker" stage, however, did not last long. Kim began to bond with other workers at the yard and a turn of events and opportunities began to forge an activist out of the *ch'ŏnyŏ* welder.

From a "ch'ŏnyŏ" welder to a labour leader

Kim's reputation as an exceptional woman and a "darn good worker" was reinforced by her reputation as an unusually "kind-hearted" person, who went the extra mile to help fellow workers in need.[38] Mrs. Chang, an *ajumma* welder and the wife of an injured KSEC worker, became a staunch supporter and friend of Kim, moved by her kindness. After noticing that Mrs. Chang, who never missed work, did not show up for several days, Kim spent her precious free time to locate and visit Mrs. Chang's house. She found the older woman ill with a severe bladder infection, and took her to a hospital to get help. In another case, Kim earned the friendship of an *ajŏssi* grinder when she gave him a letter of apology and a pair of gloves she bought for him. The previous day Kim had lost her temper with him while working in the "tank" together. The metal dust and noise from grinding had made things unbearable. It was not his fault that he and Kim were assigned to work in the same tank at the same time, and Kim wanted to apologize for her behavior. The grinder was deeply moved by her action because, as he put it, he had never received such a nice letter and present in his whole life (C. Kim 2006b). It was this same grinder who secretly gathered the thirty signatures required for Kim's candidacy in the 1986 union representatives election, and, according to Kim, the company is still baffled at how in the world Kim, who by then was under tight surveillance and prevented from meeting with her coworkers, was able to collect those signatures.

Kim also began to develop an active social life with coworkers, *ajŏssi* workers in particular, regularly joining their after-work drinking and visiting their homes on holidays. When she was not around, *ajŏssi* workers sometimes showed up at her residence, a rented room not far from the yard, to fetch her to their drinking party, usually held in one of the numerous small "hole in the wall" taverns close to the yard. When *ajŏssi* workers got drunk, she made sure each had his jacket, cigarette lighter, and shoes and helped them get home.

As Kim was an unmarried woman without male kinsmen to protect her, *ajŏssi* workers seemed to have taken her under their wings as a fictive daughter, rather than focusing on her sexuality as a young woman. Thus desexualized in her relationship to older male workers, Kim seemed to have found a way to fit in without disturbing *ajŏssi* workers' masculine identity. Considering the prevailing sexist culture at the yard, one can only imagine the complexity of negotiations and compromises involved in such a relationship. For her part, Kim seems to have wholeheartedly embraced and cherished her rapport with *ajŏssi* workers, which offered a much-needed sense of home and belonging. Asked about how she coped with the sexism of *ajŏssi* workers, including routine sexual jokes, Kim answered that she did not have a "feminist" consciousness at the time and if she had had, it would have been impossible to have good relationships with them.

Young male workers in the shop (about one third of the 144 workers there were young men), however, seemed to have had more trouble accepting Kim as a co-worker, and Kim's relationship with them was stormy at first. Not only her gender but also her work ethic, characterized by her devotion to work and the company's exaltation of her as a model worker, did not sit well with this group of workers. They called her "a loyal subject (*ch'ungsin*) of the company," and stopped their conversation when Kim approached them. Competition and jealousy might not have been the only reason they shunned Kim as "a loyal subject." Determined to prove herself and earn more money, and unfamiliar with the customs and the work ethic among shipyard workers of regulating the amount and speed of their work, Kim might have antagonized young workers as a "rate breaker." Over time, however, young male workers also warmed to Kim, especially after she began to show interest in labour activism.

As a woman production worker, sharing gender-specific grievances at work, including the insufficient provision of female restroom facilities and the sexual jokes of male workers, Kim was also able to bond with *ajumma* workers. The necessity to use the only female locker room at the yard allowed women to see each other on a daily basis. Tired from hard labour, women seldom talked for long and the competition among *ajummas* was often severe. But women workers, many of whom were neighbours in nearby working-class communities of Yŏngdo, seem to have developed a sense of community because of their similar backgrounds and positions at the yard.

In these ways, Kim Chinsuk was able to forge rich and strong social relationships with all three groups of shipyard workers over time: the *ajŏssi* workers, the young male coworkers, and the *ajumma* workers. Her unique position in-between these groups of workers made her a potential builder of a wider network of solidarity at the yard. Kim's story indicates that work culture at the KSEC contained elements that had the potential to counteract the organization of work at the yard that drove workers to competition, isolation, and division, including the division by gender. Even in the midst of cutthroat competition, KSEC workers seem to have found ways to actively negotiate a complex array of customs, values, and interests to forge a sense of community as shipyard production workers.

Model worker Kim Chinsuk's transformation into an activist came slowly over several years, but two events in particular had a major influence on her worldview. The first was the accident in which her legs were broken by falling sheets of steel. *Ajŏssi* workers arranged a rotating schedule to bring food to Kim in the hospital. Wives and children of some *ajŏssi* workers also came by to cheer her up. The accident opened her eyes to the brutal reality of labour conditions at the yard, which often forced workers not to report their injuries and pay for the medical treatment themselves (C. Kim 2004b).

The other event that changed the direction of her life was her enrollment in 1984 in the *Ŏksaep'ul* (reed) Night School, offered by a branch of the YMCA in Pusan. Believing that the school was helping workers prepare for the qualification exam for college entrance (*kŏmjŏnggosi*), she attended two hours three times a week, anxious more than anything else to learn English, one of the core subject areas tested on college entrance examinations. To her dismay, what she was taught was mostly about the Labour Standards Law. Kim harbored a certain class-based mistrust toward the teachers at the night school, called "*kanghak*" (one who teaches/learns), who were middle-class college students and thus, in her mind, did not understand the harsh situations workers faced.[39] A teacher gave her a copy of *Chŏn T'aeil p'yŏngjŏn* (The Biography of Chŏn T'aeil), the life story of the famous garment worker whose self-immolation in 1970 in protest at sweatshop working conditions became a major inspiration for labour activists, but she had no intention of reading it. She was not on good terms with teachers, but her fellow students, most of whom were young factory girls working at shoe factories in Pusan, impressed her by their dignified attitude and pride in their *"nodongja"* (worker) status, and thus, stimulated her interest in the labour movement.[40]

Kim began to see her workplace in a different light, and eventually formed a small study group with two young male coworkers in her shop, Yi Chŏngsik and Pak Yŏngje.[41] They studied the Labour Standards Law and began to look into their union's activities.[42] Kim was so encouraged by all the protective measures written in the Labour Standards Law that she began to preach workers' rights to *ajŏssi* workers whenever she had a chance. For example, she told them that overtime work should not be forced upon workers according to the law, and therefore, they should all refuse overtime work, seemingly oblivious of the fact that many workers were fighting tooth and nail to get more overtime hours. *Ajŏssi* workers, amused by her passion for labour rights, joked when she approached them: "There comes the Labour Standards Law!" *Chŏn T'aeil p'yŏngjŏn*, which she finally read around this time, also exerted a great influence on her, she later recalled (C. Kim 2007: 47–50).

Kim's open agitation for workers' rights had a role in *ajŏssi* workers' decision to send her to the union assembly, described at the beginning of this essay. The suggestion by *ajŏssi* workers surprised Kim because she and her study group members were at the time debating whether they should run for the union position or not. The main reason for their hesitation was the concern that they did not have enough knowledge to venture into union politics. In Kim's opinion, three considerations probably motivated senior workers to choose her as a candidate: first, she was a single woman with no dependents to worry about; second, she was a model worker, whose voice the company would pay more attention to; and lastly and most importantly, she was a trustworthy person who would not betray fellow workers after getting a position of power (C. Kim 2006a).[43]

The foremen in the Slip Assembly Shop were naturally very upset when Kim, Yi Chŏngsik, and another young worker announced their intention to run for the election, and managers began to harass these three workers.[44] A foreman came to Kim's house to check to see what kinds of books she had, and managers and foremen blocked her and the other two workers from approaching the shop. On election day Kim managed to sneak up to a huge room on top of a crane, which production workers from many shops used as a lunch room. The room, accessible only by a long steep ladder, was almost never visited by managers and white-collar workers, and thus afforded an ideal venue for the campaign speech Kim proceeded to give. She denounced the way union officials embezzled the dues members paid out of their precious earnings from hard work and the way the company treated production workers. She pointed at the company-issued lunch the workers ate and asked whether it was better than dog food.[45] Roaring applause burst out from hundreds of workers who were in the room when Kim finished her speech. Managers and security personnel rushed up to the room and tried to drag Kim out, but workers, *ajŏssi* workers in particular, rose up to defend her, shouting "Don't touch her! Let her go!" *Ajŏssi* workers from her shop then demanded to have a vote right then and there. Sensing that a riot might break out, managers agreed. Kim Chinsuk won the highest number of votes, and Yi and Kim Sŏngt'ae were second and third, handsomely defeating the three foremen candidates. Watching the democratic election process unfolding before their eyes, workers from other shops began to discuss ways to have a competitive election in their shops too.

Gender and worker solidarity

After winning the election, the trio attended the Assembly of Union Representatives, only to find that their opportunity to speak was systematically blocked by union officials. They distributed a flier criticizing the union, titled "After Attending the Assembly of Union Representatives." Thus did the struggle for the democratization of the union begin, but it took several years to accomplish its goals. In the process, Kim, Yi, and Pak were fired by the company, interrogated under torture by the KCIA and the police, and beaten up numerous times by company security guards.[46] But they persisted, gaining strength from the support fellow workers continued to show them.

Despite the constant surveillance and threats of grave consequences for those who had any kind of contact with Kim, *ajŏssi* and *ajumma* workers secretly slipped her small sums of money, a bottle of a popular drink, *Pakk'asŭ*, or a packet of gum. When Kim's group began producing fliers and later, a newspaper, entitled *Chogong nodongja sinmun* (KSEC workers' news; first issued in March 1987), *ajŏssi* workers donated money to the cause. Kim's study group had by then expanded to include two dozen workers under the name of the "Task Committee to Normalize the KSEC Union," and the committee members, mostly young men, secretly delivered copies of the newspaper to the yard by hiding them in their hard hats or shoes in order to go through the company gate where security guards searched workers' bodies. Newspapers and fliers were mostly left in the restrooms and outhouses production workers used, venues perfectly suited for safe delivery and circulation. The company promised informers a big sum of money (500,000 won) and promotions to 5th grade, which was a big hope for the majority of workers, who remained at the 6th grade for many years. But nobody ever reported to the company what they knew about the deliveries. Workers read and circulated the papers with great zeal, and the knowledge of that was what sustained Kim and her group during the ordeal, Kim recalled.[47] Making thousands of copies of the newspaper to match the number of union members cost a great deal of time, effort, and money, because it had to be done secretly, sometimes in other cities. She willingly used up her lifetime savings to help fund the copying.[48] According to Kim, she missed her fellow workers terribly, especially *ajŏssi* workers who used to "pat [her] back instead of saying a hundred words," and through the circulation of the newspaper she felt that she had a link to them (C. Kim 1995 and 2006b). Her involvement in labour activism transformed her perspective toward life, and a commitment to labour's cause and solidarity replaced her ardent desire to go to college and attain middle-class status.

The company responded with redbaiting tactics, portraying Kim as a communist (*ppalgaengi*).[49] The tactic, which had been a vital weapon for many other companies and the government in their efforts to repress unionists in the postwar era, did not succeed in Kim's case because *ajumma* and *ajŏssi* workers refused to believe the charge. Kim believed that if she had been an activist from outside, workers would not have trusted and supported her like they did (C. Kim 2004b).

The company then tried another tactic: provoking masculine anxiety among male workers. At the orientation for new workers, managers emphasized the fact that Kim, a woman, had been wreaking havoc on the company, and asked, "You are men, right? You know what happens when men listen to what women say?" (C. Kim 2006b).[50] A Catholic priest chimed in by delivering a sermon to the same effect. Yi Chŏngsik's father, who attended the sermon, was upset by the revelation that his son had been manipulated by a woman, and slapped Kim on the back with his cane (C. Kim 2006b). The company's blatant gender tactic did not seem to have much effect, since more young workers joined the movement started by Kim's study group, including Pak Ch'angsu. Pak, another member of Class 26, later became the president of the democratized KSEC (by then Hanjin Heavy Industries) union in July 1990, and his untimely death in May 1991, while in police custody, has galvanized the Hanjin union movement ever since.[51] Pak said in an interview that he had joined the union inspired by Kim Chinsuk's actions.[52] Despite the attack specifically targeting her gender, Kim Chinsuk continued to play a crucial role connecting diverse groups of workers beyond gender and generational divides in the KSEC union movement.[53] By the 1990s, she was already on the way to becoming a legend at the yard and in the metal workers' movement in the region.[54]

Kim Chinsuk's unique status as the only female leader who has risen from the grassroots level in the male-dominated metal workers' movement in South Korea continues to be framed by an emphasis on her exceptionality, of being an unusually selfless, kind-hearted, and capable person who was passionately committed to labour's causes. In other words, Kim was relegated to a gendered image of the self-sacrificing, desexualized, almost saint-like woman. In that regard, Kim is in the tradition of a long line of single women activists and educators in Korean history whose desexualized images pivot around their dedication to a worthy cause, which oftentimes foreclosed the possibility of marriage and pursuit of individual happiness. This deeply gendered discourse of an exceptional woman leader selflessly devoting her life for the public good came to define the relationship between Kim and her fellow unionists, and continues to condition her subjectivity and agency.

In light of her image as an exceptional, selfless, and charismatic leader for all workers, it is not surprising that her visible presence in the labour movement over the last twenty years has not provoked a serious call to revise the gender norms and practices among metal workers. Still, the challenge her gender has posed to the union movement, at the KSEC and beyond, continues. Kim Chinsuk has recently emerged as the champion of the most downtrodden of all workers, non-regular (*pijŏnggyu*) workers, the majority of whom are women. And she is becoming increasingly vocal in criticizing the masculine culture of the union movement.[55] The image and legitimacy of a devoted leader allows her to speak with a certain moral authority on behalf of her less fortunate fellow workers against the organized labour establishment. As she is an unusually gifted writer and popular union educator, her voice of dissent has the potential to be heard widely. How her gendered position as an exceptional woman leader will play out in the much-changed landscape of the South Korean economy and labour movement in the twenty-first century remains to be seen.

Notes

I thank the participants of the "Gender and Labour in Korea and Japan" workshop in July 2006 in Sydney, Australia, especially Laurel Kendall, Jong Bum Kwŏn, Elyssa Faison, Ruth Barraclough, and Hagen Koo, for critical comments and helpful suggestions on earlier drafts of this chapter.

1 A slip (or slipway) is an inclined plane leading down to the water where ships are built or repaired.
2 The case of P'aeng Chongch'ul, who served as former KSEC union president from November 1969 to January 1981 and then became the president of the National Metal Union Federation, illustrates the status of the KSEC union in the national union movement.
3 On the history of the labour movement at the KSEC yard, see Nam (2003) and Nam (2009).
4 Korean-language literature on these subjects is too large to cite here. Representative works include Kang and Sin (2000) and Cho and Chang (1994). For English-language works that discuss these issues, see S. Kim (1997), Koo (2001), and Moon (2005).
5 For example, Downs (1995), Glucksmann (1990), Milkman (1987), and Pierson (1986).
6 Temporary workers, who often formed the majority of the workforce in the 1960s, were admitted into the union in 1965 against the company's wishes (Nam 2003, 2009).
7 Jun Kim's study of Hyundai shipyard workers shows similar conditions of extreme competition among workers during the 1970s and 1980s, which, he argues, resulted in the isolated and atomized nature of their existence (J. Kim 2004).
8 Sin Wŏnch'ŏl emphasizes that the identity of machine-industry workers in South Korea in the 1960s and 1970s was primarily informed by the "ethic of competition" rather than a culture of solidarity and cooperation (Sin 2004: 149).
9 For example, a union member remarked in the pages of the March 1975 issue of *Chogong*, "The only time I feel the union's presence is when I see the pay stub on pay day [from which union dues were deducted]."
10 According to Kim Insu, General Secretary of the Hanjin Heavy Industries Union, who worked at the yard starting in the 1980s, the place had a unique work culture, quite different from the *chaebŏl* (large business conglomerate) shipyards, in that control over working time was rather loose as long as work got done by the set time. For example, a worker with a hangover could easily find a place at work to sleep. When a worker accumulated enough vacation days, he simply did not show up for work until he used up those days without incurring penalties. If a worker was on good terms with his foreman, he could skip work without even calling in sick.
11 For its skilled shipbuilding workforce, the new Hyundai yard had to rely on the pool of skilled workers that the KSEC had produced as the leader in the industry for many decades. But for semi-skilled or unskilled jobs, Hyundai preferred to hire new high-school graduates and train them in company facilities.
12 The genealogy of the family wage/male breadwinner ideal among industrial workers in Korea, which likely begins with Japanese industry practices in its colony, Korea, in the first half of the twentieth century, still awaits research.

13 The number of women union members ranged between 9 and 72 (Nam 2003: 280).
14 The Women's Department was headed by a 44-year-old hull worker, named Yi Pongho, but her involvement in union activities must have been minimal. Chŏng Ongnyŏn, who worked in the union office as a page (*kŭpsa*) from 1964 to 1969, only vaguely remembered Yi's name and did not recall ever meeting her (Chŏng 2006).
15 According to Kwŏn Odŏk, the core group of the KSEC union leadership, including himself, was formed through such connections (Kwŏn 2006, Kwŏn and Chŏng 2006).
16 The woman escaped injury. The scene left a lasting memory to participants of the strike.
17 Interest in the KSEC strike resulted in an unprecedented move by two editors of the *Pusan Daily*, the most influential regional newspaper at the time, who personally visited the strike site to talk with workers during the strike. After the visit, they wrote an editorial clearly favorable to workers (*Pusan Daily*, 18 December 1969). The paper also ran investigative reports on the KSEC strike (*Pusan Daily*, 5 and 19 December 1968).
18 The work was hard partly because of the height of the worksite (the ships), which required the use of scaffolding and ropes. Other cleaning jobs at the yard also involved removing rust with a wire brush, and the red dust the work produced caused much hardship for women. Because the red powder seeped even into underwear and did not wash away, women cleaning workers at the yard made a habit of changing into a separate set of "work underwear" before beginning the shift.
19 Chŏng Ongnyŏn testified to the same effect.
20 Kwŏn Odŏk, who claimed to have been the main author of most union documents in the late 1960s, did not recall the "equal pay for equal work" article inserted in the draft contract, when asked specifically about it (Kwŏn 2006).
21 Daewoo entered the shipbuilding industry by purchasing the Okp'o shipyard on Kŏje Island from the financially struggling KSEC in December 1978.
22 The class of 26 had twenty to thirty women and the next class had much fewer women, according to Kim Chinsuk.
23 Metal cutting work was much easier than welding, and in the early 1980s the KSEC yard employed about "14 to 16" women cutters. Other shipyards also hired women cutters.
24 For an excellent discussion of the historical process through which gendered definitions and meanings of skills were constructed in the French knitting industry, see Chenut (1996). See also Rose (1992), Downs (1995), and Caraway (2007) on the gender and skill dynamics.
25 For example, Hyundai shipyard employed 1,055 women production workers in 1990 (5.3 per cent of the total production workforce of 19,919), 291 of whom were in the category of "*kinŭngjik*," that is the skilled workforce (Hyundai Heavy Industries 1992: 1194).
26 Kim described *ajumma* workers as those who were cornered because their husbands were injured at work, sick, or addicted to alcohol or gambling. They were thus desperate for any kind of work in order to be able to feed their children.
27 Both Cho Ch'unhwa and Kim Chinsuk repeated that the work had been "really hard" numerous times during my interviews with them.
28 Cho emphasized how great an opportunity it was to become a welder because she was able to put her children through school with her earnings.
29 Statistics are from union membership records in *Chojik silt'ae pogo, 1979–81* (Report on the situation of the organization, 1979–81) in KSEC Union (various years).
30 Among the women union members in the 1980–81 period, on average 39 per cent were workers from subcontracting firms, who were organized in sub-locals of the union.
31 Kim chose Pusan because it seemed like the farthest place from her hometown, where everybody knew everything about her poverty-stricken life.

32 "Bus girls," whose duties included pushing customers into the bus when it was already filled to the brim and then blocking the doorway with their bodies by hanging onto the door with their arms outstretched, were one of the most abused and exploited groups of workers in South Korea. For working conditions of bus girls, see Chŏnghwa Kim (2002).

33 One woman was the daughter of a friend of the training institute president. According to Kim Chinsuk, they were not sincere about learning and even skipped important licensing tests.

34 Even the day she was poisoned by carbon monoxide, she reported to her shop and then collapsed (C. Kim 1995).

35 I have yet to locate the essay. According to Kim, upon reading the essay her *ajŏssi* coworkers scolded her, saying, "What is so great about our job? We are just *ttaemjaengi* [persons who mend holes or bind broken pieces together]!" (C. Kim 2004a).

36 Kim has been fighting since her dismissal more than twenty years ago to return to the yard. The two coworkers who had been fired together with Kim were finally reinstated as of 1 January 2006. See Kim's essay on the reinstatement of her coworkers, Yi and Pak, "20-nyŏn man ŭi pokchik" (Kim 2005).

37 Kim's starting wage as a production worker in the 6th grade was 136,000 won, and with over 60 hours of overtime work per month, she was able to make 180,000 to 190,000 won, which was much more than the average of 138,814 won for her grade in 1981. In other words, she was not subject to gender discrimination in wages. Wage rates of KSEC employees as of February 1981 are from *1981* in KSEC Union (various years).

38 Cho Ch'unhwa, an *ajumma* welder, remembers Kim as a "really kind-hearted" (*chŏngmal ch'akhan*) person, who sometimes gave away part of her paycheck on paydays to fellow workers in dire need.

39 An incident involving a shoe worker who came to school with a bruised cheek because a manager had slapped her in the face hardened Kim's class-based antagonism toward her college student instructors. When a teacher scolded workers for not initiating a signature-gathering campaign to submit a petition to the Office of Labour Affairs on the matter, saying that they would live like that forever if they did not rise up to fight against injustice, Kim and other students exploded in anger because in their mind the teacher did not have a clue about what it was like to live as a female factory worker, routinely subjected to abuses and violence. She felt her teachers had no idea of the risks involved in protesting workplace injustice (C. Kim 2006b).

40 There were about 20 students in her class and about 80 per cent of them were women shoe factory workers (C. Kim 2006b).

41 Kim and Pak, both members of Class 26 of the training institute, started the group and invited Yi to join, according to Kim. They named the study group "*Yangsimhoe*" (an association of conscience).

42 Church and student activists played an important role in the development of the South Korean labour movement in the 1970s and 1980s (Koo 2001: chs 4 and 5). Outside activists, however, do not seem to have had much influence on Kim and her colleagues or on the KSEC union movement in general. There was a *hakch'ul* (student-turned-labor-activist) who worked as a pipe fitter at the yard, but he did not fit in well (everybody knew that he was not a real worker, especially because he wore an expensive Burberry coat) and within just a month or so left the yard after experimenting with restroom graffiti. In the workers' understanding, he left because he could not endure hard labour (C. Kim 2004a and 2006b). For recent studies that problematize the relationship between intellectuals and workers at night schools and in the South Korean labour movement during the 1970s and 1980s, see W. Kim (2006), and Lee (2007: chs 6 and 7).

43 It is significant that the initiative for this rebellious act came from *ajŏssi* workers. Many of them had over twenty years of seniority at the yard, according to Kim. That

meant that at least some of them had witnessed the heyday of the democratic union movement at the yard, which lasted until the fall of 1969. How much and in what way the memories of the 1960s' labour movement at the KSEC yard contributed to this rebellious decision by *ajŏssi* workers in Kim's shop in 1986, and at other shipyards in the region during the massive labour upsurge the next year, called the "Great Workers' Struggle of 1987," is an important question that needs further research.

44 Among the study group members, Pak did not run because he was on a leave because of a work-related injury. Instead, Kim Sŏngt'ae, whom the three were thinking about inviting into their group, volunteered to run.

45 Information on the lunchroom incident comes from C. Kim (2006a). The poor quality of the lunch the company provided at a fee had been an issue constantly raised by workers at union meetings and labour–management council meetings at the KSEC. "Lunch boxes that contained mouse shit" became a rallying cry in the union democratization movement. For example, see Kim Chinsuk and Yi Chŏngsik, "Chohapwŏn yŏrŏbun kke tŭrinŭn yangsim sŏnŏn" (Declaration of conscience to union members), a flier they issued after their dismissal from the company, and Kim's "Hosomun" (1986), which is a letter she wrote to Cardinal Kim Suhwan, dated 7 July 1986. The quality-of-lunch question was closely interconnected with one of the central issues in the South Korean labour movement: the discrimination between white-collar and blue-collar workers. "Install a cafeteria for production workers and abolish discrimination between managerial (*kwallijik*) and production (*saengsanjik*) workers!" was one of the demands Kim's group raised in the summer of 1986, when KSEC workers "with an amazing level of solidarity" conducted a campaign to refuse lunch. The quotation comes from a handwritten flier, entitled "Uri nŭn yoguhanda!" (We Demand!). Another campaign flier, entitled "Pora!" (Look!), cried out, "Managerial employees eat cleanly prepared rice and soup in a comfortable and pleasant cafeteria. Aren't we production workers, who are exhausted from intense work and poor working conditions, also members of the KSEC family?" The chronology of events from the February 1986 election to 2000 is summarized in Kim-Kwak Commemoration Committee (2004: 506–30).

46 Kim and Yi were taken to a KCIA office on 20 May, and the company suspended them two days later as "impure elements," meaning communists. On 2 July Kim was transferred to a remote office as a clerical worker, and fired on 14 July when she refused to obey a series of transfer orders. She was arrested in May 1989, and imprisoned for 145 days from June to November in 1990 in violation of the notorious labour law prohibiting "third-party intervention" in labour disputes because of her speeches at Hanjin (KSEC) union rallies. She was again jailed in 1993 for a month and a half because she supported Pongsaeng Hospital workers, most of them women, in their 59-day strike for union recognition (C. Kim 1986, 1995, 2005).

47 Some workers corrected misspellings they found on the newspaper and returned it to the outhouse, signaling to Kim and her group that they appreciated the paper (C. Kim 2004b).

48 In 1990, the democratized Hanjin Heavy Industries (KSEC) union, under newly elected union president Pak Ch'angsu, instituted a new program that provided living expenses for union members who were arrested, wanted by the authorities, or fired. Three other unions in Pusan had similar programs at the time (Kim-Kwak Commemoration Committee 2004: 512). The monthly allowance, initially set at 100,000 won but since then increased to 1 million won (about $1,000), was for a long time Kim's main source of income as a labour activist.

49 The KCIA interrogated her three times but was unable to link her to any outside group. Therefore, she was branded as a "home-grown" communist. Kim on two occasions attended a JOC (Young Catholic Workers) meeting with Yi Chŏngsik, who was a Catholic. Kim wrote in her "Hosomun" that the company used it as proof of Kim's communist thought. On JOC activities in Korea, see Koo (2001: ch. 4).

50 She learned about this from a young male worker who had attended one of those orientation sessions.
51 Pak Ch'angsu won the union presidency with overwhelming support, 90.85 per cent of the vote. On the process of democratization of the union, see Nam (2009: ch. 10), and Hanjin Heavy Industries Union (1995). The Hanjin Union actively participated in organizing the "Alliance of Large-Firm Trade Unions" (*Taegiŏp yŏndae hoeŭi*) and the "National Congress of Trade Unions" (*Chŏn'guk nodong chohap hyŏbŭihoe*; *Chŏnnohyŏp* or NCTU), a precursor to the Korean Confederation of Trade Unions (KCTU) as the national center for the anti-FKTU, "democratic" (*minju*) unions. On 11 February 1991, Pak was arrested with two other union officials after attending a meeting of the *Taegiŏp yŏndae hoeŭi* on the strike being waged by Daewoo shipyard workers. After about three months of incarceration and interrogation, Pak was suddenly moved to a hospital on 4 May, 1991 and died there two days later. The Roh Tae Woo government's claim that Pak's death was caused by a suicide attempt when Pak jumped out of the window in his hospital room did not find a sympathetic audience. Many labour activists believe that he was tortured to death by the KCIA, whose agents were at the time pressuring him to withdraw from the NCTU. His name was added to a long list of victims of "suspicious death" at the hands of the KCIA, the police, and the military. On the arrest and death of Pak, see Hanjin Heavy Industries Union (1995: 484–88).
52 From an interview with Pak Ch'angsu (C. Pak 1991).
53 She has worked in the labour movement in the Pusan region for over twenty years and is currently working as an advisor (*chido wiwŏn*) at the Pusan Headquarters of the KCTU.
54 An interesting example of stories about her exceptional capacity circulating among the yard's workers is that Kim Chinsuk used a magic method of contracting space (*ch'ukchibŏp*), one popular in martial art stories and folk tales, to distribute news-papers and fliers simultaneously to many locations at the huge shipyard. She learned about the story from a young male worker (C. Kim 2006b).
55 Among Kim's recent speeches and lectures to that effect are "Pae Talho ch'umosa" (In commemoration of Pae Talho) (25 January 2003), "Kim Chuik ch'umosa" (In com-memoration of Kim Chuik) (9 November 2003), and her Labour Day speech at Pusan Station (30 April 2005). The first two are reprinted in Kim (2007). See also the news-paper article on Kim's lecture, "Pijŏnggyujik kwa hamkke pap mŏgki silt'ani 133" (They don't want to eat meals together with non-regular workers?), *Ohmynews*, 13 January 2005.

References

Caraway, T. (2007) *Assembling Women: The Feminization of Global Manufacturing*, Ithaca, NY: Cornell University Press.

Chenut, H. (1996) "The Gendering of Skill as Historical Process: The Case of French Knit-ters in Industrial Troyes, 1880–1939," in L. Frader and S. Rose (eds) *Gender and Class in Modern Europe*, Ithaca, NY: Cornell University Press.

Cho, Ch'unhwa (2004) Interview with the author, Pusan, 26 July 2004.

Cho, H. and Chang, P. (eds) (1994) *Gender Division of Labor in Korea*, Seoul: Ewha Wom-an's University Press.

Chŏng, Ongnyŏn (2006) Interview with the author, Pusan, 19 May 2006.

Downs, L. (1995) *Manufacturing Inequality: Gender Division in the French and British Metalworking Industries, 1914–1939*, Ithaca, NY: Cornell University Press.

Frader, L. (1996) "Engendering Work and Wages: The French Labor Movement and the Family Wage," in L. Frader and S. Rose (eds) *Gender and Class in Modern Europe*, Ithaca, NY: Cornell University Press.

Frader, L. and Rose, S. (eds) (1996) *Gender and Class in Modern Europe*, Ithaca, NY: Cornell University Press.

Glucksmann, M. (1990) *Women Assemble: Women Workers and the New Industries in Interwar Britain*, London: Routledge.

Hanjin Heavy Industries Union (1995) *Che 32-yŏnch'a hwaltong pogosŏ* [The 32nd annual activity report], Pusan: Hanjin Heavy Industries Union.

Hyundai Heavy Industries, Co. Ltd (1992) *Hyundai chunggongŏp 20-yŏnsa* [A 20-year history of the Hyundai Heavy Industries], Seoul: HHI.

Kang, I. and Sin, K. (2000) *Yŏsŏng kwa il: Han'guk yŏsŏng nodong ŭi ihae* [Women and labour: understanding women's labour in Korea], Seoul: Tongnyŏk.

Kim, Chinsuk (1986) "Hosomun" [Appeal], unpublished flier.

—— (1995) "Hangso iyusŏ" [Reasons for appeal], reprinted in C. Kim (2007: 250–76).

—— (2004a) Interview with the author, Pusan, 24 July 2004.

—— (2004b) Interview with the author, Seoul, 30 July 2004.

—— (2005) "20-yŏn man ŭi pokchik" [A reinstatement that took twenty years]; reprinted in C. Kim (2007: 13–23).

—— (2006a) Interview with the author, Pusan, 20 May 2006.

—— (2006b) Interview with the author, Pusan, 29 May 2006.

—— (2007) *Sogŭm kkot namu* [Salt flower tree], Seoul: Humanitas.

Kim, Chŏnghwa (2002) "1960-yŏndae yŏsŏng nodong: singmo wa bŏsŭ annaeyang ŭl chungsim ŭro [Women's labour in the 1960s: focusing on housemaids and bus girls]," *Yŏksa yŏn'gu* [Study of history], 11.

Kim Chuik – Kwak Chaegyu yŏlsa il-jugi ch'umo saŏp ch'ujin wiwŏnhoe [Commemoration project committee for martyrs Kim Chuik and Kwak Chaegyu on one-year anniversary; hereafter, Kim-Kwak Commemoration Committee] (2003) *85-ho k'ŭrein: Kim Chuik, Kwak Chaegyu yŏlsa ch'umo charyojip* [Crane number 85: collection of materials in commemoration of martyrs Kim Chuik and Kwak Chaegyu], Pusan: Kim-Kwak Commemoration Committee.

Kim, Insu (2004) Interview with the author, Pusan, 26 July 2004.

Kim, J. (2004) "1970-yŏndae chosŏn sanŏp ŭi nodongja hyŏngsŏng: Ulsan Hyundai Chosŏn ŭl chungsim ŭro" [Workforce formation in the shipbuilding industry in the 1970s: focusing on the Hyundai Shipbuilding], in C. Yi *et al. 1960–1970-yŏndae Han'guk ŭi sanŏphwa wa nodongja chŏngch'esŏng* [Industrialization and worker identities in Korea during the 1960s and 1970s], Seoul: Hanul.

Kim, S. (1997) *Class Struggle or Family Struggle? The Lives of Women Factory Workers in South Korea*, Cambridge: Cambridge University Press.

Kim, W. (2006) *Yŏgong 1970: kŭ nyŏ dŭrŭi pan yŏksa* [Women workers, 1970: their antihistory], Seoul: Imaejin.

Koo, H. (2001) *Korean Workers: The Culture and Politics of Class Formation*, Ithaca, NY: Cornell University Press.

KSEC (various years) *Chogong* [KSEC].

KSEC Union (various years) *KSEC Union Archive Documents*, preserved at the union office in Pusan.

Kwŏn, Odŏk (2006) Interview with the author, Pusan, May 18 2006.

Kwŏn, Odŏk and Chŏng, Ongnyŏn (2006) Interview with the author, Pusan, May 19 2006.

Lee, N. (2007) *The Making of Minjung: Democracy and the Politics of Representation in South Korea*, Ithaca, NY: Cornell University Press.

Milkman, R. (1987) *Gender at Work: The Dynamics of Job Segregation by Sex During World War II*, Champaign, IL: University of Illinois Press.

Moon, S. (2005) *Militarized Modernity and Gendered Citizenship in South Korea*, Durham, NC: Duke University Press.

Nam, H. (2003) "Labor's Place in South Korean Development: Shipbuilding Workers, Capital, and the State, 1960–79," unpublished Ph.D. diss., Seattle, WA: University of Washington.

——. (2009). *Building Ships, Building a Nation: Korea's Democratic Unionism under Park Chung Hee*, Seattle, WA: University of Washington Press.

Pak, C. (1991) "T'ujaeng ŭi pulssi rŭl sallinŭn maŭm ŭro [Caring to keep a live coal of struggle alive]," *Chiyŏk kwa nodong* [Region and labour], no. 8.

Pak Insang munjip palgan wiwŏnhoe (2004) *Yŏngwŏnhan wiwŏnjang* [Eternal president], Seoul: Tanggŭrae.

Pierson, R. (1986) *They're Still Women After All: The Second World War and Canadian Womanhood*, Toronto: McClelland & Stewart.

Rose, S. (1992) *Limited Livelihoods: Gender and Class in Nineteenth-Century England*, Berkeley: University of California Press.

Scott, J. (1988) *Gender and the Politics of History*, New York: Columbia University Press.

Shim, Y. (1988) "Nodong sijang kujo ŭi pyŏnhwa wa yŏsŏng nodong ŭi silt'ae" [The transformation of the labour market and the female wage labour in Korea: on the heavy and chemical industry], *Han'guk yŏsŏnghak* [Korean women's studies], 4: 101–54.

Sin, W. (2004) "Kyŏnjaeng yangsik kwa nodongja chŏngch'esŏng: 1960–70-yŏndae kigye sanŏp nodongja rŭl chungsim ŭro [Patterns of competition and worker identity: focusing on machine-industry workers in the 1960s and 1970s]," in Yi, C. et al., *1960–1970-yŏndae Han'guk ŭi sanŏphwa wa nodongja chŏngch'esŏng*, Seoul: Hanul.

7 The frailty of men

The redemption of masculinity in the Korean labour movement

Jong Bum Kwon

On 16 February 2001, at the behest of the state, Daewoo Motor management laid off 1,750 production workers from the Bupyŏng factory, the main manufacturing facility and union headquarters of the company.[1] The unprecedented action provoked a protracted standoff between the union and the state. The "Daewoo Motor Struggle against Mass Redundancy Dismissals" (hereafter "Struggle") was one of the most contentious and fierce challenges to the state's drive to restructure the labour market in the wake of the Asian financial crisis that began in 1997. It marked a litmus test of militant labour's strength and the state's commitment to neoliberal reform.[2]

For two years, the laid-off Daewoo workers fought to reclaim their jobs. They marched and protested on the streets, often confronted by riot police. They demanded that President Kim Dae Jung (1998–2003) step down. His administration's neoliberal agenda (to deregulate financial institutions and institutionalize a flexible labour market), they shouted, was killing workers. They warned that they would fight to the death to "return to the factory." This was the slogan emblazoned on their union vests and headbands; it was the slogan that punctuated the hammering of workers' fists into the air.

In the union culture of male-dominated heavy industries, such as at Daewoo Motor, demonstrations were the conventional vehicles of political opposition, displaying collective determination and identity and communicating grievances and demands (cf. Eyerman 2006). Elsewhere, I have described how labour protests were practices of social memory that invoked a history of manly militant struggle: from the aggressive posturing of combat through song and movement to actual physical confrontation with riot police, protesters drew from a cultural script that dramatized masculine heroic resistance against a repressive state (Kwon 2005). But even as Daewoo demonstrations reproduced a narrative of violent heroic protest, many of the rallies and other public events revealed the production of a powerful, deeply felt moral and affective economy. In this production, women, not men, were the key actors.

This essay examines the reproduction as well as contestation of normative gender identities in a male-dominated union struggle against neoliberal restructuring within the context of the social-economic upheaval of the Asian financial crisis. The social turmoil unleashed by the nation's near bankruptcy and resultant mass unemployment was enacted as a moral panic centered on the phenomenon of "family breakdown" (*kajok haeche*). Popular and official discourses of family crisis identified men as the principal victims and as privileged subjects for rehabilitation to their status as so-called "pillars" of the "traditional" family. Social activists and non-governmental organization experts did not challenge but reaffirmed those profoundly gendered moralizing scripts of the normative family. As Song (2006) trenchantly demonstrates, neoliberalism, as both policy and discursive frame of moral-economic evaluation, was produced and reproduced at multiple social sites and by a wide range of social actors outside the formal boundaries of the state.

Heavy industry unions, while posing an aggressive challenge to labour market restructuring, were one such site of the reproduction of normative understandings of masculinity and family. That male-dominated unions framed neoliberalism as the destruction of men's role and status as "breadwinners" does not surprise. My research, based on two years of fieldwork (2001–2) with laid-off Daewoo workers and their wives, demonstrates, however, that women were not only crucial to but also actively complicit in the production of this gendered framework. My analysis critically examines women's practices and understandings of their actions, in particular, their performances of "motherhood." Women were engendering agents and were integral to the constitution of normative masculine identities for the unemployed men. It was the women who redeemed the men, enabling them to reclaim their identities as respectable husbands and fathers. It was the women who enabled men to return to the factory and consequently to return home. It may be argued, then, that women's labour, their participation in labour struggle, in fact, *made* men (cf. Gutmann 1997).

Below are brief descriptions of two performances that spotlight the significance of women in the labour struggle. The first is a solidarity rally and the second is an Easter Mass held at the Sangoktong Catholic Church in Bupyŏng.

Solidarity rally

On 16 January 2002, the Korean Metal Workers Federation (KMWF), an industrial-level organization comprised of unions from the heavy industry and chemical sector, mobilized a solidarity rally at Seoul Station Square, a common downtown venue for demonstrations. The laid-off men of the Daewoo Motor Union gathered to demonstrate their comradeship and resolve to "crush neoliberal restructuring." In the slow drizzle of that winter afternoon, the men sat cross-legged on the wet pavement. At this demonstration, leaders from the Daewoo Sales and Marketing Union sat front and center on the makeshift stage. After a rousing speech of determination to fight, their heads were shaved as a symbolic gesture of commitment and self-sacrifice.

As the clippers chopped through their thick black hair, they clenched their faces, but failed to hold back tears. During the performance, a speaker paced back and forth at the foot of the stage and addressed the crowd. In a voice choked with emotion, he slowly uttered their desire to return to their homes. He spoke of "our beloved families," and announced, "We want to go home; our children, our wives are waiting for us." "We are workers but also husbands and fathers," he continued.

Listening somberly, the crowd of men lowered their heads. Some took long drags from their cigarettes, and a few openly wiped their tears away.

Easter Mass

On 15 April 2001, an outdoor Easter Mass for the laid-off Daewoo workers was held at the Sangoktong Catholic Church.[3] Laid-off men and their families, many of whom were not Catholic, congregated at the church grounds. During the service, the wife of one of the union leaders gave a testimonial. On the program, her account was entitled, "Han Ul's Mother's Sad Story." She spoke of the suffering of workers' wives and their sacrifices for the Struggle. She recounted with difficulty the story of a miscarriage experienced by one of the young mothers:

> But the miscarriage by Jae-Rong's mother is the most tragic. She tirelessly participated in demonstrations and rallies, carrying her sick four year-old son on her back. Because of her pregnancy, she was careful, cautious. Still, it must have been difficult to keep safe her unborn child as she was hauled off by the police and struck by riot police shields.
> […]
> With a sense of fear and urgency she came out to fight with us. [During the fight] we yelled out, "There is a pregnant mother!" "There is a sick child!" "Be careful!" "Don't push!" But, they didn't want to believe. I don't know if they pretended not to hear or if it was an excessive sense of duty, but when they heard the command to "push forward," to "haul them away," it seemed they became brainwashed and they grabbed and carried away a pregnant mother, a sick mother, a mother carrying her child.
> I am fighting to protect my husband's place of work, to secure a future for my children. We members of the "Emergency Family Action Committee" are fighting.
> Tears streamed down her face. The men in the crowd cried openly.

The two descriptions above illustrate the centrality of workers' wives in the Struggle. Han Ul's mother's reading testifies to the wives' participation and sacrifices. It invokes a powerful image of (lost) motherhood. In the immediate aftermath of the layoffs, fifty wives formed the "Emergency Family Action Committee." They visited the homes of laid-off husbands, consoled them for their loss of job and pride, and persuaded wives to support the fight. They pleaded their case to subway passengers; holding pictures of their husbands, they walked through the trains with children in tow, some with infants wrapped in quilts and tied to their backs. They participated in demonstrations. Dressed in union vests and with red bands tied around their heads, women fought with the riot police, pitching their fists and bodies against the policemen's shields and armored bodies. And, as at the Easter Mass, women also addressed the public with powerful and moving speeches.

The juxtaposition of the two events, however, reveals a perplexing contradiction related to the presence of women in the Struggle. The rally was rather conventional in form. Men held the stage and were the visual focus. Their performances followed a predictable script, producing iconic identities of labour militancy. Exemplary here was the shaving of the men's heads, an act of violence done to their own bodies and a bodily inscription of their declaration to fight. This rally, however, was less conventional in that it made visible an implicit theme of labour demonstrations since the onset of the Asian financial crisis. Through the invocation of wives and children, the fighting men were also identified as suffering fathers and husbands who wanted to go home. The speech signaled a profound loss – their absence from home – that brought tears to the eyes of hardened male factory workers.

The desire to return home was a common refrain voiced by laid-off Daewoo workers. This desire, however, constituted women as an absent presence and men as a present absence. While the men expressed a desire to return home, most did in fact return home each night after a day's meetings and demonstrations. Thus, while men were present at home, they were represented as absent, as "homeless" men. Conversely, while women were present at demonstrations, they were invoked as absent, as at home waiting for the men.

Labour demonstrations and other public cultural productions may be understood as engendering performances. The concept of performance I use here underscores the dramatic, emotional, and tacit dimension of collective political action. Performance communicates through embodied knowledge, dramatizing an affective and moral economy through choreographed as well as improvised movements, song, oratory and the embodied presence of deeply resonant cultural themes, motivations and identities. As the above descriptions show, labour demonstrations and similar public events were emotionally charged, for both the performers and the audience.

The analytic of performance, moreover, highlights the performativity of gender. That is to say, even as the events were performances, gender, too, was a performance. Gender, as many have argued, is a cultural construction. In terms of performance, however, gender is an emergent identity, "in need of ongoing accomplishment" (Pyke 1996: 528). Following Butler (1993, 1999), specific instantiations or materializations of gender identities are the effects of embodied reiterations of gender norms, such as through gesture, posture, and style. In this instance it was the performance of specific gender identities, in particular "motherhood," that "moved" the Struggle (Eyerman 2006).

That gender is a cultural construction, however, does not lead to a notion of "radical free agency." Rather, as Butler explains, gender performances are compelled by historically and culturally contingent norms. She states, "Those norms are the condition of my agency, and they also limit my agency" (Butler 2004). Thus, while workers' wives were engendering agents, their performances transforming unemployed men into good husbands and fathers deserving of respect, sympathy, and not least, a return of their jobs, they were complicit in the reproduction of normative gender identities. Their performances undermined their own status and experiences, displacing their own presence and suffering onto that of the men. As will be demonstrated, moreover, women performed "motherhood" at great emotional and bodily cost. Despite the centrality of their roles, women consistently cast themselves as supporting actors in the Struggle.

To say that the women were complicit in the reproduction of "motherhood" is to submit that they were self-conscious agents of their performance. This is not to say, however, that they simply misrecognized their own interests, or simply identified their interests as those of their husbands. In fact, in my interviews and discussions with the women, they revealed a high degree of awareness of gender and class inequities in Korean society, and proffered insightful analyses and alternative visions of family and gender relations. Rather, to say that the women were complicit is to shift the analytic lens to the conditions under which particular forms of agency are constituted and legitimated. Performers do not act in a cultural vacuum; performances not only draw upon culturally structured scripts but also are shaped within a context of reception (Butler 2004: 345). In the next sections, I examine the stage of women's performances, the discursive as well as practical fields that enabled and constrained women's understanding and exercise of their agency as mothers and wives.

Financial crisis as a "crisis" of men

In late November 1997 the currency shocks that leveled the economies of Southeast Asia also shocked South Korean markets. Foreign creditors refused to renew short-term loans owed by Korean financial institutions, and urged immediate repayment, resulting in a precipitous devaluation of the Korean *wŏn* and depletion of the country's foreign exchange reserves.[4] Faced with the spectre of national bankruptcy, President Kim Young Sam (1993–97) negotiated a massive $57 billion bailout from the International Monetary Fund (IMF). In return, the IMF mandated major structural and institutional reforms along neoliberal market principles that included the restructuring of labour markets.[5]

The crisis was a catalyst for far-reaching socio-cultural and economic transformations. Among them was the dramatic restructuring of labour and employment relations; notably, the breakdown of the contentious capital–labour compromise that had secured relative job stability for those employed at *chaebŏl* in return for a measure of labour peace in the aftermath of the Great Workers' Struggle in the summer of 1987. The new "flexible" labour market was not simply an outcome of neoliberal policies, but the critical objective of so-called structural adjustment. Mass layoffs were the precondition for financial reform, to attract foreign investors to acquire and recapitalize insolvent firms (B. Kim 2000: 40; see also Koo 2001). In the climate of national calamity, Kim Dae-Jung, who assumed office in January 1998, was able to extract a new "social compromise" from notoriously militant unions. Through the vehicle of the Tripartite Committee (est. 15 January 1998), composed of state, business, and labour interests, the new administration obtained heretofore unimaginable concessions such as the legalization of layoffs and the hiring of temporary workers.[6] In addition, the dogmatic application of IMF prescriptions entailed austerity measures, including interest rate and tax increases, which exacerbated the debt crisis, triggering widespread liquidity problems for prominent *chaebŏl* and bankruptcies of small and medium-sized subcontracting firms.

The consequences were devastating. During the first months of the Crisis approximately 10,000 workers a day lost their jobs; the official unemployment rate during the height of the Crisis (1998–99) was near 9 per cent, or 2 million people (Chun 2006). As alarming as those figures were, private researchers estimated that the fallout was closer to 20 per cent, an astounding increase from near full employment from before the Crisis. Workers at prestigious *chaebŏl* companies were not immune. Over the first five years (1997–2002), 236,000 workers, blue and white collar, in the top 30 largest corporations lost their jobs (Chun 2006: 78). On the street people were saying that "IMF" really meant "I-M-Fired" (K. Shin 2002: 427).[7]

In public culture, the unprecedented levels of un- and underemployment provoked widespread anxiety about families in crisis. Sensational and heart-rending stories of scattered and broken families, of the sharp rise in suicides, abandoned children, and the increasing numbers of the homeless were frequently reported in both popular and academic media (e.g. Shin and Chang 2000; Seong 1998). The central figures of these tragic narratives were unemployed men. Although women, who historically occupied the least secure and lowest paid positions in the labour market, were the first to be downsized and laid-off, it was men who were represented as the principal victims. The husband who abandoned his wife and family out of shame; the father who killed his family and himself out of despair: the desperate men who committed such acts that struck at deeply held understandings of the normative family were the desperate motifs of the financial crisis.

In both popular culture and official discourse, the iconic figure of the "IMF Crisis" was the homeless man. The middle-aged, middle-class man in his conservative blue suit, holding an empty briefcase and loitering on park benches in the middle of the day became the face of the "IMF era."[8] He was understood to be too ashamed to go home and confront his family and inform them of his ignominious dismissal. And the public commotion stirred by the high visibility of the growing numbers of homeless men at Seoul Station reinforced the equation of male unemployment with homelessness.

While men were considered the primary victims of the crisis, women occupied an ambivalent position in the cultural imaginary. They were both saints and sinners. In movies, novels, and the popular press, women were portrayed as immoral – as wives and mothers who abandon their husbands and children, demand divorce, and scandalously commit adultery (see Song 2003). But women were also potential saints, who through self-sacrifice could nurture their enfeebled, unemployed husbands and thereby preserve their families. Newspapers and television news celebrated those saintly wives and mothers. In an article, "Save Our Household Heads," for example, it was related that,

> Wives are showing lots of love for their husbands whose spirits [vitality] have been quashed as a result of IMF layoffs and pay reductions. Some use letters, telephone messages, or faxes to send their love. Still others wash their husbands' feet.

> (Kim and Finch 2002: 129)

In official discourse, the "IMF homeless" was the focus of government unemployment policies.[9] The "IMF homeless," officially specified as men who became homeless due to layoffs, became subjects of the Kim Dae Jung administration's neoliberal "productive welfare-ism," and were identified as the neediest but also most deserving of government attention (Song 2006).[10] Furthermore, President Kim Dae Jung mobilized discourses that related nation-building with manliness and "encouraged the recuperation of Korea's 'warrior culture' as a way to get South Koreans out of their economic slump" (Jager 2002: 393). In an address to the nation Kim Dae Jung stated:

> The sacred spirit of fallen patriots will watch over us – the patriots who gave their lives for national liberation, for democracy and for the Republic. United in hand, let us all rally under the banner of the "Second Nation Building." Let us all take reigns of our glorious destiny.
>
> (Jager 2003: 143)

According to Jager, Kim Dae Jung selectively borrowed from Park Chung Hee's notions of martial manliness, and he mimicked his policies, inaugurating the second *Saemaŭl Undong* (New Village Movement) as part of the *Chae 2ŭi Konkuk* (Second Nation Building) in 1998, initiatives that were originally launched by Park in the early 1970s (Jager 2003: 143).

If the crisis exposed Korea's economic vulnerability in the post-Cold War global economy, it also rendered as spectacle the "crisis" of Korean men. Discourses that articulated the financial crisis as a crisis of men and consequently as a crisis of the "traditional" family constituted a deeply resonant affective economy in which to interpret, experience and situate oneself in the economic upheaval. Such discourses formed the hegemonic gender scripts of the crisis.

Crisis and hegemonic masculinity

The position of men and women in Korean society is highly ambivalent. On the one hand, Korea is decidedly patriarchal, a place where male dominance and privilege is structurally as well as culturally inscribed. On the other hand, scholars have observed the social recognition, if not valorization, of "mother power" and "wifely power" (H. Cho 1998, 2002) and the endemic "frailty" of men. In this section, I briefly examine the historical and cultural formation of hegemonic gender norms, demonstrating that these forms were constituted and legitimated in relation to a "crisis" of the family, articulated as both an intimate private sphere and the nation.

Korea's modern organization and practice of hegemonic gender norms were configured according to spatial and ideological divisions that rendered men as providers, acting in the public sphere, and women as consumers and caregivers, acting within the private sphere. In addition, men's productive economic activity in the public sphere secured their social, moral, and legal position as household heads.

The gendered division of labour, however, did not take hold as a normative ideal until the 1960s with industrialization, urbanization, and the development of the nuclear family form. As with much of the modernization of Korea, the state played a crucial role in the production of the gendered division of labour. Seungsook Moon (2005) demonstrates that the gendered segmentation of the labour market was a state project that channeled rural men into industrial work under successive military regimes in the postwar period. In return for their consenting labour, men were rewarded materially as well as symbolically. Furthermore, to secure this transformation, the state passed policy measures that legalized and enforced gender division and male authority in the household (Moon 2002: 85).

But if the gender division became hegemonic during the rapid industrial transformation of Korean society, men were subject to sustained anxiety and repeated bouts of "crisis" regarding their identity and place in society. Gender, as a whole, has been a prominent and contested terrain where critical categories and structures of society are negotiated and transformed (Kendall 2002: 1). As Laurel Kendall observed:

> We witness the vertigo of a society that has come to question the social costs of its own swift success, posing its critiques and frustrations in gendered imagery: the avaricious middle class housewife, the alienated and ailing middle-aged father, the sexy young wife on the make.
>
> (Kendall 2002: 4)

The imagery reveals not only how the confusions and discontents of rapid social change, what many observers describe as "compressed modernity," have been inscribed onto gender identities, but also how women have been represented as villains and the men as victims. "Specifically, male loss or displacement constitutes a grammar for articulating the costs of colonialism, the Korean War, and rapid social transformation in South Korea" (Abelmann 2003: 188).

For example, in popular culture, the emasculation of men was a prominent theme in representations of colonial and post-colonial history (Abelmann 2002, Choi 1998, Em 1995). Writing about contemporary Korean film, Kyung Hyun Kim states:

> The dawning of a new modern era is normally punctuated by hope and optimism, but the weight of intense history and its attendant violence loomed so excessively large that it ended up traumatizing, marginalizing, and denaturalizing men. Wrecked and disordered was the male subjectivity after the Korean War, the subsequent division, and the continuing legacy of colonialism through military dictatorship; the metaphor of the "symbolic lack" was astutely installed as one of the primary thematic impulses in postwar cinemas.
>
> (K.H. Kim 2004: 11; see also E. Cho 2005, K. Kim 2005, Abelmann and McHugh 2005)

Popular cultural forms articulated a structure of feeling that registered the confusion, disorientation, and loss due to rapid industrialization and social transformation in terms of trauma to male subjectivity.

Even at the height of Korea's industrial development, just prior to the Asian financial crisis, men, specifically white-collar workers, were represented as carrying an unbearable, perhaps lethal, burden for society's progress. June Lee observed, for example, that in the mid-1990s, the news that Korean men had the "world's highest mortality" rates for middle-aged men shocked and captured the attention of the public (J. Lee 1996, 2002). Discourses of men's diseases and illness figured prominently in identifying men as victims and "forgotten heroes." Those discourses of bodily suffering were, moreover, inflected by narratives of the social suffering of men who had become estranged in the home due to having lost their authority after an absence brought about by longstanding sacrifice to the company and to the nation.

The recent history of state and popular discourses regarding men and masculinity suggests that "emasculation" (signified through trauma to the body or subjectivity) was a normal rather than aberrant condition (cf. K. Kim 2004: 15). The enunciation of "crisis," then, suggests less a new threat or rupture of normative ideals than a discursive effect that articulates social change as a hazard to an imagined national and social order, which in turn reproduces hegemony. The term "crisis" is often highly politicized in that it is a discourse produced by the state and reproduced by interested parties to secure their interests (Shin 2000). While "crisis" may be used as "shorthand for notions of instability and displacement of a particular (notably patriarchal) set of norms and ideals," conveying a "sense of anxiety and moral panic," the norms may be "as much imagined as real" (Chant 2001: 215n). Thus, "crisis" is a political-cultural articulation that constitutes the very normative ideals that are ostensibly in jeopardy.

With the nation and the men of the nation in a state of chronic "crisis," women assumed crucial "masculine" roles. Faced with absent husbands from war and the economic demands of nation building, women were active agents inside and outside the private realm, engaging in land and stock investment, guiding children's education, and performing a range of "status production work" (Abelmann 2003; Kendall 1996, 2002; M. Kim 1992, 1993; Moon 1990; Yi 1998).[11] Their activities in the public sphere, however, constituted ambivalent identities in the public imagination. In the late 1980s and early 1990s, for example, with the development of consumer culture, women were vilified for excessive consumption and speculation (land and capital), and were seen to embody an immoral indulgence that exacerbated tensions between the rich and poor and threatened the domestic economy (Nelson 2000: 114). More recently, "too modern" women have become the exemplars of an open and dangerous sexuality, willing actors in infidelity, or "home wreckers," treacherously blurring the lines between sexuality and motherhood (S. Lee 2002).

Women's increasing visibility and open enactment of their prowess in the public sphere in the 1990s was counterposed to men's increasing vulnerability and victimhood in both the public and private realms. But this apparent unraveling of normative gender identities and relations constituted the condition for the reproduction of hegemonic forms. "Crisis" placed the onus of "national" recovery on the family, constituting the family as a special refuge of emotional stability, and the place best suited for the care of children (and men) and the reproduction of a moral society (Sung 1998: 76). In such a manner, discourses of crisis constructed and valorized normative gender subject positions – women as mothers and wives and husbands as providers. "Crisis," then, at once condemned women's assumption of agency, when expressed as a breach of normative expectations, but also sanctioned a particular agentive subjectivity, when expressed as motherly or wifely self-sacrifice for the family.

"I want to return home a proud husband and father"

Daewoo workers occupied a precarious gender and class position. On the one hand, they were the "labour aristocracy," the most privileged of the working class. They had worked for one of the primary affiliates of the Daewoo *chaebŏl*, which prior to the crisis was one of the top five companies in the nation with an international reach and reputation. Aside from the material rewards of employment at a conglomerate, including regular bonuses, educational and housing subsidies, job security, and relatively high wages, such employment was culturally meaningful, conferring a particular status distinction readily claimed by workers themselves and generally acknowledged in the working-class community at large. They enjoyed a moral and social standing beyond the reach of most manual labourers.[12]

On the other hand, within the context of the broader Korean social and cultural hierarchy, Daewoo workers were still manual labourers. They themselves described their work as *dansunhan nodong*, or simple labour. It is work, they said, that anyone could learn in a few days, if not a few hours. The work was physically difficult and monotonous. Many complained about the drudgery, the pace of the assembly line, the noise, dirt and fumes that saturated their senses. They recognized this kind of labour as lowly and belittling. Workers at times called themselves *kongdoli*, a highly pejorative term connoting servitude, mental ineptitude, and moral dissipation, and described their work as "eating grease."[13] But perhaps just as telling, most, if not all, self-consciously avoided identification with that experience and image of work. They called themselves *hoesawŏn*, meaning company employee, or Daewoo *kŭnroja*, meaning simply Daewoo worker. Those labels dissemble the stigma of manual labour.

But within the labouring community, within the factory, and among their fellow workers, not to mention family, working at Daewoo conferred social value. Although labourers' feelings towards Daewoo Motor changed dramatically after they were laid off, many still recalled a sense of *chabushim* (pride) and *aesashim* (affection for company). Kim Kwang Ju, a young and unmarried assembly line worker, remarked:

> Of course [I had pride]. [Daewoo] is *daegiŏp* [large company]. In Korea, a *daegiŏp* is ... it's considerably ... what should I say ... should I say, an object of envy? It's to that extent. In Korea, it's like that. *Daegiŏp* ... or a civil service job is considerably ... something everyone wants. I had a lot of devotion, and my family was that proud of me, working at a company as big as Daewoo.
>
> (Personal interview, 18 October 2001)

Later in the interview, he stated, "Even the most trifling home appliances I bought were Daewoo brands. Really, even a small camping stove. … That is how much I had affection and devotion for the company."

Working at Daewoo Motor not only granted men social standing in the community, but it also signified masculine moral worth. A "Daewoo Man," as some commented, was unlike other manual labourers. He was dependable, competent, and able to live up to his full responsibilities as a respected member of the community. One man recalled that before the crisis they were treated like "kings" in Bupyŏng:

> If you wore your Daewoo jacket or uniform, wherever you went, you could eat and drink on credit because they knew that at the end of the month you were getting a paycheck and could pay. You could always get a loan from a bank. All the bank had to see was your Daewoo identification.
>
> (Field note, verbatim recording, translated by author)

The Daewoo uniform was worn like a badge of honour, and it enabled the men to claim a measure of middle-class respect and dignity. They were not manual labourers but "Daewoo Men."

The moral value attributed to a "Daewoo Man" was intimately associated with a normative masculinity – of being good providers, good husbands and fathers. A recurring gendered theme in workers' discussions expressing their social value as Daewoo employees was that of marriageability. They related that in the days before the crisis, they were "good catches," in the sense that they were desirable marriage partners. For example, Choi Man Su, a husband and father of two, stated,

> If you listen to the stories from the 1980s, the men who worked here … of course they were just *saengsanjik* (production/manual workers) and [just] high school graduates … but if you said that you work here, people used to say that you were a first-rate marriage candidate.
>
> (Personal interview, 17 December 2001)

The wives, in several interviews, corroborated this; they felt that they were marrying good and dependable men who would be able to provide a secure and stable livelihood.

Being laid-off not only stripped the men of their badge of social respectability but also undermined their claim to hegemonic masculinity. When asked about how his authority at home had changed, an elderly labourer echoed the phrase that had become common in the late 1990s and more so since the financial crisis, "*kogae sugin abuhji*" (bowed or cowed father). "In one word, '*kogae sugin abuhji*.' In Korea, maybe you don't know about Korea, but in Korea, men work at a job, and as the *kajang* (household head) they are the one who leads and controls the family." At this point in the interview a friend of his interjected, "the pillar." The elder worker continued, "The man is the pillar, but now, that is all lost, like we forfeited it to the woman" (Personal interview, 18 December 2001).[14] Another stated:

> As a man, I don't have any respect; I lost it. As the family head, I don't have respect; I lost it. My son comes to me for money for school. I tell him to go ask his mother, trying to escape explaining. … "Family head," there's nothing to say. My wife earns money now, you have to look at it that she's now the family head, since now I can't fulfill my role.
>
> (Personal interview, 18 December 2001)

No longer "Daewoo Men," workers relinquished their rights and privileges as household heads.

With the loss of authority at home, men were not at home. Home was a place for husbands and fathers, not a place for the unemployed. Not a few men admitted that they left home early in the morning and returned late at night, or spent nights at the union offices or with other laid-off labourers so as to avoid contact with their wives and children. One obvious interpretation is that men left to avoid fighting with their wives or to hide from their children that they were laid-off. For example, one man stated: "Instead of fighting [with my wife], in my heart I feel I would rather be outside, wandering around. Ironically, it's more comfortable. If I'm at home we fight, things get said, and I'd just rather be outside" (Field note, verbatim recording, translated by author).

It was not an uncommon sentiment among the men, but it would be an injustice to attribute their leaving as simply avoidance or running away from family responsibility, for in fact, men leave to claim responsibility. Men leave in order to reclaim their place at home by staking out a place in the public sphere, by participating in the Struggle.

This articulation between participation in the Struggle and the redemption of masculinity was evident in the following scene. On 10 April 2002, the men gathered in one of the larger rooms in the union offices for an early meeting with union officials. Sitting crossed-legged on the floor, they looked solemn as the current leaders announced that the union had signed a tentative agreement with management to negotiate an end to hostilities, in which an unspecified number of men (somewhere between 300 and 450) would be gradually recalled to the factory by the year's end in return for the normalization of labour–management relations and amendments to the union's collective bargaining agreement. There were no guarantees as to whom and under what conditions labourers would be reinstated. As the meeting progressed, men grumbled under their breath, and the room filled with smoke. A tall stout man with a round youthful face belying his middle age, stood up and began to speak:

> Yesterday I was too ashamed to tell my wife that the union signed the agreement. Do you know why I was ashamed? When I received the notice [of my being laid-off] and returned home to get my bags [to return and occupy the factory for the imminent standoff with management and government], I told my wife confidently that I would return home a proud husband and proud father. In our fight song, doesn't it say, "Let's return proud"? Is this returning

tall and proud? We fought for over a year. ... Do we have to crawl back in shame?

(Transcribed from personal video recording, 10 April 2002)

His voice was defiant, and after he sat down, the other men cheered in approval. It was a startling moment when the emotional and moral tenor of the Struggle came into greater focus, as the ostensible object of their Struggle – to return to the factory – seamlessly sutured onto the emotionally compelling desire to return home.

Men's participation, however, was tensely negotiated and fought over with wives, and men did not (on the whole) arbitrarily make decisions to participate. This negotiation reveals a gender relationship and dynamic in which women play a powerful part in the making of men and in the shaping of men's agency. The following interview excerpt powerfully demonstrates this tension:

> I told my wife, "Honey, until I get my job back I'm going to fight in the Strug-gle. I'm going to get my job back. So, believe in me this once, believe in me and follow me, do as I say this one time. If you do that, I'll do anything you tell me to, everything. Whatever you want me to do, I'll do. Ask me to wash your feet, okay, I'll wash your feet; so please, this one time, believe in me and do what I ask." Now, I swallowed my pride as a man to ask my wife these things. Truthfully, I asked her to please have faith in me and follow me, don't speak but just this once follow me. My wife started to cry. Crying, she said, "How did you get this way, become a miserable wretched man? How can such a proud and boastful man say something like that to me?" Seeing my wife cry, my eyes started to well up ... and tears started streaming down my own face. ... As a man, a man's pride ... [you're] not supposed to cry in front of women.
>
> (Personal interview, 16 October 2001)

The man is smallish in stature and wears small, round wire-rimmed glasses, and is on the face of it an unimposing person. But he is recognized as one of the most ardent members of the Struggle. He is often early at demonstrations, setting up the sound system, and during demonstrations, taking hold of the microphone and passionately defending the union and the Struggle.

The image of this once proud man washing his wife's feet recalls the spate of newspaper and television reports on how wives and family members "boosted" or revitalized the spirits and vitality of household heads who had lost their jobs, showing their love and welcoming the men home from the hostile world by wash-ing their husbands' feet. It is unclear if he was consciously evoking this particular image popularized in the press, but his telling reverses the social roles. He will wash her feet, if she would let him participate in the Struggle.

Performing women

The following are some scenes taken from the Daewoo union's own video record-ing of the Struggle titled *Winter Uprising: The Second Story*.[15] When discussing the Struggle, labourers often referred to the video, asking if I had seen it. They suggested that I see the video as evidence and testimony of their Struggle, their point of view, and their suffering. "Everything is in the video," they said. In a conversation with one of the union's filmmakers, he described the films and other footage as "the true history of the Struggle." The filmic reality of the videos is nonetheless a mediated construction. The representation of women in the video is emblematic of the performative role of women and children in emotionally and morally framing the Struggle.

The first scene of the video captures the riot police breaking up the union's occupation of the factory. Women fight with the riot police while their children clutch onto their coats and the men retreat and hide. Close-up shots show women's contorted and distressed faces as they yell and scream at the police. Their husbands are gone, having either fled or been caught by the police. Similar scenes of women fighting and children crying are repeated throughout the video documentary. But while the women appear to be the protagonists in the video, the actual subjects of the Struggle are the men.

Women and children in the video are the bodily conduits of suffering. Their representation draws its emotional force, on the one hand, from the evident distress of the women and children, but on the other, from cultural expectations of normative gender relations. The high profile of children in these representations identifies women as mothers and wives. The presence of women in unfamiliar and unexpected contexts, doing what is again unfamiliar, and what many may perceive as violent behavior, creates a disjuncture between place and gender relationships. Furthermore, their presence signals the absence of fathers and husbands – an incomplete configuration. Why are these mothers and wives out in the street? What has led them to fight with the police? Why are they crying? Where are their husbands? They invoke an anxiety over broken expectations: "That is, the claims they make play on and resonate with audiences' shared underlying ethical and moral beliefs" (McLagan 2003: 608). Women and children are critical in the Struggle's self-portrayal because they index not only their own distress but the injustice experienced by their absent husbands. Although we may not see their husbands, the women testify to the truth of their husbands' suffering at the hands of the government and corporations. They testify to the truth of their threatened and broken families, the truth of the crisis of family.

This representational trope of the absence of the father through the testimony of wives is evident in the video's second scene. After the introductory images of women fighting with police, the video cuts to a view of the exterior of an apartment complex. A door opens to an apartment; a small boy is waiting. The filmmaker asks from behind the camera, "Where is your father?" "At the church," the boy answers. He is the youngest son of one of the union leaders. The wife is in the kitchen, and she stirs and ladles a large pot of an herbal remedy made of Korean pears and ginger. She is in a black dress and is visibly pregnant. She explains that it is for her ailing husband. The video then cuts to her two sons eating a simple meal of rice and kimchee. The older son complains that there are no side dishes for the meal. The video cuts again, this time to a small room where the wife sits as she begins to recount what happened that day when the riot police invaded the occupied factory. As she tells her story, the video cuts back to the scene of the attack. As the wives wail helplessly, one by one, men who were unable to escape are hauled into an awaiting bus to be sent to jail. The video returns to the wife, and a close-up frames her face as she dabs at her eyes, trying to hold back tears.

Although hers is the voice and body of the scene, her husband remains a haunting and ghostly figure. Empathy and dramatic tension is created by the absence of her husband and the portrayal of the woman as a loyal wife, mother, and caregiver, feeding her children what she can, and preparing a remedy for her husband. She waits for her husband's return home.

Women were also prominently featured at demonstrations. A small number of the wives of unemployed Daewoo men often participated in the larger, more public demonstrations. They sat with the men in loose columns on the street or sidewalk, their voices and raised fists following the military cadence of the songs and speeches. They brought their children who sat drowsily in the nest of their crossed legs or stood restlessly, looking here or there, sometimes self-consciously mimicking the militant postures and fist-raising of their parents. In between songs and speeches, men played with the children, holding their hands, holding them in their arms, talking to them, and feeding them snacks. The wives, some wearing red headbands and union vests and holding their children, were tangible reminders of what was at stake in the Struggle: the survival of families and the redemption of the men.

Strong women

The representation of men and families that women produced through their performances were poignant and appealing. But it is problematic to assume that all the men were indeed good husbands and fathers, and that the women, too, were simply good wives and mothers. Such interpretations are readily susceptible to hegemonic gender narratives of the hardworking family man and the long-suffering Korean wife.

The women had endured much both before and during the Struggle. Interviews and casual conversations with both men and women revealed that many families were in fact troubled even prior to the mass layoff. A few of the women divulged that they had been thinking of divorce. These same women would go on to participate in the Struggle at great cost to their own mental and physical well-being. Like many of the men, the women also complained of social alienation, fear for their future and worry for their children, and numerous physical ailments. Many, for example, stated that their heads ached, that they were unable to think, that their bodies were constantly fatigued and that their legs and backs cramped up. They reported that they couldn't sleep at night, or when they did fall asleep they had terrifying dreams of riot police attacking their husbands. They woke up only to find themselves alone, their husbands out fighting or imprisoned at the church. One wife stated that she felt like screaming out loud; she said, "My head just hurts. When my head feels heavy, I can't think at all, but when I'm frustrated, feeling suffocated, my head feels ready to crack, I feel I have to bang my head against the wall or just scream."[16]

The emotional and physical pain that wives experienced was not simply due to their husbands' unemployment. It was also due to the burden of "traditional" wifely duties of taking care of the house and children. Many of the wives were young, in their early to mid-thirties and with young children. Not only did they work for the Struggle, visiting families and participating in demonstrations, but they also had to somehow manage the household on little or no income and with little or no outside support. One wife stated:

> The most difficult thing is my body. The children are difficult, too. After I come out here and go home, there is housework to do. Children are at the age when they just mess up the whole house. I have to make them dinner, prepare snacks. When I go home I just want to rest but I can't.

Another explained:

> In the beginning, I woke at four, five in the morning. Three or four days a week there was a morning demonstration at the factory gates. I thought I was going to go crazy. It was too hard. For about two months, when I went home I just wanted to lie down, not clean the house, just sleep.[17]

On top of their involvement in the Struggle, these women must also work a second shift at home.[18]

Some of the wives were further burdened by employment outside the home. With unemployment compensation and savings dwindling, a few sought employment and some began networking enterprises, selling commercial products from their home or door-to-door. The following is a statement from one working mother:

> Before, I understood the father [husband]; because he has to return to the factory, I thought I would endure everything; but now, since I'm working, I can't take it. Although in my mind I understand, my body doesn't follow. I cry when I go to work, I cry when I watch my children … yesterday was so hard … it's not just hard, it's so hard that I can't even hold my child.

She continued:

> But since I have to raise the children, I continued to take my child along with me. I should've said something to my husband, but that was also distressful. It would cause my husband pain. Because I know how hard it [the Struggle] is … if I didn't take part in the Struggle, I would've probably nagged and complained. But because I know how hard it really is I couldn't say anything. I suffered alone. Yet, I chose to work and it is difficult. Because of the circumstances of being laid-off, all of the burdens are put on a woman's shoulders. Raising the children, earning money, all of this.[19]

If women created the image of good, wholesome families victimized by the crisis, it appeared that they did so at the cost of suppressing their disappointments and frustrations as mothers and wives.

The complexity of women's agency, the apparent contradictions between their performance and their experience, may be understood, as suggested by Taylor (1994: 292; 1997) in her study of the protest theatrics of *Las Madres de la Plaza de Mayo*, by differentiating between performance and essentialized notions of motherhood that are instantiated by performance. The difference lies in that women self-consciously performed *as* mothers: "That *as* marks the conceptual distance between the essentialist notion of motherhood […] and the self-conscious manipulation of the maternal role – understood as performative" (Taylor 1994: 293; 1997). In other words, women were not mothers by nature, but drew upon culturally valorized scripts of motherhood in order to solicit public attention and sympathy for their husbands' plight.

The women were not simply passive victims of the media and union representational strategies. They were quite astute in understanding the effects of their performances. They were cognizant of the media value of their role, that their presence solicited public sympathy. As the wife depicted above, who was at the time pregnant with her third son, stated, "The media pays attention. Compared to when only men come out, when the entire family comes out … they take at least one more picture" (Personal interview, 12 March 2002). They understood that their presence aroused powerful emotions for the public as well as for their own husbands.

Even in interactions with the riot police, women proceeded with an understanding of societal expectations surrounding gender relations. The ranks of the riot police were composed of young men fulfilling their mandatory military service. Thus wives acted with the understanding that the riot police who were many years their junior would be less liable to retaliate against them; as one woman remarked, "So, since we're women, we don't get hit as much as the men" (Personal interview, n.d.). In their protestations, women drew attention to their status as mothers and wives and to the suffering of their absent husbands. Banging on metal shields, women chastised the young recruits with, "Our baby's father"; "He's a father"; "Save our fathers."

While they may have performed as vulnerable and suffering wives and mothers, they understood themselves to be strong, purposeful individuals. Women uniformly stated that they were fighting to save their families. As one wife stated, "Restructuring, layoffs, are ruining families. Because of that, the entire family has to band together and fight … to protect my family. So this is my fight, too" (Personal interview, 12 March 2002). Her statement reiterated the gendered script of the crisis, but it also intimated at her agency, and complicated, self-positioning. It was *her* family, *her* fight, too.

It was women's actions, their performances, that would save their husbands, their families, their gendered class investments. They were the wives of "Daewoo Men." If employment at Daewoo Motor conferred upon men "kingly" value, women, too, gained both material and moral benefits. At a group interview session at one woman's apartment, their class and gender identification was evident.

Many of the women were, like their husbands, from working-class backgrounds with high school educations. When I inquired about their work history, many said that they were simply housewives, although a few had worked at small factories. Our discussion revealed their sense of having acquired a degree of class mobility, many answering my query about their class identity with middle-class identifications prior to the layoffs.

Furthermore, the wives were highly aware of gender inequality in the job market and in Korean society as a whole. They were aware that women like them were the first to be laid off and that the only jobs available were in the low-paying service sector. They asked me, rhetorically, as housewives educated at high school, what jobs were they qualified for, what could they do to preserve their families and social position? For the women, the threat of downward mobility was palpable. In participating in the Struggle, they were also fighting for their class and gender interests, but to do so, they had to fight to sustain their faltering husbands.

Although they may play the subordinate role in the Struggle, as mothers, they emphasized that they understood that it was the women who were strong, not the men. As one woman remarked, "When it comes to family matters, aren't women stronger? From a long time ago ... I don't know what it is like it in the West, but from a long time ago people said that Korean women are strong." Reversing the domestic/public dichotomy, the women argued that they are strong because their everyday lives were full of struggle and confrontation. It was the men who were actually sequestered and inexperienced in confrontation, their lives bound by the routine of going to and from work. In the same interview, another woman stated,

> In actuality, women have to face more confrontations ... in our daily lives. Women experience more pain from not having money. Children ask us for money, right? They don't ask their fathers. We have to go out and buy food for the family. Men don't buy food for the family. ... Women have to directly confront people, and it is difficult. So, at bottom, women cannot but be strong. Because in reality, it is women who fight everyday [in society].
>
> (Personal interview, 12 March 2002).

Another woman pointed out that if women didn't participate, neither would the men. She stated:

> But, if women don't participate, they [men] not only don't understand the real situation ... they only care for their own. They only see that they don't have money, so they go out and work day jobs ... they do day labour and get hurt, and they don't fight with us. But, I'm telling you that then their families become ruined faster. Those families ... husbands and wives fight more ... because husbands want to fight but their wives try to stop them.
>
> (Personal interview, 12 March 2002)

It was a striking comment. She voiced a common belief among the women I interviewed: it was the women who were strong, who enabled the men to continue to fight, and consequently return home as good husbands and fathers. Although women may on occasion dissuade men from fighting, women should understand the "real situation," the real threat to their families and livelihood – the frailty of the men.

Interviews with women revealed that wives were not only critical of but also distraught over what they perceived as weakness in their husbands. Significantly, they attributed this frailty to men's inability to let go of society's patriarchal expectations. Women revealed a degree of insight into hegemonic gender norms. Many women readily expounded upon their experiences of favouritism for sons in their own family, unequal employment opportunities, and the legal authority over property and household headship held by men.

However, they recognized that while the patriarchal system may privilege men, it also made great demands upon them, expectations, they argued, that men found difficult to fulfill, particularly in their current circumstances. Commenting on her experience of her husbands' job loss, one woman stated,

> Women, too, can become household heads. There are instances when women become household heads when they lose their husbands, but even with husbands, men and women can exchange roles. I think that it has to happen, so that both can live comfortably. But then, men are too tightly wrapped up with it [patriarchal expectations]; they needlessly suffer alone.
>
> (Personal interview, 12 March 2002)

Since the layoffs, women observed troubling transformations in their husbands. Their husbands drank more, often drinking alone at home, and they smoked more. When not at the union or on the streets demonstrating, they were at home restlessly watching television, or doing nothing at all. These were not the same men that they had married. They were listless and prone to volatility. For example, one woman observed the changes that she saw in her husband's behavior and personality. Her husband was a shop-floor union representative and departmental leader. She said,

> He cursed me as he would curse a man. It seemed as though the stress and anger he couldn't express at work he took out on me. Seeing that, I felt scared. So I thought I needed to join in the fighting. Men, they change a lot, their personality. They can't deal with the situation, with themselves.
>
> (Personal interview, 12 March 2002).

Women agreed that men were the pillars of the family, but they also knew that these pillars were fragile. After a long exchange about the mistreatment of women in Korean society, one woman in my interview volunteered, "Because that's the way the culture is, men can't let go of the idea that they have to feed the family and make a living. Because they can't fulfill their duty, they lose their confidence, their sense of themselves as men. That's the biggest problem." I asked if it was because wives pressured the men. She replied, "Women may nag, but that's not the biggest reason. They [the men] do it to themselves." The last statement is telling: the men do it to themselves. They are unable to function "normally" outside of the patriarchal order, unable to operate outside the role of normative masculinity. Thus, it is the women who preserved the men's place in the patriarchal order, who redeemed the men.

Conclusion

In this chapter I examined the conditions that informed gender performance in the Daewoo Struggle. The performances revealed not only the reproduction of normative masculinity in the labour movement but also its complex linkages with gendered discourses of family breakdown in the aftermath of the Asian financial crisis. In my analysis, I argued that women's participation and performance were critical to this reproduction. In the Daewoo Struggle, workers' wives were in fact self-conscious agents of their performance of motherhood. However, in describing women's actions as a form of agency my intent was not to ascribe a radical free agency. Rather, by using the lens of performance, I suggest that women's performances were in a sense overdetermined by the discursive and performative field they occupied – wives and mothers of laid-off husbands at a time of national, economic, and family "crisis." Furthermore, their self-description as agents in the social drama – strong wives and mothers – was also culturally structured. Agency (and the theoretical implication of authenticity) is also historically and culturally contingent; that is, it is embedded in distinct kinds and ideologies of motivation, such as the presumed authenticity of women's devotion to their husbands and families.[20]

The complicated structure of women's agency suggests the intricate entanglements between class and gender identities at the juncture of Korea's neoliberal turn. The financial crisis exposed the socio-cultural vulnerability of Korean men, the intimate connection between patriarchal and economic structures and their deep dependence upon those structures to sustain normative masculine identities. With the sudden deprivation of job security that accompanied the imposition of flexible labour markets, men found themselves at a loss – figuratively, and sometimes actually, "homeless." Men's actions for their class interests, in this case the preservation of their relatively privileged class position, entailed the reproduction of hegemonic gender norms. Women's actions for their class interests, too, entailed the reproduction of hegemonic gender norms. It was the labour of women that enabled the self-described hapless and enfeebled men to reclaim their social and moral position. It was the women who redeemed the men in order to preserve the normative family order.

Notes

1 Daewoo Motor was the flagship enterprise of the Daewoo Group *chaebŏl* (family-owned conglomerate). It was the third largest auto manufacturing firm in Korea and the twenty-fifth largest car maker in the world in the 1990s. In late 1999, Daewoo

collapsed under the weight of debts of over US $10 billion, and was put in court-receivership. In return for emergency loans from private and state creditors, the carmaker agreed to radically downsize its workforce.

2 In 1998, the state failed to carry out the threat of large-scale redundancy dismissals at Hyundai Motor, the country's largest automaker and also the stronghold of the largest and reputedly the most militant labour union, because of fierce labour resistance. Afterwards foreign investors widely questioned the government's will to face down militant labour and enforce a flexible labour market.

3 The riot police violently drove union leaders and workers from the factory on 19 February 2001. Many of the union leaders and several of the workers were wanted by the police, and they found sanctuary within the church walls. From that time on, the church served as the operational headquarters of the Struggle.

4 According to Doowon Lee (2000: 10), of the total liabilities of US $158 billion, approximately 40 per cent was short-term debt.

5 According to Wade and Veneroso (1998:11), the mandates set by the IMF went "well beyond standard IMF programs, calling for structural and institutional reform, even though they are not needed to resolve the crisis." Although wary of conspiracy theories, the authors argue that the reforms were intended to "make the financial system operate like a Western one, though without actually saying so." The Crisis was rendered as the inevitable outcome of the irrationality of so-called Confucian, or more pejoratively, crony, capitalism (cf. Kang 2002), and the mandates foreclosed upon the development-state model of economic growth (state mediation of capital accumulation and distribution in which large, "national" firms are nurtured and protected from competition). Left-leaning analysts described the Crisis as the fallout of the breakup of the Cold War economic pact between Korea and the United States, in which the United States provided privileged access to its markets and protected Korean markets in order to buttress Korea against possible social dissent, read communism (see Cumings 1998, Gowan 1999, Harvey 2003).

6 As noted by Koo (2000), one of the peculiarities of Korea's labour laws is that despite the draconian legislation suppressing, often violently, union activity, employers did not have a clear right to lay off workers until the agreement reached in 1998.

7 In addition, the numbers of non-standard or irregular workers – those in temporary, contract, or day labour – rose astronomically, superseding the number of regular workers by the year 2002 (55.7 per cent or 7.37 million) (Chun 2006: 87).

8 The public concern for male household heads was primarily directed towards the middle class, and there was considerable fear regarding the destruction of that symbol of national development.

9 For a detailed analysis of the relationship between neoliberal governmentality and "IMF homeless" see Jesook Song (2003, 2006).

10 Historically, the Korean state has depended upon the family to provide the social safety net. In times of such "crisis," conservative ideologies of the family, in particular Confucian, were mobilized to legitimate the state deferral of social responsibility. See Jung Shi Sung (1998: 76). Furthermore, the family was instituted as the basic unit of survival and mobility through the colonial and developmental periods. Song (2003) also observes that during the "IMF Crisis" under the management of the Kim Dae Jung regime, the discourse of "family breakdown" may be understood as a "crucial technology for managing unstable society." Propagated by the government and NGOs, crisis discourse was a "rhetorical strategy for opening new social spaces and pursuing diverse interests that resulted in the amplification of (neo)liberal governmentality" (Song 2003: 88–89).

11 The studies of women have primarily focused on the middle and upper-middle class. Notable exceptions include Abelmann's (2003) study of women's life history narratives of gender, class, and social transformation, Kim Seung-kyung's study of women factory workers, and Kendall's (1996) study of changes in marriage rites – all of which include the experiences and stories of working and lower class women.

12 For a discussion on the class distinctions between small and large firms in Japan see Dorinne Kondo (1990: 53–57) and Roberson (2003: 129).
13 On the symbolic weight of the terms *kongdoli* and *kongsuni* (factory girl) see Koo (2001: 126–36); S. Kim (1997).
14 On the "pillar" as a metaphor of normative masculinity in Japan, see Thomas Gill (2003: 44–45).
15 *Winter Uprising: The Second Story*, Daewoo Motor Union, 2002. Since the late 1990s, the union's video team documented union activities, including demonstrations and meetings. It produced two hour-long documentary videos of the Struggle. The videos were produced for internal consumption by union members, their families and other affiliated organizations, and outside civic organizations. The first documented the union's efforts to mobilize opposition to the impending layoffs. The second captured the Struggle after the layoffs, focusing on the plight of the laid-off men and their families. It was this second video that the men referred me to as the documented "truth" of the Struggle.
16 Interview (2001) conducted by Dr. Jin Joo Chung, chief researcher Wonjin Institute for Occupational and Environmental Health. Dr. Chung kindly granted permission to access and use her interview materials conducted with the Daewoo workers' wives. My own interviews corroborated her findings.
17 Interview (2001) conducted by Dr. Jin Joo Chung.
18 It was difficult to accurately gauge the extent to which men do or do not help with childcare and household chores, and how men's domestic work changed or did not change with unemployment. In casual conversation, the majority of the men I asked said that they did some kind of household work, be it washing dishes or taking care of the children. In discussing this with women, however, the majority stated that their husbands did little or no work; or if men were willing to help around the house, they were more an encumbrance than help.
19 Interview (2001) conducted by Dr. Jin Joo Chung; also personal interview (12 March 2002).
20 For an incisive discussion on the question of agency, see Desjarlais (1997: 201–5) and Abu-Lughod (1990).

References

Abelmann, N. (2002) "Women, Mobility, and Desire: Narrating Class and Gender in South Korea," in L. Kendall (ed.) *Under Construction: The Gendering of Modernity, Class, and Consumption in the Republic of Korea*, Honolulu: University of Hawai'i Press.
—— (2003) *The Melodrama of Mobility: Women, Talk, and Class in Contemporary South Korea*, Honolulu: University of Hawai'i Press.
Ablemann, N. and McHugh, K. (2005) "Introduction: Gender, Genre, and Nation," in N. Abelmann and K. McHugh (eds) *South Korean Golden Age Melodrama: Gender, Genre, and National Cinema*, Detroit, MI: Wayne State University.
Abu-Lughod, L. (1990) "The Romance of Resistance: Tracing Transformations of Power through Bedouin Women," in *American Ethnologist*, 17: 41–55.
Butler, J. (1993) *Bodies That Matter: On the Discursive Limits of Sex*, New York: Routledge.
—— (1999) *Gender Trouble: Feminism and the Subversion of Identity*, New York: Routledge.
—— (2004) *The Judith Butler Reader*, Malden, MA: Blackwell Publishers, Inc.
Chant, S. (2001) "Men in Crisis? Reflections on Masculinities, Work and Family in North-West Costa Rica," in C. Jackson (ed.) *Men at Work: Labour, Masculinities, Development*, London: Frank Cass.

Cho, E. (2005) "The Stray Bullet and the Crisis of Korean Masculinity," in K. McHugh and N. Abelmann (eds) *South Korean Golden Age Melodrama: Gender, Genre, and National Cinema*, Detroit, MI: Wayne State University.

Cho, H. (1998) "Male Dominance and Mother Power: The Two Sides of Confucian Patriarchy in Korea," in W.H. Slote and G.A. de Vos (eds) *Confucianism and the Family*, Albany, NY: State University of New York Press.

—— (2002) "Living with Conflicting Subjectivities: Mother, Motherly Wife, and Sexy Woman in the Transition from Colonial-Modern to Postmodern Korea," in L. Kendall (ed.) *Under Construction: The Gendering of Modernity, Class, and Consumption in the Republic of Korea*, Honolulu: University of Hawai'i Press.

Choi, C. (1998) "Nationalism and the Construction of Gender in Korea," in E. Kim and C. Choi (eds) *Dangerous Women: Gender and Korean Nationalism*, New York: Routledge.

Chun, J. J. (2006) "The Symbolic Politics of Labour: Transforming Employment Relations in South Korea and the United States," PhD dissertation, University of California, Berkeley.

Cumings, B. (1998) "The Korean Crisis and the End of 'Late' Development," in *New Left Review*, 228: 43–72.

Daewoo Motor Union (2002) *Winter Uprising: The Second Story* [video], Bupyŏng: Daewoo Motor Union.

Desjarlais, R. (1997) *Shelter Blues: Sanity and Selfhood among the Homeless*, Philadelphia, PA: University of Pennsylvania Press.

Em, H. (1995) "'Overcoming' Korea's Division: Narrative Strategies in Recent South Korean Historiography," in *positions: east asia cultures critique*, 1, 2: 450–85.

Eyerman, R. (2006) "Performing Opposition, or How Social Movements Move," in J.C. Alexander and B. Giesen (eds) *Social Performance: Symbolic Action, Cultural Pragmatics, and Ritual*, Cambridge: Cambridge University Press.

Fuller, N. (2001) "Work and Masculinity among Peruvian Urban Men," in C. Jackson (ed.) *Men at Work: Labour, Masculinities, Development*, London: Frank Cass.

Gill, T. (2003) "When Pillars Evaporate: Structuring Masculinity on the Japanese Margins," in J.E. Roberson and N. Suzuki (eds) *Men and Masculinities in Contemporary Japan: Dislocating the Salaryman Doxa*, London: RoutledgeCurzon.

Gowan, P. (1999) *The Global Gamble: Washington's Faustian Bid for World Dominance*, London: Verso.

Gutmann, M.C. (1997) "The Ethnographic (G)ambit: Women and the Negotiation of Masculinity in Mexico City," in *American Ethnologist*, 24, 4: 833–55.

Harvey, D. (2003) *The New Imperialism*, Oxford: Oxford University Press.

Jager, S. M. (2002) "Monumental Histories: Manliness, the Military, and the War Memorial," in *Public Culture*, 14, 2: 387–409.

—— (2003) *Narratives of Nation Building: A Genealogy of Patriotism*, Armonk, NY: M.E. Sharpe.

Kang, D.C. (2002) *Crony Capitalism: Corruption and Development in South Korea and the Philippines*, Cambridge: Cambridge University Press.

Kendall, L. (1996) *Getting Married in Korea: Of Gender, Morality and Modernity*, Berkeley: University of California Press.

—— (2002) "Introduction," in L. Kendall (ed.) *Under Construction: The Gendering of Modernity, Class, and Consumption in the Republic of Korea*, Honolulu: University of Hawai'i Press.

Kim, B. (2000) "The Politics of Crisis and a Crisis of Politics: The Presidency of Kim Dae-Jung," in K. Oh (ed.) *Korea Briefing 1997–1999: Challenges and Change at the Turn of the Century*, Armonk, NY: M.E. Sharpe.

Kim, K.H. (2004) *The Remasculinization of Korean Cinema*, Durham: Duke University Press.
—— (2005) "Lethal Work: Domestic Space and Gender Troubles in *Happy End* and *The Housemaid*," in N. Abelmann and K. McHugh (eds) *South Korean Golden Age Melodrama: Gender, Genre, and National Cinema*, Detroit, MI: Wayne State University.
Kim, M. (1992) "Late Industrialization and Women's Work in Urban Korea: An Ethnographic Study of Upper-Middle-Class Families," in *City and Society*, 6, 2: 156–73.
—— (1993) "Transformation of Family Ideology in Upper-Middle-Class Families in Urban South Korea," in *Ethnology*, 32, 1: 69–85.
—— (1995) "Gender, Class, and Family in Late-Industrialization South Korea," in *Asian Journal of Women's Studies*, 1: 58–86.
Kim, S. (1997) *Class Struggle or Family Struggle? The Lives of Women Factory Workers in South Korea*, Cambridge: Cambridge University Press.
Kim, S., and Finch, J. (2002) "Living with Rhetoric, Living against Rhetoric: Korean Families and the IMF Economic Crisis," in *Korean Studies*, 26(1): 120–39.
Kondo, D. (1990) *Crafting Selves: Power, Gender and Discourses of Identity in a Japanese Workplace*, Chicago: University of Chicago Press.
Koo, H. (2000) "The Dilemmas of Empowered Labour in Korea: Korean Workers in the Face of Global Capitalism," in *Asian Survey*, 40(2): 227–50.
—— (2001) *Korean Workers: The Culture and Politics of Class Formation*, Ithaca: Cornell University Press.
Kwon, J.B. (2005) "In the Crucible of Restructuration: Violence and Forging 'Workers of Iron' in the Transition to a Neoliberal Democracy in South Korea," Ph.D. dissertation, New York University.
Lee, D. (2000) "South Korea's Financial Crisis and Economic Restructuring," in K. Oh (ed.) *Korea Briefing 1997–1999: Challenges and Change at the Turn of the Century*, Armonk, NY: M.E. Sharpe.
Lee, J. (1996) "Health food as gendered commodity: Body, health, and sexuality among the middle-class Korean men: An analysis of health food," in *International Journal of Politics, Culture, and Society*, 10, 1: 73–94.
—— (2002) "Discourses of Illness, Meanings of Modernity: A Gendered Construction of Songinbyong," in L. Kendall (ed.) *Under Construction: The Gendering of Modernity, Class, and Consumption*, Honolulu: University of Hawai'i Press.
Lee, S. (2002) "The Concept of Female Sexuality in Korean Popular Culture," in L. Kendall (ed.) *Under Construction: The Gendering of Modernity, Class, and Consumption in the Republic of Korea*, Honolulu: University of Hawai'i Press.
McHugh, K. and Abelmann, N. (eds) (2005) *South Korean Golden Age Melodrama: Gender, Genre, and National Cinema*, Detroit, MI: Wayne State University.
McLagan, M. (2003) "Principles, Publicity, and Politics: Notes on Human Rights Media," in *American Anthropologist*, 105, 3: 605–12.
Moon, O. (1990) "Urban middle class wives in contemporary Korea: Their roles, responsibilities and dilemma," in *Korea Journal*, 30: 30–43.
Moon, S. (2002) "The Production and Subversion of Hegemonic Masculinity: Reconfiguring Gender Hierarchy in Contemporary South Korea," in L. Kendall (ed.) *Under Construction: The Gendering of Modernity, Class, and Consumption in the Republic of Korea*, Honolulu: University of Hawai'i Press.
—— (2005) *Militarized Modernity and Gendered Citizenship in South Korea*, Durham, NC: Duke University Press.
Nelson, L. (2000) *Measured Excess: Status, Gender, and Consumer Nationalism in South Korea*, New York: Columbia University Press.

Pyke, K. D. (1996) "Class-Based Masculinities: The Interdependence of Gender, Class, and Interpersonal Power," in *Gender and Society*, 10, 5: 527–49.

Roberson, J.E. (2003) "Japanese Working-Class Masculinities: Marginalized Complicity," in J.E. Roberson and N. Suzuki (eds) *Men and Masculinities in Contemporary Japan: Dislocating the Salaryman Doxa*, London: RoutledgeCurzon.

Seong, K. (1998) "Massive Unemployment and Social Disorganization: A New Face of High-Risk Society," in *Korea Journal*, 38, 4: 229–55.

Shin, G., and Chang, K. (2000) "Social Crisis in Korea," in K. Oh (ed.) *Korea Briefing 1997–1999: Challenges and Change at the Turn of the Century*, Armonk, NY: M.E. Sharpe.

Shin, K. (2000) "The Discourse of Crisis and Crisis of Discourse," in *Inter-Asia Cultural Studies*, 1, 3: 427–42.

Song, J. (2003) "Shifting Technologies: Neoliberalization of the Welfare State in South Korea, 1997–2001," PhD dissertation, University of Illinois, Urbana-Champaign.

—— (2006) "Family Breakdown and Invisible Homeless Women: Neoliberal Governance during the Asian Debt Crisis in South Korea, 1997–2001," in *positions: east asia cultures critique*, 14, no. 1.

Sung, S.J. (1998) "IMF sidae kajokchŭi tamlonŭi tŭngjanggwa sŏng jŏngch'esŏngŭi wigi," Yŏsŏnghak Yŏnguso, 8.1: 75–91.

Taylor, D. (1994) "Performing Gender: Las Madres de la Plaza de Mayo," in D. Taylor and J. Villegas (eds) *Negotiating Performance: Gender, Sexuality, and Theatricality in Latin/o America*, Durham, NC: Duke University Press.

—— (1997) *Disappearing Acts: Spectacles of Gender and Nationalism in Argentina's "Dirty War"*, Durham: Duke University Press.

Wade, R., and Veneroso, F. (1998), "The Asian Crisis: The High Debt Model versus the Wall Street-Treasury-IMF Complex," *New Left Review*, 228: 3–24.

Yi, E.K. (1998) "'Home is a Place to Rest': Constructing the Meaning of Work, Family and Gender in the Korean Middle Class," *Korea Journal*, 38, 2: 168–213.

8   Gender and ethnicity at work

Korean "hostess" Club Rose in Japan

Haeng-ja Sachiko Chung

What is it like working at a club in Japan, particularly if you are a transnational migrant or a man at a presumably feminine workplace? This chapter highlights the fluidity and multiplicity of workers' gender roles and ethnic identities by closely examining the discrepancies between the job content and job title as well as ethnic diversity within the presumed singular category of "Korean" through a case study of Korean Club Rose (*Kankoku Kurabu Rōzu* in Japanese) at the European Village (*Yoroppa-mura*) in the Minami district of Osaka, Japan.[1] This chapter is based upon my participant observation as a hostess in 2000–2001 and is part of my larger ethnographic research on Korean hostesses in Japan (cf. Chung 2004).

In this study I aim to contribute to labour studies, gender studies, and ethnic studies: first by investigating the gap between job content and title; second by including an examination of ethnic/migrant male workers, whom past studies have largely ignored by calling the space "hostess" clubs; third by closely examining how the precarious gender and ethnic positionalities (defined, for example, by visa status and language use) complicate relationships within the club environment; and fourth by addressing issues of diversity within the ethnic group. Since more than 90 per cent of Koreans (attempt to) pass as Japanese in Japan and more and more Koreans naturalize as Japanese, identifying ethnicity is a daunting and problematic but still necessary process to problematize the ethnic category. Therefore, I use language as an ethnic identification marker. If a person is a Korean native speaker, I tentatively categorize her as "Korean." If a person is a native speaker of Japanese, I group him as "Japanese" unless other supplementary information indicates otherwise.[2]

The category of "hostess club," which is actually an invention of Western academics, also has similar homogenizing effects. In Japan, a hostess club is simply called a club (*kurabu*). Past scholarship considered the "hostess club" to be a place where hostesses entertain customers by commodifying their femininity and sexuality, and where customers reinforce their sense of masculinity through male bonding and by showing off their wealth, social status, and power (Allison 1994). In this kind of analysis, male club workers and their relationships with customers and female workers get little attention if any. Adding the word "hostess" to modify "club" increases the danger of neglecting workers other than hostesses in the club.

In addition to gender difference, ethnic diversity within a club is often erased, too. Korean clubs, Chinese clubs, Russian clubs, Thai clubs, and Filipino clubs (cf. Faier 2007, Suzuki 2003) in Japan are marked as ethnic clubs, and it is often assumed that only migrant Koreans, Chinese, Russians, Thais, or Filipinas respectively work there. This is not always the case, however. For example, some Filipinas work at Korean clubs in Osaka. In many Japanese clubs, too, such as Club Fuji, Japaneseness is often assumed to the extent that it does not need to be ethnically marked as Japanese. Club Fuji is very ethnically diverse. A Korean-Japanese mama employs Chinese, Taiwanese, Japanese Brazilian, and Japanese-born Korean workers (Chung 2004). But such Japanese clubs are still called by the generic, unmarked name of "club," suggesting it is "Japanese."

These generalizations of titles, gender roles and ethnic categories within the workplace prevent us from looking at more complex and intertwined relationships among them. A micro-level examination of the inter- and intra-ethnic and gender relationships at "Korean" "hostess" Club Rose challenges the prevailing assumptions of ethnic homogeneity, male supremacy (represented by job titles, for example), and Japanese dominance over Koreans in Japan. I will illuminate how ethnic relationships are negotiated between Koreans and Japanese, how the border between women's and men's jobs is blurred, and how Club Rose is ethnically and linguistically diverse.

Titles and *effects* at Club Rose

Club Rose provides different sets of job titles based upon gender and ethnicity. The job titles for females emphasize the nurturing nature of the service they perform (e.g., mama, kitchen staff, hostess, and show member), and the job titles for males are generic corporate job titles (e.g., director, manager, and chief). For example, among stage performers, Korean women are categorized as "Show Member" (*Shō Dan* in Japanese and Korean), and a Japanese man is called "Master" (*Sensei* in Japanese). These job titles obscure the managing elements of female work and the entertainer elements of male work. They also reinforce the illusion that there are clear gender and ethnic boundaries between Korean female workers and Japanese male workers: women are entertainers, and men are their superiors.

The deceptive "Male Manager/Female Entertainer" scheme widely applies to other situations, too. Male workers have titles, such as director (*tenchō* or *senmu* in Japanese), manager (*maneejaa* in Japanese), or chief (*shunin* in Japanese). In contrast, female workers are often grouped as "girls" (*onnna no ko* in Japanese and *agassi* in Korean), and even the female club proprietor and managers are called Mama, which means "mother." The title Mama connotes the "non-professional" and the "domestic" and allows her labour (both at home and work) to go unrecognized as labour. Calling someone by the category of sex is an act of domination. These gender-based job titles imply that men have managerial ability and authority, and women lack such ability and rarely have access to authoritative *effects* (cf. Bourdieu 1980: 130–31; 1984: 22–26, 161–62). The two-track job titling system legitimizes sexual difference and inequality by reinforcing fictitious sexual categories as if "men" and "women" are naturally occurring categories (cf. Butler 1990: 115). Below, I explore job titles, their *effects*, and the discrepancies between job content and title.

Contrary to the image associated with the infantilized, yet sexualized category of "girls," female workers are required to have managerial and professional skills. Among thirty-nine Korean female workers at Club Rose, thirty-seven women are considered to be entertainers, and two are kitchen staff. Each woman is further categorized according to her expertise. Among thirty-seven female entertainers, twenty-four women in their twenties, thirties, and forties are categorized as hostesses. Six women in their thirties, forties, and fifties are called mama. And eight women in their twenties are identified as show members. These show members hold work visas that only allow them to sing and dance on stage inside Club Rose. However, their employers often expect them to sit down with customers between their shows, thus requiring them to work in capacities beyond their job title of show member.

Visa status imposes another set of legal limitations among workers. The tourist-visa hostesses, for example, go back and forth between South Korea and Japan every two weeks or so in order to stay in Japan legally. But their work at Club Rose is illegal since foreign "tourists" should not work at all in Japan. Six Korean tourist-visa hostesses work about half of each month at Club Rose. Club Rose also hires a number of student-visa hostesses, but their visas do not permit them to work at a club either. Visa status often causes keen anxiety among migrant workers and makes them extremely vulnerable to law enforcement. Visa status also contributes to create heterogeneity among Koreans' experiences in Japan, as I have discussed elsewhere (Chung 2004).[3]

Another two Korean women with student and spousal visas in their twenties and thirties are kitchen staff called "Dishwasher" (*Arai*, which is shortened from *Araiba* in Japanese) and "Chef" (*Chubang-jang* in Korean) respectively. They work behind the bar counter and do not entertain customers at tables at all. Female entertainers and kitchen staff have very little direct contact with each other – male workers work between them.

Two Korean waiters called "Chief" (*Chiifu* in Japanese) fill in this gap as the most mobile workers. They take food orders from customers' tables and bring dishes, plates, and glasses from the kitchen to the tables and from the tables to the kitchen. They also move around inside the club between tables where female entertainers talk with customers over drinks. The waiters also convey messages from the director or the mama, and instruct the entertainers to move from one table to another. Therefore, the waiters also function as busboys and messengers, too, rather than the leader or supervisor that their job title "Chief" suggests. In income and rank they are also lower placed than most other workers at Club Rose. Consequently, the gap between job title and content is quite significant.

Addressing a Japanese male musician as Master (*Sensei* in Japanese) is another example of an authoritative male title. Although the overuse of such authoritative titles and the gap between the titles and contents can undermine the value *of* titles, we cannot underestimate the *effects* of the authoritative titles (cf. Bourdieu 1984: 161–62). Female singers and dancers cannot claim such an aura of authority when they are simply grouped together as "show members." For outsiders to the business who may not know the specific function and position within the club hierarchy of those holding certain titles, the titles themselves may lead to misperceptions of an employee's status among his or her coworkers.

Korean female show members and a Japanese male musician

Usually Korean female show members arrive at Club Rose around 7:30 p.m., and like Mamas and male workers, they serve multiple functions within the club. Their visa status as stage performers does not permit the show members to entertain customers at tables. However, in reality a club often expects them to sit down and entertain customers at tables between the shows. After all, each female show member appears on stage for only ten minutes of dancing, singing, or drumming once or twice per evening. Although they spend some preparation time backstage changing their costumes, retouching their make-up, and rearranging their hair for the stage performances, they spend most of their time entertaining customers at tables at Club Rose. Therefore, they bear multiple roles as hostesses as well as singers, dancers, and drummers.

Similarly, a Japanese male musician called Master also assumes multiple roles. He not only performs on stage, but is also responsible for lighting and sound effects when the female show members perform on stage or a customer sings a song on stage. When a customer or female entertainer sings a song, Master plays the keyboard and synthesizer to accompany the singer. Since Master does not change his clothes for his stage performance, he does not have backstage time. His performing time on stage, therefore, is much longer than that of the female entertainers. Furthermore, he occasionally entertains customers at their tables at their own request. He drinks with, chats with, and listens to the customer just like female entertainers. However, his occupational title of "Master" implies that he enjoys higher status than "show members" or "girls."

Mamas

Unlike waiters with job titles that suggest authority, female managers are called merely *mama*. However, a mama needs to effectively manage other female entertainers at and beyond the customers' tables in order to increase her sales as well as the club's profits. Late one evening, Yuka Mama calls a hostess, Mitsuko, to her Japanese customer Mr Honda's table. Yuka Mama learns that Mr Honda likes Mitsuko and has brought a $1,000 Missoni sweater as a gift, hoping he can have dinner with Mitsuko and Yuka Mama after their official work hours. Although Mitsuko attentively listens to Mr Honda and even smiles at him occasionally, she is not enthusiastic about spending more time with him after work. Sensing Mitsuko's lack of interest in him, Yuka Mama gently says to Mitsuko after retreating to the locker room, "All you have to do is come to dinner with me and Mr Honda (Honda-san)." When Mitsuko still keeps looking down at the locker room floor without agreeing, Yuka Mama reminds Mitsuko in a firmer tone that he has given her a very expensive gift and asks her, "What are you going to do with it? Are you going to return it? How?" After pondering for a few more seconds, Mitsuko reluctantly agrees to go to a restaurant, and Yuka Mama appreciates that Mitsuko has changed her mind. Yuka Mama plays the role of liaison between her customer and his favourite hostess Mitsuko. The mama uses various techniques to manage both customer and hostess by sensing their needs, pampering them, and pressuring them if necessary.

Six such mamas work at Club Rose. Big Mama (*Ō Mama*) owns Club Rose. The other five mamas are called Small Mama (*Chii Mama*), and Yuka Mama is one of these small mamas. Each small mama individually runs her own business operations by renting the space and staff of Club Rose from Big Mama. The Japanese-born Korean customer, Mr. Kaneko,[4] characterizes this mama system of the club as follows: "Mamas are like small-business owners. They are like tenants (*tanako*) of the club. They operate their own business inside the club and pursue their profits." A small mama utilizes the services of entertainers, male managers, and support staff such as waiters, the chef, and the dishwasher of Club Rose and splits the profits she makes with Club Rose. Each small mama solicits her own clients to come to the club, and entertains them with hostesses and show members so that her customers come back and spend money at Club Rose. Capable small mamas skillfully perform the roles of manager, entertainer, and liaison to generate profits.

Club Rose itself has multiple roles: it leases space and staff and also lends money to the employees. Club Rose may offer to loan tens of thousands of dollars in advance in order to recruit a small mama and a hostess to the club. The large sum of loaned money gives an incentive for a candidate to move to Club Rose from another club. She can use the money to pay back debts to her current club, purchase new clothes and jewelry, or move to a new apartment. She negotiates the loan amount with Director Hong (Hong *Tenchō*) based upon her needs and potential.

A small mama may look for better opportunities, while a director scouts for better talent for his club. For example, if Director Hong hears a rumour that a small mama who has a solid sales record is not happy at her current club, he may call her up and chat with her to get a sense of whether she might consider leaving her current job. Or he may attempt to scout a mama with great potential if he can ascertain whether she has a job or not. Director Hong headhunted Hiromi Mama. Hiromi Mama shared her experience with me about how she landed at Club Rose while we were waiting for the first customers to arrive for the evening:

> I used to run my own Korean club, but it went out of business. I was embarrassed and did not want to see or talk with people in the industry for a while. But one day Director Hong called me, asked how I was doing, and invited me for a cup of coffee. There, he asked me if I was interested in working as a small mama at Club Rose. My wounds and feelings of shame caused by losing my own club had not fully gone yet, but I decided to take this opportunity because I had heard great things about Director Hong. He is one of the most

respected directors of Korean clubs in the area. I would also eventually have to work, too.

Hiromi Mama also knew that Club Rose would hire the type of hostesses and show members her customers enjoy: "The girls at Club Rose are not only pretty but also well mannered because both Director Hong and Big Mama value these characteristics. My customers appreciate these traits." A mama manages and attracts her customers by catering to her clientele's tastes. A mama wears the multiple hats of entrepreneur, entertainer, and manager along with her beautiful feminine costumes and the effects her mama title delivers: as a "mama," she is expected to take care of her customers' needs. In other words, the title "mama" successfully obscures the professional and economic transactions of love and care as effects.

The name of Korean "hostess" Club Rose itself illustrates the gap between title and content. Despite the word "Korean" that implies that everything is Korean at Club Rose, and the word "hostess" that hides the existence of other kinds of workers, the club is much more hybrid in terms of ethnicity, gender, and job types. The English loan word "Rose" (*Rōzu* in Japanese), which is so naturalized into Japanese that even those who do not speak English know what it means, underscores this point. The following section further examines the hybridity of Club Rose by taking an in-depth look at several employees.

Multi-national, multi-gendered, and multi-lingual

Club Rose is a multi-national, multi-lingual, and multi-gendered space in spite of its designation – both self-identified and externally-imposed – as a Korean club. While the majority of the workers (95.7 per cent) were born in South Korea, thirty-seven (80 per cent) live in Japan (semi-)long term (more than three months). Some of them have even been naturalized as Japanese citizens or obtained Japanese permanent residency, long-term residency, or spousal visas. Therefore, "Korean" club workers are not homogeneously "Korean," and some of them are (or have become) Japanese citizens. Big Mama at Club Keiko epitomizes this category. She married a Japanese man, had a daughter, and became naturalized as a Japanese citizen.

As for gender, too, "hostess" is not the only job at Club Rose despite the fact that this type of establishment is referred to as a "hostess club" in the West. Both women and men work at Club Rose, and their work often overlaps. At Club Rose, like many other hostess clubs in Japan, female entertainers, such as mamas, hostesses, and show members, are more visible because they take the central role in serving customers, unlike most corporate jobs where a woman is often expected to work as a subordinate to men or work in peripheral roles (e.g., Kondo 1990, Ogasawara 1998). The importance of female workers is shown in their sheer numbers at Club Rose. Female workers outnumber (85 per cent) male workers at Rose. Thirty-nine out of forty-six workers are women. Only seven (15 per cent) are men. Nonetheless, both women and men work there, and they often cross the assumed occupational gender boundaries. For example, Executive Director Suzuki works as a mama, and as such he also manages workers and runs the club, as we will see below. This type of gender-crossing in work creates other types of gender, which cannot be captured within the frame of a dichotomous gender system, and therefore I call Club Rose a "multi-gendered" space.

Club Rose is also a multi-lingual space. Many workers speak Korean, Japanese (as well as some dialects within each language), and a "language" that is a mix of Korean and Japanese in spite of the fact that the native language of all the workers (except for two Japanese males) is Korean. Some others have lived in English-speaking countries as students or migrants and can speak English. Because of its geographical location in Osaka, many Korean workers also pick up the Osaka dialect in addition to the Tokyo dialect taught at Japanese language schools and through textbooks. All Korean workers are expected to be able to communicate in both Korean and Japanese.

Japanese–Korean bilingualism is more strongly enforced for women than men and for Koreans than Japanese – more specifically for Korean female entertainers than for Japanese male workers. Korean female entertainers are expected to entertain customers through conversations in Japanese because the first (and often the only) language the customers speak is Japanese. However, not all the female entertainers are fluent in Japanese when they start working at the club. In fact, many struggle to improve their Japanese communication skills on the job. A newly arrived Korean dancer, Sayuri, emphasizes how stressful it can be to entertain customers in Japanese by contrasting another challenge of appearance management, more specifically weight loss:

> I usually go back to the club dormitory by 1 a.m. if I do not need to eat out with customers. Then, I eat something at the dormitory. Then I take a bath and chat with my dorm mates until 3 a.m. After that, I study Japanese until 5 a.m. After sleeping for six or seven hours, I wake up around 11 a.m. or noon. I go to the gym and spend three hours doing exercise, water aerobics, and showering every-day. Although I want to lose some weight, my primary stress is not my weight. It is Japanese language! It is so stressful that I get drunk and eat too much. Then, I feel self-hatred and more stress. I am in the middle of a vicious circle.

Sayuri's effort to improve her Japanese extends to business hours. She always carries a small notebook and pen along with her business cards, lighter, and handker-chief inside her small purse during work at Club Rose. Every time she learns some new words and expressions, she writes them down. Sayuri often tries to sit next to me and asks me various questions about Japanese words, phrases, and culture while we sit at our waiting area until one of us is summoned to a customer's table:

> I want to learn proper Japanese. Other Onni [literally "older sister" in Korean, often used to refer to older women with respect and/or affection] were willing to teach me Japanese. But they are not native speakers. They could give me wrong information, and their Japanese occasionally sounded vulgar to me. That is why I ask you many questions about Japanese language. That's OK, right?

At the same time, Club Rose expects female entertainers to most clearly embody the Koreanness that the club commodifies, just as in many other societies in which women are disproportionately burdened to embody certain ethnic cultures by wearing ethnic costumes, performing traditional dance, and cooking ethnic food. At Club Rose, women wear Korean costumes, perform Korean dance, and cook Korean food. They should be able to speak Korean, in addition to Japanese, in order to communicate with other Koreans and to entertain those customers who want to practice their Korean or simply enjoy a Korean aura with female entertainers. On the contrary, Japanese male workers are exempted from the requirement of bilingualism and the knowledge of Korean traditions.

Two Japanese male workers at "Korean" Club Rose, Executive Director Suzuki (Suzuki *Senmu*) and a musician called Master (*Sensei*) do not speak Korean. Although Club Rose commodifies Koreanness and therefore the majority of workers are migrant Koreans, "those Japanese who have lots of customers or are good musicians are welcomed to work at Club Rose," according to Director Hong. However, language requirements are unevenly applied based on gender and ethnicity.

Most Japanese-born Koreans do not have adequate Korean language skills to make them appropriately bilingual at a club setting. Even those Japanese-born Koreans who are educated in Korean language at the North Korean schools in Japan (See Ryang 1997) are not linguistically and culturally proficient enough to work at Club Rose according to Vice Director Lee: "A couple of months ago, we hired a Japanese-born Korean hostess who graduated from a North Korean high school in Japan. But she could not last too long here. She quit a couple of weeks later." Those Japanese-born Koreans educated at North Korean schools often speak Korean flavored with a Japanese accent mixed with Pyongyang dialect. Therefore, their Korean often differs from the South Korean dialect that most migrants speak. The Korean language requirement prevents and discourages even Japanese-born Korean females from working at Club Rose.

Several factors contribute to this uneven application of the language requirement. First, Club Rose primarily caters to Japanese-language customers. Second, Executive Director Suzuki and Master can fulfill their job responsibilities without having to coordinate with other migrant Koreans. Third, if they have to communicate with other employees, they can do so in Japanese. And most of all, those who belong to the most naturalized category of "Japanese men" seem to be exempt from the daunting task of learning Korean even though they work at a Korean club. These taxing requirements make it difficult for Director Hong to find not only capable Japanese hostesses but also retain Japanese-born Korean hostesses.

Korean maleness at work: military experience and staff dinners

Language and nationality affect working styles, too. Executive Director Suzuki and Master work more autonomously than Korean male workers. They work as contract employees with a higher income than Korean workers who have similar status within the club, but they have less job security and sense of belonging. In contrast,

Korean males work in more intertwined and hierarchical relationships influenced by their compulsory military service.

In South Korea, Korean males, with a few exceptions due to medical or family conditions, are required to serve in the military for a couple of years. All the Korean male workers at Club Rose served in the military before they left South Korea.[5] Director Hong refers to the relationships among the male workers at Club Rose as "military style." A "military style" hierarchical relationship includes obedience to the boss and acceptance of even physical punishment. Director Hong describes his relationship with his Korean male subordinates as follows:

> The Korean male workers are connected by obligation (*giri*) in Minami. We are family (*famirii*). Family members usually range from five to ten in number. The junior must follow the senior even if he has to go through hardship. The senior is obliged to take care of the junior. For example, I have known Mr Yu and Mr Choi for three years since they came to Japan. I have been planning to retire from the club business. At my retirement, I will eventually hand over my family to Mr Yu.

In contrast, two Japanese workers, the executive director and the keyboard accompanist, do not have full membership in Director Hong's "family," which would require the experience of having been drafted for a couple of years of military service in South Korea. Therefore, they are exempt from explicitly conforming to this military-style chain of command and have a certain degree of autonomy at work.

The staff dinner reinforces this patriarchal, homosocial, and ethnic family relationship every night before business hours. Club Rose provides dinner for Korean male workers and the female kitchen staff every workday, but men and women do not eat together. While the Korean male workers eat at one of the booths where customers are entertained during business hours, Korean female Chef and Dishwasher eat by themselves behind the kitchen counter.

Around 6 p.m., the staff dinner starts. Manager Yu and Senior Waiter Choi and Junior Waiter Hyun bring dishes prepared by Chef and Dishwasher. Steamed rice, Korean miso soup, kimchee, Korean barbeque, and Korean pancakes fill the table. Junior Waiter Hyun places small glasses of water on the table for everyone except for Director Hong whose glass is a large one used for customers during business hours. Everyone else drinks from small glasses used for hostesses and mamas during business hours. The Director's larger glass symbolically reflects his highest position and even distinguishes him from other management staff, such as Vice Director Lee and Manager Yu. Gender and ethnic divisions extend to other workers, too. Hostesses, mamas, entertainers, and Japanese male workers do not participate in the staff dinner; instead, they eat dinner on their own. The hierarchical bonding among Korean male workers through the exclusion of Korean female workers and Japanese male workers becomes most obvious at dinnertime inside Club Rose.

Qualities valued in workers

At Club Rose, where multiple ethnicities, languages, and genders crisscross, what kinds of qualities are valued in workers? Director Hong explains:

> The hostess club industry values women and men in different ways. The woman's value depends upon how many clients she has. The man is valued by how many capable hostesses and their customers he can headhunt. In addition, as a Director (*tenchō*), I need to be able not only to recruit resourceful hostesses, [small] mamas, and show members to Club Rose, but I also have to maintain a good relationship with the support staff [other directors, managers, waiters and kitchen staff] in order to maintain my "family" functionally. A mama – whether she is the owner of the club or not – is also required to be able to manage the girls.

Director Hong emphasizes the different expectations of female and male workers but at the same time, he hints that the requirements merge as the positions go up to Director and Mama. Female kitchen staff and waiters are least valued because they have little direct contact with customers in spite of their physically strenuous labour and long working hours. Below, I describe the invisible labour of female kitchen staff and male workers by examining the activities before the staff dinner. I ethnographically scrutinize Director Hong's gender specific characterizations: women's value depends upon the profitability of their clientele and men's value depends upon how well they can headhunt and manage income-producing female workers.

Korean female kitchen staff and male workers

At 3 p.m., Korean female Chef, who has long straight hair and is in her early thirties, comes to Club Rose. Her slender arms carry a couple of white plastic shopping bags full of vegetables, fruits, and eggs from a nearby supermarket. She wears blue jeans, a white sweater, and metal-framed eyeglasses. She unlocks the backdoor and walks through a storage hallway to a kitchen to prepare for the evening. After putting on an apron, she stores tomatoes, onions, carrots, celery, potatoes, beef, strawberries, oranges, melons, and eggs in a refrigerator under the sink. These groceries are for both the staff dinner before business hours (6 p.m. to 6:30 p.m.) and snacks for customers during business hours (7:30 p.m. to midnight). Quietly, she starts cooking for the staff dinner.

Around 5:00 p.m., Korean conversation echoes at the elevator hall of the 4th floor occupied by Club Rose. Chef's husband, Manger Yu, who is also in his thirties, enters the club accompanied by two younger waiters, Mr Choi and Mr Hyun in their twenties. All of them are around the same height (5'10") and keep their hair short. Mr Choi is skinny and friendly, and Mr Hyun is chubby and shy. Manager Yu is in good shape somewhere in-between. Because all of them already wear their club uniforms (white dress shirts, black bow ties, and black dress pants) under their coats and they do not need to retouch make-up or hair-do like female entertainers, they can jump into preparing for business straight after taking off their coats.

They assist the entertainers so that the entertainers can focus on interactions with customers at the tables. The male workers dress much more formally than the female kitchen staff because they walk around inside the club during business hours unlike the female kitchen staff who stay behind the kitchen counter. The male workers are inevitably more mobile, but they try to keep a low profile by wearing similar black dress pants and white shirts that look alike.

A hierarchy and division of labour exist among these three male staff workers, however. Manager Yu, who wears black-rimmed eyeglasses, keeps the books of the club and orders snacks, cigarettes, drinks, and other miscellaneous club items on the phone. He also distributes monthly salaries to the staff. He mostly stays in a cashier's office behind the counter near the entrance. Manager Yu has a double function as a manager and waiter, and his position falls between that of director and waiter.

The two other waiters move around from the storage space to the hall. Thin Senior Waiter Choi cleans three bathrooms (two of which serve female workers next to a locker room), sits down at a booth and rolls up damp washcloths (*oshibori*) for customers to wipe their hands, and organizes customers' reserved bottles of whiskey. Chubby Junior Waiter Hyun vacuums the large hall, dusts the booths, and wipes the tables. Cleaning responsibilities, particularly cleaning the women's bathrooms, clearly reveals the supporting nature of their labour vis-à-vis the female workers. Although the male workers hardly speak to one another, the atmosphere is more relaxed during these pre-business hours than during business hours.

In contrast, Chef chats with Dishwasher, and they even giggle occasionally. Female Dishwasher in her twenties with short hair joins Chef soon after the three male workers arrive at Club Rose. Dishwasher assists Chef in cooking, too. Chef and Dishwasher stay inside the small kitchen area. They stay physically close to each other unlike the male workers who strategically scatter inside the club. Because Chef and Dishwasher become fairly invisible behind the kitchen bar counter once the center of the activities moves to the hall during business hours, they can wear casual work clothes that are very different from the ones that female entertainers and male workers wear. Their invisible domestic femininity (represented by cooking and washing dishes) makes a stark contrast to the decorative professional femininity (wearing fancy clothes and elaborate make-up) that the thirty-seven female entertainers embody.

At 5:30 p.m., Director Hong in his late thirties comes in, Director Lee in his mid-thirties following on his heels. Both wear dark business suits and regular long ties that serve as their uniforms. Director Hong is shorter and thinner than Director Lee. Although they share the regional accent of the southern part of Korea, the timbre of their voices is different. Director Hong has a soothing soft voice while Director Lee's voice is husky. While both their employer (Big Mama) and other employees usually address them as Director Hong (Hong *Tenchō*) and Director Lee (Lee *Tenchō*), Director Lee is more specifically a vice director.

Their status difference becomes apparent through the kinds of jobs they do. Director Hong is often on his cellular phone receiving calls from female entertainers in Korean or talking with customers in Japanese. Every time he answers the phone, he lowers his voice and says "hello" in Korean (*yoboseyo*) or in Japanese (*moshimoshi*) as if to confirm his authority and masculinity. Vice Director Lee joins Manager Yu near the cashier space and exchanges information. Director Hong is in charge of the hiring, managing, and firing of all workers, including the executive director. He has much more power than Executive Director Suzuki, and influences owner Big Mama of Club Rose.

In the meantime, male contractors from Japanese stores drop by Club Rose. A young florist wearing an apron comes in and takes care of the plants and flowers his store leases to Club Rose. He waters and trims the large plants and changes the water in flower vases at the hall and entrance. A liquor store clerk brings in cases of beer and whiskey. He confirms the order with Manager Yu in Japanese at the cashier's office. Soon after, a general store clerk brings in boxes of dry snacks and cartons of various Japanese and American cigarettes. The cigarettes are stored in a cabinet of the cashier's office for customers as well as employees who run out of their own cigarettes, and snacks are stored in the kitchen space until placed on dishes by the kitchen staff and served at customers' tables. After each worker finishes a segment of his own assignment, the staff dinner starts. After dinner, they resume their preparations for business hours.

Once the first customers arrive at Club Rose around 7:30 p.m., the waiters serve food, replace glasses, bring cigarettes, and clean the tables. Upon a customer's request, a waiter brings a bill to a table from the cashier area usually occupied by Manager Yu. While waiting for the receipt prepared by Manager Yu, the waiter goes back to his other duties. Mr Choi collects empty dishes, used glasses, and ashtrays containing cigarette butts that were stacked under each table and brings them back to the kitchen where the female kitchen staff clean them. Mr Hyun moves from one table to another and refills the ice pails. When the receipt is ready, the waiter brings the receipt (along with change or a credit card) to the customer. After the customer leaves, the waiter brings back used glasses to the kitchen, cleans the table, and brings clean glasses and ashtrays.

Once the club gets busy, even the directors and manager assume multiple roles, including waiters and entertainers. But Japanese Executive Director Suzuki works less as a waiter than as an entertainer and entrepreneur. Contrary to the assumed division of labour based upon gender, Executive Director Suzuki – who holds the most high-sounding rank among male workers at Club Rose – functions both as a director and as a mama. Therefore, I call him "Mr Mama." The term "Mr Mama" epitomizes the multiple gender roles performed by workers at Club Rose. The following section closely examines how male workers entertain customers like a mama or hostess – or how they avoid such work.

Director Hong: top management (and waiter)

Director Hong would rather wait tables than drink with customers. He avoids entertaining customers at tables – one of the important responsibilities of a director. I have seen him sitting at customers' tables a number of times, but his smile and posture suggest that he is not very comfortable in this role. Consequently, he subtly but strategically allocates such undesired jobs to other male workers by hiring Korean Vice Director Lee and Japanese Executive Director Suzuki:

> Both like drinking, and they are good at talking with customers. Me? I cannot drink, you know. If I drink half a glass of beer, I am done. I would get red and drunk. But when I sit next to customers, I can't say that I drink no alcohol as a director. So, many customers do not know that I cannot actually drink alcohol, and they even invite me to other clubs and bars after work. If I liked drinking like Executive Director Suzuki and Director Lee, I might appreciate the invitations. Accepting these invitations and spending more time with customers are good for our business. But for me, the offering of more drinks and invitations to other clubs are nothing but unwelcome favors (*arigata meiwaku*).

Director Hong's statement clearly reveals entertaining customers inside and outside the club is an important segment of their work. However, as the head of the migrant Korean male militaristic hierarchy at Club Rose, Director Hong cannot afford to get inebriated, weakened and consequently "feminized" in front of his subordinates.

Executive Director Suzuki: Japanese "Mr Mama" at a "Korean" club

The relationship between Director Hong and Executive Director Suzuki, in his fifties, is particularly intriguing. First, the title of executive director would normally denote that he is higher in rank and more powerful than the director. Second, executive directors of Korean clubs in Minami are usually older and have worked as directors. Third, Executive Director Suzuki speaks with Director Hong in casual Japanese while Director Hong responds in polite Japanese to Executive Director Suzuki. And finally, as a "Japanese," Executive Director Suzuki has a longer career in the club business in Japan. However, Director Hong has more actual power than the executive director. This is another example of the gap between job title and content.

Executive Director Suzuki stands in a liminal position, which crisscrosses ethnic and gender lines at Club Rose (cf. Turner 1995). He is presumed to be ethnically Japanese, he is fluent in Japanese language and culture, he lacks Korean language ability, and he holds the most authoritative job title. He does not, however, have the most power. He assumes a feminine role as Mr Mama at tables, and he has a sales quota like the female entertainers at the club. Executive Director Suzuki brings his own clients to the club, entertains them by matching them with female entertainers as small mamas do, periodically visits clients' companies (*aisatsu mawari*) to solicit their business, collects overdue bills, and substitutes for Director Hong if necessary.

Suzuki's partial participation in the staff dinner symbolically reflects upon his marginal position. Around 6:30 p.m. as the dinner is ending, Japanese Executive Director Suzuki shows up and sits down at the dinner table. After the dinner, Manager Yu and the waiters clean the dinner table, stand up, take back the dishes to the kitchen, and bring coffee to Director Hong and Executive Director Suzuki. While Director Hong and Executive Director Suzuki keep talking at the table over coffee, Manager Yu and the waiters return to their tasks without having coffee. Coffee after dinner at the table is a luxury only allowed to the directors.

Contrary to what one might expect from their job titles, Executive Director Suzuki reports to Director Hong what kind of business he has taken care of for Club Rose during the daytime. Today, Executive Director Suzuki has collected the accounts due (*tsuke no kaishū*) from a couple of customers. He also informs Director Hong what he has accomplished in terms of his own customer management, such as visiting clients' companies and soliciting their business.

According to Director Hong, Executive Director Suzuki does not join the staff dinner because he eats at home with his wife and two children. But other reasons, such as his lack of language ability in Korean, which is the primary language at the staff dinner table, as well as his unique position as a Japanese Mr Mama, which does not neatly fit into Director Hong's military-style chain of command, may also contribute to his absence from the dinner.

Director Hong's deference to the executive director is another twist, which probably comes from the fact that the executive director is much older than the director and is a Japanese who has not shared military experiences in South Korea. This deference puts the executive director outside of the explicit "military style" hierarchical relationship. The same rule applies to the Japanese keyboard accompanist. Partially due to the isolated nature of his work from other male workers, he too, as a musician, is exempt from the hierarchies among the male workers.[6]

Once I observed Executive Director Suzuki requesting the benevolence of Director Hong soon after Executive Director Suzuki started working at Club Rose:

> Since my sales may fluctuate month to month, I hope you look at my performance in the long term. If the owner Big Mama gets impatient when my sales are not good enough, please make her understand that I will do well overall.

Director Hong vividly describes the feminized side of Executive Director Suzuki's job by using the case of conflict with female Small Mama Yang:

> Both Executive Director Suzuki and Small Mama Yang respectively claim that Mr Kitano's account (*kōza*) is theirs. Executive Director Suzuki says that Mr Kitano is his long-time customer, and Small Mama Yang insists that Mr Kitano has begun coming to Club Rose because of her.

This type of dispute related to which customer's account belongs to which hostess or Mama is quite common among female entertainers. And this is a serious matter since money spent by a customer directly reflects on the salary of the worker who "owns" the account.

Unlike all other male workers, including Directors Hong and Vice Director Lee who are guaranteed to receive fixed monthly salaries ($6,800 and $5,200 respectively), Executive Director Suzuki is paid like small mamas based upon his sales. The average monthly income of five small mamas (between $3,600 and $14,744) is $10,260, and Executive Director's monthly income is around $10,000. As for income ranking, Executive Director Suzuki is fourth among six small mamas. Executive Director Suzuki is primarily evaluated by his sales like female entertainers although his "executive" title can incorrectly suggest that he is immune to such competition with female entertainers.

Versatile Vice Director Lee as substitute hostess

By contrast, Vice Director Lee enjoys more stability with a comfortable but smaller income. He stands as number two within Director Hong's military-style chain of command, supports Director Hong, and often entertains customers at tables. He was born in South Korea, brought up in Oceania, migrated to Japan, attended a university in Japan, and is planning to emigrate to the United States to start his own business in the future.[7] His Korean wife is a former small mama at another club in Minami and lives in South Korea with their son. As his diasporic upbringing and family as well as future plans suggest, he travels a lot internationally. Vice Director Lee speaks multiple languages (Korean, English, and Japanese), embodies multiple ethnicities, and assumes multi-gendered roles at Club Rose.

One evening, Vice Director Lee was drawn into a contentious love triangle. Two customers (resident Korean Mr Taoka and Japanese Mr Hayashi) competed over a migrant Korean hostess Tomoko. On that particular night, Mr Taoka and Mr Hayashi were at Club Rose around the same time. When Tomoko was busy going back and forth between the tables of Mr Taoka and Mr Hayashi to keep them both happy, Vice Director Lee dropped by Mr Taoka's table in order to soothe Mr Taoka's frustration over Tomoko's divided attention. Suddenly, Mr Taoka tightly embraced Vice Director Lee at the table.[8] Mr Taoka even kissed him, exclaiming, "You are cute (*kawaii*)!" Considering Vice Director Lee's marital status, management position, and masculine deportment, this was quite unexpected. To my surprise, he endured the whole process with a wry smile and stiff posture without explicit resistance. Vice Director Lee was keenly aware that he had to do pretty much anything in order to reduce Mr Taoka's frustration.

There may have been several motivations for Mr Taoka's behavior. First, he may have been acting silly as a way to release the tension building up at his table. Kissing a male director with whom he was well acquainted would have been less problematic than kissing a female entertainer. Sexually explicit behavior towards female entertainers is prohibited at Club Rose, as it is in many other high-end clubs. Mr Taoka's comical mannerism and tone of voice as well as timing further suggest that he wanted to make the people at the table laugh, to make Tomoko jealous by showing that he could have a good time without her, and to make her eager to stay longer with him than his rival Mr Hayashi. Therefore, Mr Taoka's actions appeared to be part of a strategy to get Tomoko back. At the same time, they may also have suggested an actual homosocial and/or homoerotic interest in Vice Director Lee as the following case implies.

Mr Shin: metrosexual former model, waiter, and candidate for host

I include Mr Shin's intriguing story, although he worked as a junior waiter at another Korean Club called Chaplin in Minami, because it highlights the blurred gender and ethnic lines of club work. Mr Shin in his mid-twenties commuted to his Japanese-language school for a year while living with his aunt who had been living in Minami for quite some time.

Mr Shin has had ties to Japan since his childhood in South Korea. Although he was born and brought up in South Korea, his father was born in Japan. Mr Shin was exposed to Japanese products and popular culture throughout his childhood, from Japanese-style kitchenware to comic books. Mr Shin himself does not think he is a typical Korean male in terms of his way of thinking or his appearance:

> Japanese immigration officers assume that I am Japanese. Even when they stop and interrogate my Korean colleagues and friends, I have never been stopped and asked for my identification card. I believe that I look more like a Japanese person. Don't you think? Actually my nickname during my school days was taken from a Japanese comic book character, "Anthony."

As a Korean-born boy, Mr Shin embodied the hybridity of the European character Anthony, depicted in the Japanese comic book *Candy Candy.*

Even in adulthood Mr Shin embodies this hybridity. Mr Shin modeled for TV, magazines, and fashion shows of Euro-American style clothes in South Korea during his high school and college days. His favorite designer is Tom Ford who used to be a chief designer for Gucci. For these reasons, he fits quite well with the Western-originated concept of "metrosexual."[9]

Mr Shin's striking appearance and friendly personality enabled him to find a job at Club Chaplin. He quickly became close to newly hired Korean showgirls and enjoyed working there. Both female and male colleagues treated him well by giving him gifts, offering him dinner, taking him to other clubs and bars, and even celebrating his birthday. He became particularly intimate with the most popular showgirl. Mr Shin was popular among his colleagues as well as some of the male customers there.

While most of his experiences at Club Chaplin were "fun," he also had some "puzzling" encounters with male customers:

> One middle-aged male customer grabbed my waist when I was walking down the hall with a tray. I was so surprised that I almost dropped the tray. When I looked at him, he pulled my hand and whispered to me "You are beautiful. Sit down next to me."

A few other customers also made homoerotic suggestions to Mr Shin. The customers' behavior and proposals made Mr Shin perplexed and uncomfortable, and eventually he left Club Chaplin.[10]

Host as male hostess

While the above examples show Executive Director Suzuki, Vice Director Lee, and Mr Shin, a waiter, entertaining customers as part of their jobs, male hosts who work at host clubs are hired specifically to entertain female customers. This gender inversion causes a strong aversion among some Korean male club workers. Director Hong explains his view of Korean hosts in strongly negative terms:

> Hosts are the worst kind of men! They take away money from the hostesses who came all the way to Japan to make money. Hosts also interfere with our business. When a hostess gets crazy about a host, she sometimes loses perspective. She not only wastes her money on a host, but also skips work without notice. A host does more harm than good! Therefore, if I find out that one of our hostesses is involved with a host, I attempt to break them up.

Considering that both hosts and male workers at clubs depend heavily upon hostesses for their living, generally calm Director Hong's strong and emotional condemnation surprised me.

Furthermore, even metrosexual Mr Shin shares his disgust towards Korean hosts. Mr Shin states that being solicited to work as a host was much more disturbing to him than the homoerotic advances he experienced from the customers at Club Chaplin:

> I was scouted to become a host more than once. When I was walking the streets in Minami, a stranger approached me and asked whether I was interested in working as a host at his club. When I responded, "No, thank you," he still handed me his business card and insisted that I contact him if I ever changed my mind. I was also solicited to become a host when I went to bars with my colleagues. No matter how much I need money, a host is the last thing I want to be!

Both Director Hong and Mr Shin dismiss or fail to acknowledge the consolation hosts offer to female customers, such as Korean female hostess club entertainers. While Director Hong's concerns may have some valid points, both Director Hong and Mr Shin ignore how the hostess' emotional and sexual needs are taken care of by hosts.

A hostess' attraction to a host is not unique to Koreans. A host club is one of the few spaces where a female club worker can feel relaxed and empowered and have her emotional needs catered to. Almost half of the customers at host clubs in Japan are hostesses (Kadokura 2007: 41). Erika, a 33-year-old hostess, told me her experiences and observations. A host obeys a hostess' orders (such as drinking and sometimes even stripping), serves her (lighting a cigarette and making drinks), and pampers her ego (complimenting her appearance/possessions and listening to her).[11] In other words, a host both undermines and reinforces the sense of masculinity of some Korean males, such as Director Hong and Mr Shin. On the one hand, the idea of a host subordinated to a hostess causes aversion among some men. On the other hand, some male club workers who feel ashamed of their work feel better about themselves compared to hosts who are "the worst kind of men" and "the last thing" they want to become. While Korean male club workers and hosts profit from female labour, their titles also obscure the similarities.

Conclusion

Two systems of gender and ethnicity collide at Korean Club Rose in the "European Village" in Japan. Micro-level examinations of the complex gender and ethnic relationships at Club Rose challenge prevailing assumptions of male supremacy (represented by job titles of the workers) and Japanese dominance over Koreans in Japan, and demonstrate the heterogeneity of the workers in terms of ethnic and gender roles.

A successful Korean female entertainer has good entertainment and good management skills. According to Director Hong, the size of her clientele influences her value as reflected in her wages, the bonuses and loans she may receive from the club, and her job title. Her charisma, youth, experience, appearance, talent in conversation, singing, and dancing, along with many other attributes, matter only if they contribute to her sales. Mamas, in particular, should have the ability to scout and manage entertainers and customers who contribute to the overall sales of the club. Most female workers hold multiple functions as managers and as entertainers.

Unlike in corporate work where women are often expected to work as assistants to men (Ogasawara 1998), women play conspicuous roles with assistance from male workers in the daily operations of Club Rose. Male workers take various orders from female entertainers. Waiters accept drink and food orders, replace used ashtrays with stacks of clean ashtrays, serve food and drinks, bring wet towels, refill ice pails and water pitchers, and clean the tables after customers leave. They even run to a convenience store to purchase pantyhose and stock sanitary napkins in the bathrooms for female entertainers. Waiters have to be willing to take these subordinate roles, so that female workers can focus on customers' needs and give them their full attention at the tables.

Directors also assume multiple tasks. Directors not only manage the club and the workers but also play the role of hostess by sitting next to customers, mixing drinks, lighting cigarettes, and chatting in order to elevate a customer's status at a club. If the club gets busy, directors also function as waiters. Directors are expected to be versatile, and I call them "Mr Mamas," to signify their liminality in terms of gender roles. Male directors are valued for attracting customers just as female entertainers are, as in the case of Japanese Executive Director Suzuki.

The positions and functions of Executive Director Suzuki and Master illuminate how ethnicity intervenes in gender liminality. Being born and brought up in

Japan provides them with clear advantages in terms of Japanese language skills, the ability to cultivate a solid clientele, and familiarity with Japanese customs and culture. These traits get them jobs at Club Rose. At the same time, their lack of Korean language skills and military experience puts them in an outsider position with regard to ethnicity. The most telling example of this liminality is their exclusion from Director Hong's chain of command to which five Korean-born male workers belong, sharing meals together every working day.

Finally, we must consider the heterogeneity of presumably "Korean" "hostess" Club Rose. Not only Japanese workers, such as Executive Director Suzuki and Master, offer examples of ethnic heterogeneity, but there is also heterogeneity among "Koreans." There is the owner Big Mama who married, naturalized as Japanese, and raises her daughter; Small Mama Yuka who obtained Japanese permanent residency; Tomoko who received a Japanese spousal visa; and Sayuri who just arrived in Japan for the first time recently. Their different backgrounds, positions, and goals illuminate their Koreanness (and Japaneseness) quite differently even though they are often grouped as "Korean women." Among Korean males, experiences of work at Korean clubs vary. While Director Hong avoids sitting at customers' tables, Vice Director Lee does not seem to mind such jobs. Mr Shin and Director Hong differentiate themselves from hosts by harshly denigrating them.

By scrutinizing the gaps between such categories as job titles, gender and ethnicity and the content of such categories, it becomes clear that titles can be very misleading and do not necessarily reflect the realities of authority, status, work assignments, or nationalities in the club. Job titles based upon gender often do not encompass the multiple roles each worker assumes. Such categorizations, in which all males are given authoritative titles, like director and master, while females are grouped into the explicitly gendered categories of "girls" and "mamas," privilege men at least in terms of job titles. And the careless imposition of ethnic grouping, such as "Korean clubs" and "Korean migrant workers," tends to ignore the diversity within the group. This essay has closely examined labour in the entertainment industries to illuminate the fluid and multiple gender roles and ethnic heterogeneity that exist within individual clubs in Japan. By untangling the title of jobs from their actual content and value I have shown how ethnicity and gender intersect in ways that reflect the complicated nature of Japan and Korea's colonial history in Japan's contemporary eroticized service industry.

Notes

1 All the proper names used in this chapter are pseudonyms unless otherwise noted in order to protect informants' identities.
2 In particular, ideas about ethnic fixity or homogeneity need further scrutiny because ethnic passing by Koreans as Japanese is so prevalent that "native" fluency in the Japanese language does not mean that a person is Japanese, particularly at a Korean establishment. And the ability to pass itself challenges ethnic boundaries. If a Korean can pass as a Japanese, what distinguishes "Japanese" from "Korean"?
3 Beginning in 2006, Korean tourists no longer need to obtain a visa to come to Japan. How this new visa law affects migrant Koreans is a future research topic.

4 "Kaneko" is a Japanese name he uses in his daily life in order to pass as Japanese like many Koreans in Japan. He is still legally Korean with a South Korean passport, and his legal Korean name is Kim, which he hardly uses even with his Korean relatives living in Japan.
5 See Moon (2005) for a discussion of the militarization of Korean society and militarized masculinity.
6 I often saw Master joking and playing with the waiters before the clients came. But other than that, I hardly saw him interacting with other workers. I was one of the few people who talked with him casually since he could talk to me in Japanese.
7 Vice Director Lee actually emigrated and started his business in the United States within a year from the time I interviewed him.
8 "Embracing" a powerful director literally and symbolically illuminates Mr Taoka's importance and power at Club Rose.
9 "metrosexual" refers to a man who pays attention to his appearance (and more broadly his lifestyle) and spends time and money to improve his image. The term has been used from the mid-1990s in Japan. This English word was imported and transliterated into Japanese as *metorosekshuaru*.
10 In addition to the solicitations he experienced from male customers that made him uncomfortable, he found his job less enjoyable and lost interest after the showgirls including his girlfriend left Club Chaplin at the end of their contracts. He was also concerned with his student visa status, which did not legally permit him to work at hostess clubs. In addition, his former boss at Club Chaplin, Mr Chang, invited him to work at his new Korean cyber café (called *PC Pang* in Korean) as a receptionist.
11 Some hosts manage their female customers with physical violence. In other words, Erika's observation does not apply to all the host–customer relationships.

References

Allison, A. (1994) *Nightwork: Sexuality, Pleasure, and Corporate Masculinity in a Tokyo Hostess Club*, Chicago: University of Chicago Press.
Bakhtin, M. (1968) *Rabelais and His World*, trans. H. Iswoldsky, Cambridge, MA: MIT Press.
Bourdieu, P. (1980) *The Logic of Practice*, Stanford, CA: Stanford University Press.
—— (1984) *Distinction: A Social Critique of the Judgment of Taste*, Cambridge, MA: Harvard University Press.
Butler, J. (1990) *Gender Trouble: Feminism and the Subversion of Identity*, New York: Routledge.
Chung, H.J. (2004) "Performing Sex, Selling Heart: Korean Nightclub Hostesses in Japan," Ph.D. Dissertation, Department of Anthropology, University of California, Los Angeles.
Faier, L. (2007) "Filipina migrants in Rural Japan and their Professions of Love," in *American Ethnologist* 34, 1: 148–62.
Hochschild, A.R. (2003) *The Managed Heart: Commercialization of Human Feeling*, Berkeley: University of California Press.
Kadokura, T. (2007) *"Yoru no Onna" wa ikura kasegu ka?* [How much does it pay to be a "woman of the night"?], Tokyo: Kadokawa shoten.
Kondo, D. (1991) *Crafting Selves: Power, Gender, and Discourses of Identity in a Japanese Workplace*, Chicago: University of Chicago Press.
Moon, S. (2005) *Militarized Modernity and Gendered Citizenship in South Korea*, Durham, NC: Duke University Press.
Ogasawara, Y. (1998) *Office Ladies and Salaried Men: Power, Gender, and Work in Japanese Companies*, Berkeley: University of California Press.

Ryang, S. (1997) *North Koreans in Japan: Language, Ideology, and Identity*, Boulder: Westview.

Suzuki, N. (2003) "Of Love and the Marriage Market: Masculinity Politics and Filipina-Japanese Marriages in Japan," in J. Roberson and N. Suzuki (eds) *Men and Masculinities in Contemporary Japan: Dislocating the Salaryman Doxa*, New York: RoutledgeCurzon.

Tsuda, T. (2003) *Strangers in the Ethnic Homeland: Japanese Brazilian Return Migration in Transnational Perspective*, New York: Columbia University.

Turner, V. (1995) *The Ritual Process: The Structure and Anti-Structure*, Piscataway, NJ: Transaction.

Index

For Product Safety Concerns and Information please contact our EU
representative GPSR@taylorandfrancis.com
Taylor & Francis Verlag GmbH, Kaufingerstraße 24, 80331 München, Germany

www.ingramcontent.com/pod-product-compliance
Ingram Content Group UK Ltd.
Pitfield, Milton Keynes, MK11 3LW, UK
UKHW021610240425
457818UK00018B/472